PAMELA MORGAN'S FLAVORS

PAMELA MORGAN'S FLAVORS

What's New, What's Hot, What's Cooking
from New York's Premier Catering Shop

Pamela Morgan
and Michael McLaughlin

Viking

Credits

Design	Jaye Zimet
Production	Roni Axelrod
Photography	Lisa Charles Watson
Prop Styling	Mark Chandler for The Art Dept.
Food Styling	Roscoe Betsill
Make-up	Ina Vistica

Special thanks to Charles Bumgardner for his support, and to Navin at CYMK Lab, New York, for his generosity.

Props courtesy of: **Aero Limited**, 132 Spring Street, New York—*pp. 24–25,* bowls, underliner, table; *pp. 124–25,* square bowls, table; *pp. 140–41,* tray, porcelain cups and dishes; *pp. 158–59,* ironstone spoon; *pp. 180–81,* cake plate, tray, Lucite highball glasses. **Paula Rubenstein Antiques**, 65 Prince Street, New York—*pp. 24–25,* antique liners; *pp. 124–25,* antique linen; *pp. 140–41,* antique linen; *pp. 158–59,* antique linen, antique ironstone. **Global Table**, 107–9 Sullivan Street, New York—*pp. 62–63,* plates, underliners, square dish, round bowl; *pp. 104–5,* nesting bowls, small bowls, large plate, small plate; *pp. 124–25,* flatware.

VIKING
Published by the Penguin Group
Penguin Putnam Inc., 375 Hudson Street,
New York, New York 10014, U.S.A.
Penguin Books Ltd, 27 Wrights Lane,
London W8 5TZ, England
Penguin Books Australia Ltd, Ringwood,
Victoria, Australia
Penguin Books Canada Ltd, 10 Alcorn Avenue,
Toronto, Ontario, Canada M4V 3B2
Penguin Books (N.Z.) Ltd, 182-190 Wairau Road,
Auckland 10, New Zealand

Penguin Books Ltd, Registered Offices:
Harmondsworth, Middlesex, England

First published in 1998 by Viking Penguin,
a member of Penguin Putnam Inc.

1 3 5 7 9 10 8 6 4 2

Copyright © Pamela Morgan and Michael McLaughlin, 1998
Photographs copyright © Lisa Charles Watson, 1998
All rights reserved

LIBRARY OF CONGRESS CATALOGING-IN-PUBLICATION DATA
Morgan, Pamela.
Pamela Morgan Flavors: what's new, what's hot, what's cooking from New York's
premier catering shop / Pamela Morgan and Michael McLaughlin.
p.   cm.
Includes index.
ISBN 0-670-87062-5
1. Cookery. 2. Flavors (Catering shop). I. McLaughlin, Michael.
II. Title.
TX715.M8444   1998
641.5—dc21   97-37839

This book is printed on acid-free paper.
∞

Printed and bound in Great Britain by Butler & Tanner Ltd.
Set in Adobe Garamond

TO THE MEMORY OF MY FATHER, ROBERT T. MORGAN

Acknowledgments

This book is the result of the collaboration of many talented and special individuals whom I would like to thank from my heart:

My precious son, Zachary, for his patience, love and exceptional palate; Michael Trokel, my earthly angel, who has helped make so many of my dreams come true; my dear mother and father for their love, support, encouragement and belief in my abilities; my sister, Elizabeth, and brother, Tommy; my Aunt Jeanne for her special recipes; Christine Moore, who helped raise me and made our Friday-night dinners so special with her fabulous fried chicken; Michael McLaughlin, my talented co-writer, whose special friendship since our Silver Palate days helped me to pursue my catering and cookbook dreams; Dawn Drzal, my editor, who has worked tirelessly on this project and, in the process, has become my good friend—without her clear vision, this book could not have come together as it has; Sarah Jane Freymann, my patient, spiritual and gifted agent; Peggy Tagliarino, my friend and public relations diva, whose support and passion for Flavors since the day our store opened have sustained us over the years; Christopher Siversen, our dedicated and talented executive chef, whose passion, energy and drive have enabled Flavors to soar to new heights; the extraordinary staff at Flavors for all their hard work and enthusiasm—this book could not have been written without them; Rhonda Stieglitz, ace recipe tester and friend, whose attention to detail is awe-inspiring; Judy Lukas, my patient personal assistant and office manager, whose sense of humor and great attitude keep us on track; Lisa Charles Watson for her outstanding food photography, Roscoe Betsill, the book's creative food stylist, and Mark Chandler for his well-chosen props; special thanks to Charles Bumgardner for his creative support, and to Navin at CYMK Lab, New York, for his generosity; Jaye Zimet and Roseanne Serra, who designed this beautiful book and its jacket; Steve Miller, whose creativity and wonderful eye have made our store so very beautiful and reflective of the seasons; Larry Bogdanow, our architect, for giving me the exact vision for the Flavors Store; Frederica Biggs, our gifted interior designer; Mitchell Maxwell, who was with me from the inception of Flavors Catering—his encouragement gave me the confidence to move forward; Herb Maxwell for his delicious family meals and special recipes; John Gottfried for introducing me to the *exotic* foods of life; Alan Marks, whose belief in my artistic ability enabled me to live out my New York City dreams; Beth Hirsch for her incredible pastries and recipes; Lorena Stearns, and past Flavors chefs, for their contributions; Sheila Lukins and Julee Rosso, creators of The Silver Palate, for all they taught me; Madeleine Kamman for her gifts as teacher and mentor; Florence Fabricant, Suzanne Hamlin, Carol Shaw, Gillian Duffy and Beth Carrey for repeatedly recognizing Flavors in their reporting; Martha Stewart for her inspiration; my dear friend Dr. Dean Ornish, whose twenty-five-year friendship has sustained me through the years; my dear friends Ellen Hart, Gael Greene, Beth Landman Keil, Dr. Robert and Nancy Lee Giller, Denise Spatafora and Michelle Rago at Calabria for their beautiful flowers, always; Anjali Albert and Ammachi for their guidence, inspiration and love.

FINALLY, I THANK EVERY ONE OF OUR LOYAL CATERING AND RETAIL CUSTOMERS WHO HAVE BEEN SO RECEPTIVE TO FLAVORS' FOOD. YOU'VE SUSTAINED AND SUPPORTED US, ALLOWED US TO GROW AND DEVELOP, HONORED US BY SERVING OUR FOOD IN YOUR OFFICES AND HOMES AND AT YOUR CELEBRATIONS, AND YOU'VE ENABLED ME TO DO WHAT I LOVE DOING MOST—MAKING DELICIOUS FOOD FOR PEOPLE TO ENJOY.

Contents

Introduction

Food is amazing. The textures, aromas, tastes, colors and all the complex and creative ways ingredients can come together fascinate me—and they always have.

I grew up in Wichita Falls, Texas, in the heart of oil and cattle country. My mother was a wonderful cook, and the family ate every breakfast and dinner together. My fondest food memories are of Friday-night dinners and our housekeeper Christine's fabulous fried chicken, served with okra from our garden and Mom's salad of romaine lettuce and Texas grapefruit with poppy-seed dressing. I'll never forget the Sunday-supper ritual of steaks brought sizzling from the grill by my father, to be carved and napped with his homemade barbecue sauce. To go with the steaks my mother made her Caesar salad, first chilling the plates and the forks in the freezer in order to serve the salad ice-cold—great on a hot Wichita Falls evening. The food we ate was uncomplicated but delicious.

For parties, Mom used her beautiful china and silverware, and dessert was often her coffee angel-food cake frosted with whipped cream and decorated with sliced almonds. It was an unsophisticated childhood, but our family bonding occurred around the dining-room table, and family meals were the core of our connection to one another.

My love of food and entertaining came not only from my father, who adored good food, but also from his mother. My grandmother lived to be a healthy one hundred years old, watched all the cooking shows on television, and loved to entertain lavishly. We talked about food and recipes endlessly, and I know her genes contributed to who I am as well as what I do.

I had always wanted to attend an eastern college, but all of my mother's family had gone to the University of Texas, beginning with my grandfather, who graduated from the University of Texas Law School; so my mother prevailed on me to continue the tradition. After graduating from college, I became a member of a new modern-dance troupe in Austin. Our director, from New York City, wove tales of the "Big City" dance world, and I started fantasizing about dancing and living in the Big Apple. My friend Dean Ornish took me on my first trip to New York City, and I was hooked.

To my parents' dismay, I came to New York in my twenties to try my luck as a dancer, and expected to have a career on the stage. The city—a new and delicious world—had other plans. I savored my first veal piccata, polished off my first zabaglione and sipped my first espresso. The culinary diversity was overwhelming and I reveled in the possibilities: I was fascinated and full. While I still managed to dance my way into plenty of commercials and industrial shows, I made sure I waltzed through many restaurants as well.

Gradually I realized that, career-wise, something was lacking. I missed a genuine connection with the work and I felt no creative spark or sense of control. Dancers, as a rule, go where they're directed and do what they're told. Independent me felt increasingly stifled and unfulfilled. As a break from one brutal audition after another, I began to try new recipes and cook for friends. Part-time employment with one acquaintance who owned her own catering company showed me an exciting new possibility—cooking could be creatively challenging, maybe even financially rewarding!

My curiosity piqued, I signed up for a cooking class at a restaurant called Le Petit Robert. There I was taught the basics of French cuisine and I fell in love with learning how to cook. I read countless food magazines, tried to duplicate at home the recipes I sampled in restaurants and eventually started serious cooking classes at The New York Restaurant School. I also learned a lot about food chemistry and the magic of French cooking from the incredible teacher Madeleine Kamman. I was inspired by her passionate dedication to cooking and awed by her talents.

As I learned my craft and gradually left the dance scene, I was transformed. Through cooking, through the sheer process of touching food, creating recipes and making meals for others, I was connecting with a deep and undiscovered part of myself. It was a joyous process. I realized that catering, whether parties for crowds or intimate dinners, is really about celebrating the good times in life.

My earliest business venture was cooking for bachelors and leaving the food in their apartments with instructions on how to heat and serve it. *The Silver Palate Cookbook* had just been published, and inspired by the food and by the owners' story, I decided that I wanted to work with Julee Rosso and Sheila Lukins. On a whim, I called their offices and Sheila herself answered the phone. I explained my desire to learn, and a few days later, after a quick interview, I was hired. This was a very exciting time to be discovering food. American chefs like Alice Waters and Larry Forgione were earning international respect, gourmet grocers Dean & DeLuca were changing our ideas about ingredients, there were quick and stylish Pasta & Cheese stores selling fresh tortellini all over New York's East Side, Martha Stewart and Lee Bailey had begun writing books about the good life, and the whole world, it seemed, was beating a path to the door of the tiny Silver Palate shop on Columbus Avenue.

There I met my coauthor, Michael McLaughlin, and behind the counter, between selling the likes of foie gras, chocolate chip cookies and tarragon-walnut chicken salad to the likes of Yoko Ono, Sigourney Weaver and Geoffrey Beene. We tasted and analyzed everything that came from the store's kitchen and talked endlessly about food. Also there, where French pâtés, English cheeses, Italian pastas, Russian-style pumpernickel breads and prune-and-olive-studded chicken Marbella happily coexisted, I first began to dream about opening my own business.

By the time I eventually left The Silver Palate, my bachelor-feeding operation had segued neatly into Flavors, a full-service catering company with one employee—me. I had married, and, luckily, my husband, who was a theatrical producer, owned a restaurant in Greenwich Village near our first apartment. In the beginning I did it all—shopped, planned menus, interviewed clients, cooked and cleaned up. The cooking was accomplished in my husband's restaurant kitchen after the staff and customers had gone home. This lonely, late-night one-woman show did not last long, because I knew the business couldn't grow under such limited conditions. Soon I employed others, and eventually, through word of mouth and a great deal of effort—far more than any dance audition, really—the business began to grow.

This is not to imply that all was immediately smooth sailing. I remember my first really big job, for a friend who for some reason trusted me implicitly to cater his sister's wedding. Having no idea how long it took to produce food in quantity, I worked literally all night, heading straight to the event without even a moment's rest.

And then there was the glorious daylong rededication of the Statue of Liberty. We cooked three separate meals (breakfast, lunch and dinner), each for twelve hundred guests invited by E. F. Hutton to witness the festivities in New York Harbor. That night, after this heroic effort, I had to walk home (nearly twenty blocks; traffic was blocked off in the Wall Street area), my tired feet forgotten as fireworks lit up the Manhattan sky. Somehow, catering always involves sore feet; usually, it's worth the pain.

I made time to travel to France during these years, in order to continue my education. I worked in the kitchens of Roger Vergé's Moulin de Mougins and became friends with his chef de cuisine, Serge Chollet. I drove all over southern France, met many chefs and worked in many kitchens. I was very lucky to be able to see, smell and taste the Provençal cooking of the finest restaurants. To this day it remains my favorite regional food, and is certainly reflected in this book by the many uses of olives, artichokes, capers, saffron, rosemary, thyme and garlic.

My son, Zachary, was born in 1984, and I purposely kept my business small for the years when he was a baby. Although I worked a great deal (now at home in a wonderful new professionally equipped kitchen), I also made time to spend with him. He is truly a chip off the old block, and obviously inherited his mother's, grandmother's and great-grandmother's genes, asking for smoked salmon and Perrier when he was only two.

Eventually Flavors outgrew even the new kitchen. Separated from my husband by then, I took a trip during the Thanksgiving holiday, and used the time to reflect. I woke one morning after a dream vision of a food store like no other. This vision was so clear, I couldn't put it out of my mind. I wrote down the details and began planning to make it a reality.

In 1994, with the help of my friend and new partner, Michael Trokel, the vision came into being. In New York City's historic Flatiron District, a bustling downtown neighborhood of lofts, photographers' studios, light industry and wonderful restaurants, in an airy, high-ceilinged space, Flavors, the food store, was joined with Flavors, the catering business. In response to my own changing tastes and way of eating, it is a new kind of food store. At its heart is The Market Table—a grand buffet of fifteen to twenty seasonally varying meatless room-temperature dishes, many of them low in fat or even oil-free. Others, like our famous Caesar salad and our garlic mashed potatoes, are another story altogether, existing for the sheer pleasure of eating.

In addition to The Market Table, every day we serve homemade soups, unusual sandwiches, carved meats, hearty entrée dishes, home-baked desserts and coffees, juices and teas of all kinds. Lean or lavish, the food at Flavors has plenty of big, bold flavor, much of it inspired by cuisines of the world—"Texas and Tuscany" as one reviewer noted, along with plenty of Provence, oodles of Italy, a touch of Thailand and more than a morsel of Morocco. Although it is more casual than much of what we prepare for our corporate catering clients, the food at the store is produced with the same care and from the same high-quality, market-fresh ingredients, many of them organic.

To my delight, the response from our customers has been overwhelming. They, too, are looking for simpler, more healthful alternatives that keep the emphasis on taste, and they seem to have discovered, as I have, that fresh, vividly seasoned food is inherently more satisfying. They welcome the opportunity to choose from a wide and balanced array and to combine foods in any way they please each day, depending on their mood, the weather, their diet—whatever.

Each morning, around eleven-thirty, I get a familiar feeling of anticipation and excitement, not unlike that which I feel when the curtain on a stage production is about to go up. This is the magic time when the Flavors kitchen has finished its preparations and we bring out all of our sparkling white platters and bowls, brimming over with the season's best, to set up The Market Table for the day. That same food—and that same sense of excitement—are the inspiration behind many of the recipes you will find in this book.

Cooking is love. My fondest memories are of meals with family and friends. There is nothing in my life that is better than connecting with people over a beautiful table, eating the best food and drinking wonderful wines. Anyone who has ever asked for a recipe and everyone who shares my passion for food, this book is for you.

What the Icons Mean

 The history and true story behind
favorite classic dishes

 How to transform simple, casual dishes through
presentation into something suitable for company

 Certain flavors influence almost everything I cook.
Changing seasonally, these flavors are celebrated
throughout the cooking year.

 How to shop for, cook with and store dried
or otherwise preserved ingredients

 Professional or just practical technical advice
to make your job in the kitchen easier

 How to shop for, cook with and store
fresh ingredients

 How to improvise variations
on the recipes given

PAMELA MORGAN'S FLAVORS

Left to right: Olive and
Tomato Tapenade; Cumin-
Scented Pumpkin Dip;
Smoky White Bean
Spread with Roasted
Garlic and Basil

Spreads, Dips and Casual Starters

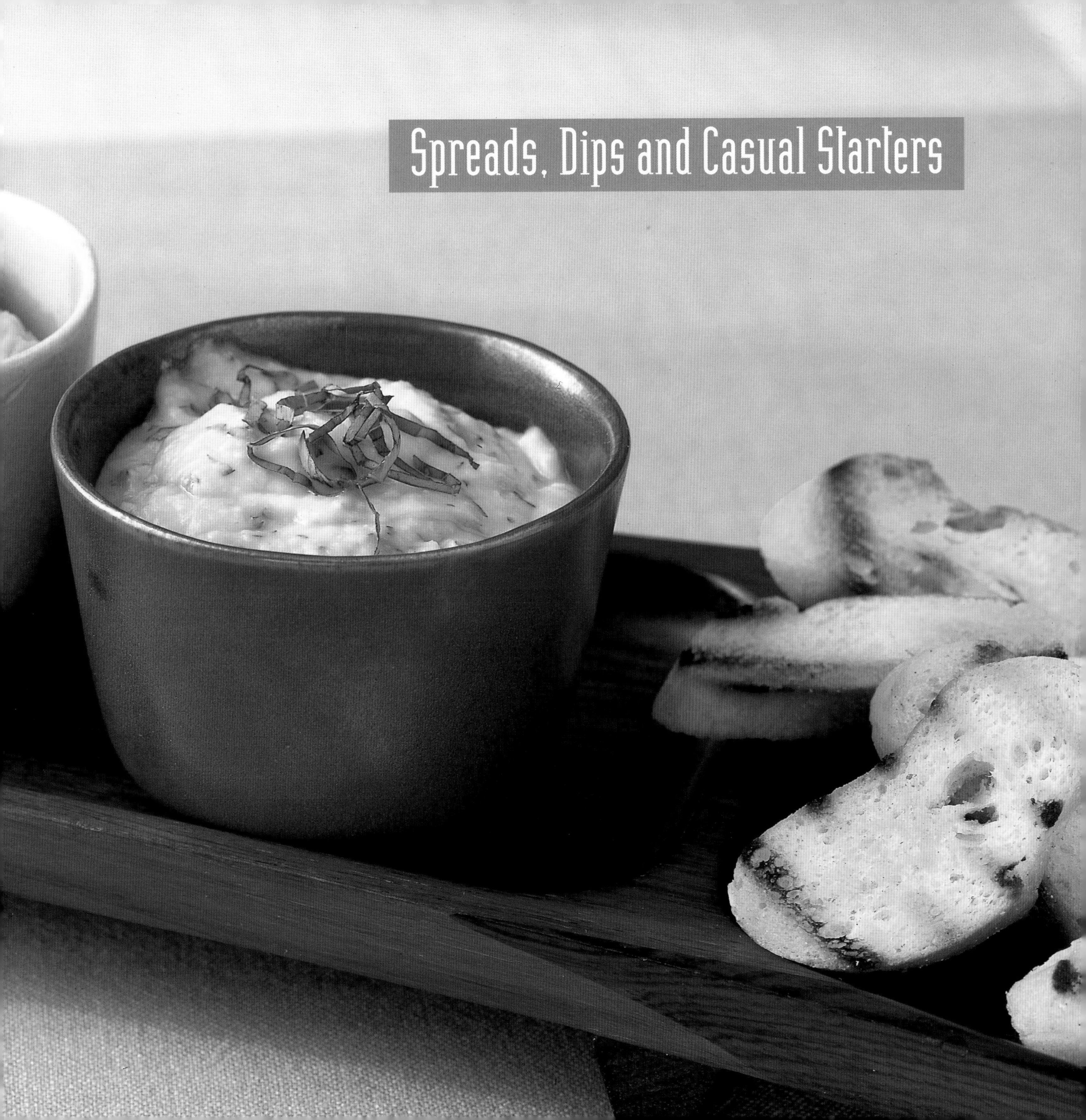

Fanciful hors d'oeuvres are fine for catered events, but when I'm entertaining at home, I prefer a lower-tech approach. These vivid, casual starters, many of them taking their inspiration from Provençal France and Italy, where cooks do effortless elegance better than anyone, are light and frequently meatless. They're served help-yourself fashion, allowing diners to take as much or as little as they like. They're also nearly always the kinds of dishes that are best made well in advance, leaving me that much more time to spend with guests. First impressions are essential, but having a relaxed good time at your own party is the most important detail of all. **Smoky White Bean Spread with Roasted Garlic and Basil • Cumin-Scented Pumpkin Dip • Olive and Tomato Tapenade • Oven-Baked Pita Chips with Za'atar • Goat Cheese and Caramelized Onion Spread with Herbes de Provence • Grilled Eggplant-Tomato Dip • Chile Pita Chips • Marcella's Fava Bean Spread • Flavors' Sweet and Spicy Cocktail Nuts • Two Tomato-Basil Bruschettas • Olive Mélange with Fennel and Orange • Crab and Corn Cakes with Chipotle Rémoulade • Pernod-Scented Artichokes with Black Olive Aioli • Baja Beach Clams Steamed in Beer • Lavash with Herbed Cream Cheese and Smoked Salmon • Gravlax with Sweet Mustard-Dill Sauce**

Smoky White Bean Spread with Roasted Garlic and Basil

Here is one of our most delicious, most unusual and most flexible appetizers. Created by Flavors' chef, Chris Siversen, it originally called for actually smoking the cooked beans in one of those metal stove-top devices. As we began turning out what seemed like hundreds of pounds of the delicious stuff, the recipe evolved to use pure liquid-smoke flavoring. The taste is exactly the same (trust me, I didn't want to tamper with success), with far less work. Just don't overdo the liquid smoke or the spread will become acrid. We serve it with pita chips (pages 7 and 11) or bruschettas (page 14), and spread it on cold lamb sandwiches (page 60). I always include it in a big spread of mezze (page 5).

Makes about 6 cups

1 pound dried white beans, such as cannellini or Great Northern, picked over, see Note
2 cloves
½ small yellow onion, plus ½ cup chopped onion
1 carrot, peeled and cut crosswise into 3 pieces
4 sprigs fresh thyme
2 garlic cloves, peeled and chopped
3 tablespoons fresh lemon juice
4 teaspoons salt
1 tablespoon liquid hickory smoke flavoring
1 teaspoon freshly ground black pepper
10 large basil leaves, chopped
1 tablespoon finely chopped sage, optional

In a medium bowl, cover the beans with cold water and let soak for at least 4 hours, or overnight for convenience.

Drain the beans. In a large pan, cover them with fresh cold water. Push the cloves into the onion half. Add the onion half, carrots and thyme sprigs to the pot with the beans. Set over medium heat and bring to a simmer. Cover tightly, lower the heat, and cook gently, stirring once or twice, until very tender, about 50 minutes (bean cooking times vary widely; add additional boiling water and continue to cook as necessary). Reserve 1 cup of the cooking water. Discard the onion half, carrot pieces and thyme sprigs. Drain and cool the beans.

In a food processor, combine the beans, chopped onion, ⅔ cup of the reserved cooking water, garlic, lemon juice, salt, smoke flavoring and pepper. Process until smooth, stopping several times to scrape down the sides of the work bowl and adding additional cooking liquid if the mixture seems too thick. Transfer to a bowl and stir in the basil and sage. Adjust the seasoning. The spread can be used immediately or covered and refrigerated for up to 3 days. Return it to room temperature before serving.

Note: Canned beans can be substituted. Four 15½-ounce cans, drained, will yield 6 cups. Use the canning liquid in place of the cooking water in the bean spread. Reduce the salt slightly, since canned beans are nearly always well salted.

Cumin-Scented Pumpkin Dip

I came up with this easy dip as an appetizer for an autumn cocktail party. The rich color and the unexpected intriguing flavors just say "fall" to me (although we serve it all year long). A bowlful, accompanied by pita chips (pages 7 and 11) or plain toasts for scooping, always vanishes with amazing speed.

Makes about 3 cups

2 tablespoons unsalted butter
¾ cup finely chopped yellow onion
¾ cup finely chopped sweet red pepper
1¾ teaspoons ground cumin, preferably toasted
¾ teaspoon Hungarian sweet paprika
½ teaspoon sugar
¼ cup whipping cream
2 ounces cream cheese, cubed, at room temperature
1 (16-ounce) can solid-pack pumpkin
  (not pie filling)
1½ tablespoons finely chopped flat-leaf parsley
1¾ teaspoons salt
¾ teaspoon freshly ground black pepper
¼ teaspoon Tabasco Pepper Sauce

In a medium skillet over moderate heat melt the butter. Add the onion, sweet pepper, cumin, paprika and sugar and cook uncovered, stirring occasionally, until golden brown, 8 to 10 minutes.

Add the whipping cream to the skillet and bring just to a simmer. Add the cream cheese and cook, stirring, just until the cheese has melted. Remove from the heat.

In a medium bowl, combine the warm cheese mixture and the pumpkin. Stir in 1 tablespoon of the parsley, the salt, pepper and Tabasco. Adjust the seasoning and stir again. Sprinkle the remaining parsley over the dip. Serve at room temperature.

The dip can be prepared up to 3 days in advance, letting its flavors intensify slightly. Cover tightly and refrigerate, returning the dip to room temperature and sprinkling the remaining ½ tablespoon parsley over it just before serving.

The recipe is delicious made with store-bought ground cumin but for a richer, nuttier, flavor dry-toast whole seeds by putting a quantity (¹/₃ cup or so) dry in a small, heavy skillet over low heat. Cook, stirring often, until the seeds are evenly and richly browned and beginning to pop, about 8 minutes (don't overcook or the cumin will be bitter). Remove the seeds from the skillet and cool. Store airtight at room temperature and grind the seeds, in a spice mill or in a mortar with a pestle, just before using.

A MEZZE SPREAD—Mezze are the wonderfully varied and flavorful appetizers of the Middle East. Dips, spreads, marinated vegetables and even light salads can be included, along with olives, crumbled feta cheese, fresh seasonal produce, lemon wedges, flavored oils and herbs, herbs, herbs. One or two mezze may do for a family supper or small gathering, before moving on to the main course, but at a party, the more the merrier, and you can hardly offer too many. In fact, during hot weather, such an array, accompanied by a variety of good breads, plenty of wine and a light seasonal dessert, all served on rustic terra-cotta, can be the basis for a dazzling buffet supper. The vivid flavors of the mezze awaken appetites like few other foods, and my guests love the lightness and the freedom of choice. Consider serving the following dishes in this book at a mezze party (see the index for page numbers): Olive Mélange with Fennel and Orange; Cumin-Scented Pumpkin Dip; Olive and Tomato Tapenade; Goat Cheese and Caramelized Onion Spread with Herbes de Provence; Smoky White Bean Spread with Roasted Garlic and Basil; Marcella's Fava Bean Spread; Grilled Eggplant-Tomato Dip; Chile Pita Chips; Two Tomato-Basil Bruschettas; Oven-Baked Pita Chips with Za'atar; Tuscan White Bean Salad; Lentil and Roasted Red Pepper Salad with Walnuts and Grilled Green Onions; Chickpea and Brown and Wild Rice Salad with Moroccan-Spiced Dressing; Lemony Herbed Orzo with Tomatoes, Olives and Feta; Flavors' Bread, Tomato and Mozzarella Salad; and Cucumber and Tomato Salad with Olives, Feta and Mint.

HUNGARIAN PAPRIKA—For too many cooks, paprika is a flavorless red dust, traditionally sprinkled onto deviled eggs for a "touch of color." Hungarians know better. In Hungary, sweet to hot red peppers (transplants from the New World and related to nearly all the great culinary chiles) are dried and ground into a deeply flavorful spice that is the soul of Hungarian cuisine. At Flavors, Hungarian sweet paprika adds both color and flavor to a number of dishes, occasionally even standing in for pure unblended medium-hot chile powder when we simmer up a pot of the Texas national dish, chile con carne. Lately there has been some question about adulteration of the Hungarian product and cooks have turned to equally flavorful Spanish paprika (pimentón). Either way, store your paprika as other spices and dried herbs should be stored—in a cool, dry place away from direct sunlight. Toss out a can or jar more than six months old and start over with a fresh one.

Olive and Tomato Tapenade

Here is the Flavors version of tapenade, the ubiquitous (and utterly delicious) Provençal spread. Interestingly, though it is olive-based, the name tapenade *comes from the Provençal word for capers. In southern France, there are as many recipes for* tapenade *as there are cooks, the results ranging from thick, inky purees that are the very essence of black olives, to lighter, looser and more colorful approaches like this one. Set it out in a cool, heavy crock, and offer bruschettas (page 14) or pita chips (pages 7 and 11) for spreading—a great, casual appetizer.*

Makes about 3 cups

8   sun-dried tomato halves
1   cup boiling water
¼   cup cold-pressed extra-virgin olive oil
1   cup finely diced fresh fennel bulb
¾   cup finely chopped yellow onion
¼   cup tomato paste
½   teaspoon balsamic vinegar
¼   teaspoon Tabasco Pepper Sauce
    Freshly ground black pepper
¼   pound drained pitted Greek black olives
    (Kalamatas)
12 large, brine-cured Spanish or Italian green olives
    (such as Sicilian), about ¼ pound, drained and
    pitted
¼   cup drained small (nonpareil) capers
⅔   cup diced seeded ripe plum tomatoes

¼   cup finely chopped flat-leaf parsley
¼   cup finely chopped fennel fronds

In a small, heat-proof bowl, combine the dried tomato halves and boiling water. Let stand, stirring once or twice, until plump, tender and cool, about 30 minutes. Drain, reserving 1 tablespoon of the tomato soaking water. Coarsely chop the soaked tomatoes.

In a medium skillet over moderately high heat, warm 2 tablespoons of the olive oil. Add the diced fennel and onion and cook uncovered, stirring occasionally, until lightly browned, 8 to 10 minutes. Remove from the heat and stir in the tomato paste, reserved tomato soaking water, balsamic vinegar, Tabasco and a generous grinding of black pepper. Cool to room temperature. In a food processor, combine the black and green olives, sun-dried tomatoes and capers. Pulse

TABASCO PEPPER SAUCE—Red chile-based Tabasco is one of this country's oldest condiments, produced on a salt mountain called Avery Island that rises out of the Louisiana bayou. It's also one of our hottest condiments and will certainly wake up both a plate of breakfast eggs and the sleepy diner sitting before it. At Flavors, however, Tabasco is used mostly in quantities too small to make the dish in question actually fiery, adding tartness, salt and just a bit of heat, and enhancing the flavor of the dish. Like any seasoning, Tabasco fades with time. Buy the small bottle, store it in the refrigerator, and discard it, preferably *before* it starts to lose its zip.

several times, scraping down the sides of the work bowl between pulses, until the olives are just roughly chopped. Add the fennel mixture, the fresh tomatoes and the remaining 2 tablespoons olive oil. Pulse again, just to blend; the tapenade should be coarse and chunky.

Cover tightly and refrigerate for at least 2 hours, or up to 3 days (the tapenade will improve upon standing).

Let the tapenade come to room temperature. Adjust the seasoning and stir in the parsley and fennel fronds just before serving.

 If your Kalamatas do not come pitted, use a cherry pitter, or gently crush the olives with the bottom of a glass and then pick out the pits. You will need to start with about ⅓ pound olives to achieve the necessary ¼ pound after pitting. To pit green olives, stand them on end, then cut downward with a paring knife following the curve of the pit as closely as possible, removing as much of the flesh as you can.

Oven-Baked Pita Chips with Za'atar

Za'atar—also spelled, less entertainingly, zatar—is a spice blend made of hyssop (an herb in the mint family), sesame seeds and tangy sumac. We buy it at a fascinating upstairs Middle Eastern shop on the second floor of a building on lower Broadway in Manhattan, and use it to season these crisp, oven-baked pita wedges. Good wherever pita scoopers are good, these are especially appropriate when tahini is involved, particularly with Grilled Eggplant-Tomato Dip (page 9), but they are quite tasty on their own.

Serves 6 to 8

6 6-inch white or whole-wheat pita breads, each
    cut into 6 equal wedges
¼ cup olive oil, see Note
4 tablespoons za'atar
⅛ teaspoon salt

Position a rack in the middle of the oven and preheat to 400° F.

Lightly brush the pita wedges on both sides with olive oil, transferring them to a baking sheet as you go (the wedges need not lie in a single layer). In a small bowl, stir together the za'atar and salt. Sprinkle this mixture over the chips, stirring and turning them several times as you do so to coat them evenly on both sides.

Set the baking sheet in the oven and bake the chips, stirring occasionally, until lightly browned and crunchy, about 15 minutes.

Cool the chips on the pan on a rack. Store airtight at room temperature. Rewarm the chips for serving if desired.

Note: Roasted garlic–flavored olive oil, available in specialty food shops and some supermarkets, makes a nice substitution here.

Goat Cheese and Caramelized Onion Spread with Herbes de Provence

Long-cooked, sweetly caramelized onions and slightly tangy goat cheese are wonderfully complementary in this nicely textured mixture. It keeps well, and has many uses, which makes it a Flavors essential. Spread it on bruschettas (page 14) as an appetizer, use it in sandwiches (the browned onion mixture can be omitted here, if desired), stuff it under the skin of a grill-smoked chicken (again without the onions, see page 68). The fresher and smoother the goat cheese the better the spread. I recommend Coach Farms, if you can locate the product of this excellent upper New York State cheese maker.

Makes about 2 cups

Caramelized Onions
11 ounces soft, mild goat cheese, at room temperature
2 tablespoons Roasted Garlic Puree (page 162)
2 tablespoons crème fraîche, optional
¾ teaspoon crumbled herbes de Provence
   Freshly ground black pepper
¼ cup julienned drained oil-packed sun-dried tomatoes, optional

In a medium bowl, combine the onion mixture, goat cheese, garlic puree, crème fraîche if you are using it, and the herbes de Provence. Season generously to taste with pepper and stir again. The mixture can be used immediately or covered and refrigerated for up to 3 days. Let it come to room temperature before using.

Scatter the sun-dried tomatoes over the goat cheese spread just before serving.

Caramelized Onions

Makes about 1 cup

2 tablespoons olive oil
4 cups thinly sliced yellow onion (from 2 8-ounce onions)
¾ teaspoon herbes de Provence, crumbled
½ teaspoon sugar
½ teaspoon salt

In a large, heavy skillet over low heat, warm the olive oil. Add the onions, herbes de Provence, sugar and salt. Cover and cook, stirring occasionally, until the onions are golden and juicy, about 30 minutes. Uncover the skillet and cook, stirring occasionally, until the onion juices have evaporated, 15 to 20 minutes. Raise the heat slightly and cook, stirring often, until the onions are lightly and evenly browned, another 10 to 15 minutes. Remove from the heat and cool slightly.

Grilled Eggplant-Tomato Dip

On a trip through Turkey, I found some version of this classic eggplant dip (a close cousin of baba ghanoush) on the table of virtually every restaurant I visited. Easy to make ahead, it's very good indeed, spread onto slices of crusty baguette (as I found it in Turkey) or scooped onto pita chips (pages 7 and 11) or bruschettas (page 14) and accompanied with a glass of cold white wine. It's also an essential part of a mezze spread (page 5). A bit of toasted sesame seed oil nicely reinforces the flavor of the tahini.

Makes about 4 cups

2 cups wood chips, preferably hickory, optional

2 medium eggplants (1½ pounds total), trimmed and sliced ½ inch thick

2 large ripe tomatoes, about 1½ pounds total, trimmed and cut horizontally into thirds

¼ cup olive oil

3 tablespoons tahini

2 tablespoons fresh lemon juice

2 tablespoons Roasted Garlic Puree (page 162) or minced fresh garlic

2 teaspoons soy sauce, preferably tamari

1¼ teaspoons salt

1¼ teaspoons Asian sesame oil, from toasted seeds

1 teaspoon Tabasco Pepper Sauce

½ cup finely chopped flat-leaf parsley

2 teaspoons coarsely ground toasted cumin seeds (page 4)

Prepare a hot charcoal fire or preheat a gas grill (medium-high). When the fire is hot, distribute the wood chips if you are using them. Position the grill rack about 6 inches above the heat.

Lightly brush the eggplant and tomato slices on all sides with the oil. Lay the vegetables on the rack. Cover and grill, turning the vegetables once, until the eggplant is well browned and the tomatoes are lightly browned and very tender, about 10 minutes total. Remove from the grill and cool to room temperature.

Roughly chop the eggplant and tomato. In a food processor, combine the chopped vegetables, tahini, lemon

HERBES DE PROVENCE—Each time I crumble this fragrant herb mixture into a dish (and I use it often), I'm transported back to the South of France. Like any convenient prefabricated seasoning blend, herbes de Provence varies with the brand. Shop for one that includes the greatest number of herbs (a favorite of mine combines tarragon, chervil, savory, sage, marjoram, thyme, parsley, basil and lavender flowers). This last ingredient is essential. If you have ever seen and smelled a field of lavender blazing purple under the Provençal sun, you will know that a blend without it can only be a pale shadow of the real thing. As always, store the herb mixture in a cool, dry place, away from direct sunlight, and use it up or replace it often.

TAHINI—The rich sesame seed paste known as tahini is an essential element of hummus and is used in a number of other Mediterranean sauces, soups and desserts. It is increasingly available, particularly in health-food stores, usually stocked with the peanut butter. (Don't buy the boxed hummus mixes, though Chinese sesame paste, the kind used on authentic sesame noodles, can be substituted.) Tahini made from toasted seeds has more flavor. The paste is oily and it separates. Spoon the contents of the jar into a bowl and work it with a spoon until homogenized and smooth before measuring out the quantity the recipe requires. Return the remaining tahini to the jar and refrigerate. It will keep for several months.

juice, garlic puree, soy sauce, salt, sesame oil and Tabasco and process until almost smooth. Transfer to a bowl, cover and let stand at room temperature for 1 hour. (Or, cover tightly and refrigerate overnight or for up to 3 days. Return to room temperature if chilled.)

Stir in the parsley. Adjust the seasoning. Spoon the eggplant mixture into the center of a platter. Sprinkle evenly with cumin. Serve at room temperature.

Note: Though the smoky accent of the grill makes this spread particularly delicious, the vegetables can also be roasted in the oven. Preheat it to 450° F., brush the eggplant slices and tomatoes with oil and roast until browned and tender, 20 to 25 minutes. Cool and then proceed with the recipe.

Always looking for that extra boost of flavor, I like to add wood chips to the fire when grilling. Here's how: Depending on your grill manufacturer's directions, the chips may first need to be soaked in water, then drained. When the fire is hot, they are then scattered over the coals or firestones or transferred to the grill's wood-chip compartment. Their fragrant smoke bathes the food as it cooks and adds robust flavor that a plain charcoal or propane fire can't. Choose lighter mesquite for seafood, sweet fruitwoods like apple or cherry for pork or poultry, and pungent nut woods such as hickory or pecan for beef. A limited selection of smoking chips is sold in good supermarkets, while a gourmet range can usually be found in a fancy food shop or catalog.

Chile Pita Chips

Plain wedges of pita bread work efficiently enough as scoops, but when brushed with chile paste and then grilled over a smoky fire, they become downright exciting. We make what seem like tons of these for parties every week.

Serves 6

2 cups wood chips, preferably hickory,
    optional
⅓ cup olive oil
1 tablespoon Italian red chile paste
⅛ teaspoon salt
6 6-inch white or whole-wheat pitas,
    each cut into 6 equal wedges

Prepare a hot charcoal fire or preheat a gas grill (medium-high). When the fire is hot, distribute the wood chips if you are using them. Position the grill rack about 6 inches above the heat.

In a small bowl, stir together the olive oil, chile paste and salt.

Brush the pita wedges lightly on both sides with the olive oil mixture. When the wood chips are smoking, lay the wedges on the rack. Cover and grill, turning once, until lightly marked by the rack, 3 to 4 minutes total. Transfer to a napkin-lined basket and serve hot or warm.

Note: For extra-crispy chips, transfer them after grilling to a sheet pan and bake in a preheated 200° F. oven for 10 to 15 minutes. Leftover chips will keep, tightly bagged and stored at room temperature, for several days. They're great for snacking and a lifesaver when company drops in.

ITALIAN RED CHILE PASTE—Among the most useful flavor boosters in my kitchens, both at work and at home, is Italian red chile paste. Olive oil–based and fairly fiery, this paste not only makes our pita chips terrifically addictive, it is also an essential ingredient in the croutons for our famous Caesar salad (page 144) and, a modest dollop at a time, adds savory heat to soups, dips and pasta sauces. Of the three brands commonly available—Dal Roccolto, Amore and Colavita—Dal Roccolto is my favorite, but they can all be made to work. Or, in a pinch, chile-flavored olive oil (but not Asian chile oil) can be substituted, though the effect will be slightly muted.

Marcella's Fava Bean Spread

Though I had enjoyed favas often in Italy and France, I had never really cooked with them until a batch turned up in the market on the same day I spotted a recipe for this spread, from Marcella Hazan. Unlike Marcella, I like to cook the beans for a very few minutes before I puree them—it makes them easier to digest. Though guests can never guess exactly what the spread is made of, they never fail to eat every bit. Serve the rustic mixture on bruschettas (page 14) or toasted Tuscan sourdough bread.

Serves 4 to 6

1 pound fresh fava beans in the pod
⅓ cup freshly grated Parmigiano-Reggiano cheese
⅓ cup cold-pressed extra-virgin olive oil
3 tablespoons finely chopped fresh mint
2 tablespoons finely chopped fresh basil
2 tablespoons fresh lemon juice
2 garlic cloves, peeled and chopped
¼ teaspoon salt
Freshly ground black pepper

Remove the beans from the pods; you should have 1½ cups beans.

Bring a small pan of water to a boil. Add the beans and cook, stirring once or twice, for 3 minutes. Drain, rinse with cold water and cool to room temperature.

In a food processor, combine the beans, cheese, oil, mint, basil, lemon juice, garlic, salt and pepper to taste. Process, scraping down the sides of the work bowl several times, until smooth. Adjust the seasoning. Serve immediately, or cover tightly and hold at room temperature for up to 2 hours. The dip is best if never refrigerated.

FAVA BEANS—Eaten in a good part of the world, fava beans are nearly unknown in this country, although heightened interest in things Mediterranean has increased their availability somewhat. Really good specialty produce stores or farmer's markets that cater to chefs are your best sources for the big green pods, which begin to appear in early spring. Once removed from the pod, the beans need to be individually peeled and then, if young and tender, can be eaten raw. Lazy cooks (or those faced with more mature favas, a common state of affairs on this side of the Atlantic) can resort to a brief blanching. Looking rather like lima beans, favas are used in spreads, salads, stews and soups, like the one on page 34. Favas are also available dried, and then are often cooked until tender, mashed and served with a drizzle of olive oil and pita for scooping. You can even find crunchy deep-fried fava beans, an addictive snack, in Middle Eastern groceries.

Flavors' Sweet and Spicy Cocktail Nuts

These are our signature cocktail nibble, one that appears at virtually every catered event. Addictively sweet and hot, with a nice background flavor of spices, they get people's attention right away. The nuts disappear quickly, but any leftovers can be stored airtight at room temperature, and will keep for at least a week.

Makes about 12 cups

1¾ cups water

1¾ cups sugar

2 cups (about 7 ounces) unsalted pecans

2 cups (about 7 ounces) unsalted walnuts

1½ cups (about 7 ounces) unsalted shelled pumpkin seeds

1 cup (about 5½ ounces) blanched almonds

1 cup (about 5 ounces) unsalted shelled sunflower seeds

1 cup (about 4½ ounces) shelled unsalted pistachios

5 teaspoons curry powder

4¼ teaspoons ground cumin, preferably from toasted seeds (page 4)

4 teaspoons kosher salt

2 teaspoons Hungarian sweet paprika

1¼ teaspoons ground cinnamon

1¼ teaspoons ground coriander

1⅛ teaspoons cayenne pepper

¾ teaspoon ground cardamom

½ teaspoon ground allspice

⅛ teaspoon freshly grated nutmeg

In a small, heavy saucepan, combine the water and sugar. Set over high heat and bring to a boil, stirring to dissolve the sugar. Lower the heat slightly and simmer briskly until the mixture registers 230° F., about 30 minutes. Remove from the heat and cool slightly.

Position a rack in the middle of the oven and preheat to 375° F.

In a large bowl, toss together the nuts and seasonings. Add the sugar mixture and stir well. Spread the nut mixture evenly onto a jelly-roll pan. Bake, stirring occasionally, until the nuts are crisp and brown, about 30 minutes.

Cool the nuts on the pan on a rack for 5 minutes, then scrape into a large bowl. Break up the larger clumps of nuts, then return all of the nuts to the pan and cool completely.

Store at room temperature in an airtight container.

Note: If desired, 1½ cups cashews can be substituted for the pecans and an equal amount of peanuts can replace the pistachios.

Two Tomato-Basil Bruschettas

At Flavors, bruschettas are thin ovals of good bread, lightly brushed with olive oil and grilled. Served with an almost endless array of fresh zesty toppings, they are among our most popular catered appetizers. They are also ideal for home entertaining, since they are so undemanding to make and so deliciously satisfying. Here are two of our most popular tomato-based toppings to get you started, though improvisation is ultimately the name of this game.

Serves 8

Bruschettas
1 thick baguette, about 22 inches long, ends trimmed, loaf angle-cut into 36 ½-inch slices
⅓ cup olive oil

Tomato-Caper Topping with Lemon
2 large, ripe tomatoes, about 1 pound total, trimmed, seeded and diced (¼-inch)
¼ cup finely chopped fresh basil
2 tablespoons drained small (nonpareil) capers
1 tablespoon cold-pressed extra-virgin olive oil
1 tablespoon minced lemon zest (colored part of peel, removed with a zester and finely chopped)
2 garlic cloves, peeled and crushed through a press
Salt
Freshly ground black pepper

Yellow Tomato-Smoked Mozzarella Topping with Olives
2 large ripe yellow tomatoes, about 1 pound total, trimmed, seeded and diced (¼-inch)
3 ounces smoked mozzarella, diced (¼-inch), at room temperature
¼ cup chopped drained pimento-stuffed green olives
¼ cup chopped fennel bulb
¼ cup finely chopped fresh basil
1 tablespoon cold-pressed extra-virgin olive oil
2 garlic cloves, peeled and crushed through a press
Salt
Freshly ground black pepper

For the bruschettas, light a charcoal fire and let it burn down until the coals are evenly white, or preheat a gas grill (medium). Brush the bread slices lightly on both sides with the olive oil. When the fire is hot, lay the bread on the rack. Cover and grill, rearranging the position of the slices on the rack to create attractive markings and turning them once, until they are crisp and lightly browned, 3 to 4 minutes total. Remove from the heat and cool. The bread slices can be grilled several hours in advance.

For the tomato-caper topping, in a medium bowl, stir together the tomatoes, basil, capers, oil, lemon zest, garlic, ½ teaspoon salt and a generous grinding of pepper. Cover and let stand at room temperature for 30 minutes.

For the tomato-smoked mozzarella topping, in a medium bowl, stir together the tomatoes, mozzarella, olives, fennel, basil, oil, garlic, ¼ teaspoon salt and a generous grinding of pepper. Cover and let stand at room temperature for 30 minutes.

Adjust the seasoning on both tomato mixtures. Serve them, accompanied by the grilled bread slices, letting guests top their bruschettas to taste.

Note: Bruschettas are natural starters for a grill meal. Don't hesitate to toast them over a wood chip–boosted fire for extra flavor, if you're proceeding on to some grilled main course. Conversely, the ovals of bread can be brushed with oil and toasted under a preheated broiler.

Olive Mélange with Fennel and Orange

I grew up in Texas in the sixties, and at that time I thought olives were either green, from a jar (and went into potato salad and martinis), or black, from a can, and were festively worn by my sister on her fingertips. It wasn't until my first trip to France and my first stroll through the open-air market in Nice, where stall after stall featured dozens of crocks of olive varieties—small, large or huge, smooth or wrinkled, glistening with oil, dappled with herbs, redolent of garlic and chiles, in a rainbow of muted colors—that I really began to understand and appreciate this ancient food.

Serves 12 or more

2 pounds drained assorted black and green imported olives

2 garlic cloves, peeled and lightly crushed

2 tablespoons cold-pressed extra-virgin olive oil

2 tablespoons fresh lemon juice

2 tablespoons fresh orange juice

2 tablespoons fresh orange zest (colored part of peel, removed with a zester and minced)

1 tablespoon fennel seeds, lightly crushed

¾ teaspoon crushed red pepper

In a strainer under cold running water briefly rinse any brine-cured olives (don't rinse any oil-cured or flavored ones); drain well.

In a medium bowl, combine all the olives, the garlic, olive oil, lemon juice, orange juice, orange zest, fennel seeds and red pepper.

Cover and refrigerate, stirring occasionally. The olives should marinate for at least 24 hours and will keep at least a week. Return them to room temperature before serving.

Olives are such a natural finger food (something my sister obviously realized) that we nearly always serve them in a casual setting. At one al fresco party, we spooned the mélange out of a big bowl into small cones of parchment paper, recreating the way they are sold in French markets, and let guests stroll and nibble as the sun began to set. (Don't do this if you will be bothered by pits in your flower beds.) If you prefer a dressier presentation, divide the olives and a bit of their dressing among individual ramekins or small dishes and set one at each diner's place. Be sure to provide extra small bowls for pits.

Crab and Corn Cakes with Chipotle Rémoulade

The addition of tender corn and roasted red pepper reinforces the natural sweetness of the crab, which is in turn offset some-what by the smoky, slightly fiery mayonnaise that tops these extra-tasty crab cakes. Undergoing a renaissance these days, crab cakes turn up with remarkable regularity at most parties and in many restaurants. I think you'll find these among the best ever.

Serves 4

¼ cup mayonnaise

1 large egg

½ teaspoon Tabasco Pepper Sauce

1 pound crabmeat, preferably jumbo lump, picked over for pieces of shell

1 cup fine, fresh bread crumbs

½ cup sweet tender corn kernels and juices, cut and scraped from 1 small ear

⅓ cup finely diced roasted sweet pepper (page 28), preferably red

3 tablespoons olive oil
Chipotle Rémoulade, recipe follows

In a medium bowl, whisk together the mayonnaise, egg and Tabasco. Add the crab, bread crumbs, corn and roasted pepper. Mix well, breaking up some of the lumps of crabmeat. Cover and refrigerate for 1 hour.

Divide the crab mixture into 8 equal portions, then pat and squeeze each portion into a ¾-inch-thick cake, transferring the cakes as formed to a flat plate or a flat baking sheet. (The cakes will be fragile and will need careful handling until they begin to cook.)

In a large, heavy nonstick skillet (work in batches or use a second skillet if desired), warm the olive oil over medium heat. With a spatula, carefully slide the crab cakes into the skillet. Cover and cook until golden brown and crisp, about 5 minutes. Carefully turn the cakes, cover the skillet and cook until golden brown, crisp and just cooked through while remaining moist, 4 to 5 minutes. Drain on paper towels.

Set 2 crab cakes on each of 4 plates. Spoon a dollop of the rémoulade beside the cakes and serve immediately.

CHIPOTLE CHILES—Chipotles are red-ripe jalapeños, smoked and then either dried or canned in a vinegary sauce (adobo). The latter are more readily available and more useful. Many supermarkets now stock them (in fact, I have seen a new, larger-size can), or they can be found in specialty food shops. Very hot and very smoky, chipotles are usually minced to distribute the flavor and fire throughout a dish. Brands vary in heat, flavor and thickness of the adobo; shop around and taste-test to find a favorite. Transfer unused chipotles to a tightly covered storage container. They can be refrigerated for up to one month.

Chipotle Rémoulade

This hot and smoky mayonnaise is also good as a dip for grilled shrimp, or on a turkey sandwich or a big, juicy hamburger.

1 cup mayonnaise
4 teaspoons finely chopped green onion (tender tops included)
1 tablespoon minced chipotle chiles en adobo (page 16)
2 teaspoons sauce from the chipotles
2 teaspoons fresh lime juice
1 teaspoon Dijon mustard

In a medium bowl, stir together the mayonnaise, onion, chipotles, chipotle sauce, lime juice and mustard. Cover and refrigerate for up to 3 days. Return to room temperature before using.

Saffron Aioli

2 tablespoons medium-dry white wine, such as Chardonnay
¼ teaspoon packed saffron threads
1 cup mayonnaise
2 teaspoons Roasted Garlic Puree (page 162) or 2 medium garlic cloves, peeled and crushed through a press
Freshly ground black pepper
Salt

In a small saucepan, or in a small bowl in a microwave oven, bring the wine to a boil. Remove from the heat and add the saffron threads. Cool to room temperature. In a small bowl, whisk together the mayonnaise, saffron mixture, Roasted Garlic Puree or 2 garlic cloves, a generous grinding of black pepper and a pinch of salt. Refrigerate overnight before using; the mayonnaise can be prepared up to 3 days in advance. Return it to room temperature before using.

REMOULADE SAUCE—We use the term <u>rémoulade</u> rather freely at Flavors, applying it to any number of bumpy, flavorful mayonnaise-based toppings or dips for all kinds of cold or hot seafood, meats and other catered nibbles. The authentic French version, including chopped sour pickles, maybe minced hard-cooked egg, plus capers, herbs such as tarragon and a bit of anchovy, would certainly not include smoked Mexican chiles! Perhaps a Creole rémoulade, spiked with a bit of cayenne pepper, comes closer to the mark. And certainly tartar sauce is a close cousin. For all our mayonnaise-based sauces, no matter what they're called or to what they are applied, we use mayonnaise from a jar (Hellmann's or Best Foods, actually), rather than risk salmonella contamination, a sure party-wrecker. Low- or nonfat or reduced-calorie mayonnaises can be substituted; some of these are rather sweet and may require that you modify the recipe slightly in compensation.

Pernod-Scented Artichokes with Black Olive Aioli

I never tire of making this simple appetizer, and family (especially my son, Zach) and guests are never bored with eating it. I do vary the artichokes by serving them with a different sauce or flavored mayonnaise each time. In addition to the aioli here, those that work the best are Chipotle Rémoulade (page 17), Pesto Mayonnaise (page 61), Lemon Mayonnaise (page 171) and Saffron Aioli (page 17).

Serves 4

4 large artichokes
2 cups white wine
1 small yellow onion, peeled and thinly sliced
1 lemon, thinly sliced
2 tablespoons olive oil
1 garlic clove, peeled and thinly sliced
1 teaspoon whole black peppercorns
2 teaspoons Pernod
2 bay leaves
¼ teaspoon salt
Black Olive Aioli, for serving

Trim ½ inch off the stem and top ends of the artichokes. Pull off the toughest outer leaves. With kitchen scissors cut off the prickly points of the remaining leaves.

In a large, nonreactive pot, combine the artichokes, wine, onion, lemon slices, oil, garlic, peppercorns, Pernod, bay leaves and salt. Add water to cover the artichokes and set over medium heat. Bring to a boil, then lower the heat slightly and simmer briskly until the artichokes, when tested with the tip of a paring knife from the stem end, are tender, about 50 minutes.

Drain well and serve warm, with a small bowl of the aioli, for each diner, for dipping.

Black Olive Aioli

Makes about 1 cup

1 cup mayonnaise
12 pitted black Greek olives (Kalamatas), halved
2 garlic cloves, peeled and crushed through a press
2 teaspoons fresh lemon juice
Freshly ground black pepper

In a small food processor, combine the mayonnaise, olives, garlic, lemon juice and a generous grinding of pepper. Process with short bursts of power just until thoroughly mixed; good-sized pieces of olive should remain. Transfer to a bowl, adjust the seasoning and stir to mix. Use immediately or cover and refrigerate for up to 3 days. Return to room temperature if chilled before using.

Baja Beach Clams Steamed in Beer

If you have only enjoyed clams dipped in melted butter in a shack near the Connecticut shore, or perhaps steamed open in white wine with garlic in Little Italy, you are going to be pleasantly surprised by how deliciously colorful and different they are in this Mexican-inspired preparation. Digging into a briny bowl of these spicy bivalves, their broth mopped up with good bread, the whole business washed down with plenty of cold beer, is the best kind of festive, laid-back outdoor eating I know.

Serves 4 as an appetizer, 2 as a main course

2 tablespoons olive oil

1 small, fresh jalapeño chile, stemmed, and seeded if desired, and sliced into thin rounds

3 garlic cloves, peeled and minced

2 large plum tomatoes, trimmed and finely chopped (1 cup)

⅓ cup thinly sliced green onion, tender tops included

2 cups light lager beer, such as Corona

24 small hard-shelled clams (littlenecks), well scrubbed and rinsed

⅓ cup finely chopped cilantro

Wedges of lime, as optional accompaniment

In a large, heavy pot over low heat, warm the olive oil. Add the jalapeño and garlic, cover and cook, stirring once or twice, for 3 minutes. Add the tomatoes and green onion, raise the heat slightly and cook uncovered, stirring occasionally, for 3 minutes. Add the beer and clams. Cover the pan and raise the heat. Cook the clams, stirring them occasionally, and transfer them with a slotted spoon as they open to shallow serving bowls. (The time will vary, from only a few minutes to as long as 20.) Discard any clams that have not opened after 20 minutes. Pour the broth through a fine-mesh strainer set over a deep bowl or measuring cup. Spoon the tomato mixture from the strainer over the clams, dividing it equally. Let the broth settle briefly, then spoon it over the clams, leaving the sandy residue behind.

Sprinkle the cilantro over the clams and serve immediately, accompanied by lime wedges for squeezing if desired.

AIOLI—Aioli is not only a powerfully garlicky mayonnaise, but also a traditional Friday—sometimes also Christmas Eve—eating event in which poached fish, cold boiled beef, beets, carrots, sweet peppers, potatoes, cauliflower, artichokes, chickpeas, even octopus or snails are all slathered with the potent stuff. Conquering _le grand aioli_ requires a Provençal stomach and soul—not to mention a cleansing shot of brandy at the approximate halfway point—and in any case is better experienced at the source. Garlic mayonnaises, on the other hand, are endlessly useful and we use them in soups, on sandwiches and as dipping sauces for a variety of zesty nibbles.

For a completely different but equally satisfying summertime clam preparation, lay medium-sized hard-shells (cherrystones) on a medium-hot grill. Cover and cook without turning for 5 to 10 minutes, transferring the clams in their shells as they open to plates lined with a layer of coarse salt. Spoon a dollop of one of the bruschetta toppings on page 14 into each clam and serve immediately.

Lavash with Herbed Cream Cheese and Smoked Salmon

Lavash, a thin, round, Middle Eastern–style flatbread, has been the basis for many of the Flavors appetizers and sandwiches since opening day. Some lavash are crisp and crackerlike but the ones we use, which come two to a package and are about the size of a round bathmat—no kidding—are flexible and taste rather like pita. (Lately, sandwiches using a similar bread are turning up everywhere under the accurately descriptive term "wraps.") Trimmed into a more manageable rectangle, each lavash is spread lightly (for hors d'oeuvre use) or more heavily (for sandwiches) with some savory preparation or other, then rolled and sliced into rounds like a jelly roll. What goes into the lavash is very improvisational; one successful pairing is this one, featuring smoked salmon, cream cheese and dill.

Makes about 24

⅔ cup Herbed Cream Cheese, recipe follows, at
     room temperature
4 teaspoons minced fresh dill, plus sprigs of dill as
     optional garnish
1 lavash shepherd's bread, about 7 ounces, uneven
     sides trimmed to produce a 9-by-17-inch
     rectangle
   Freshly ground black pepper
10 ounces thinly sliced best-quality smoked salmon

In a small bowl, stir together the cream cheese mixture and dill.

Cut the rectangle of lavash crosswise (across the short way) into two smaller rectangles. Evenly spread each rectangle with half the cream cheese mixture. Season generously with pepper. Arrange the salmon over the cream cheese, overlapping the slices slightly, if necessary, and trimming any overhang.

Working from a long side of the rectangle, tightly roll up 1 piece of lavash. With a serrated knife, trim the ends of the roll, then cut it crosswise into ½-inch pieces, transferring the pieces to a serving platter as you go. Repeat with the remaining lavash roll.

The lavash can be served immediately, or tightly cover the plate with plastic wrap and refrigerate for up to 3 hours. Garnish with sprigs of dill if desired before serving.

Herbed Cream Cheese

Top each round of lavash with a dollop of salmon caviar just before serving.

This cream cheese is also good as an omelet filling (along with some chopped ripe tomato) and it's wonderful on a toasted bagel.

Makes about 1½ cups

8 ounces low-fat cream cheese, at room temperature

⅓ cup plain fat-free yogurt

½ cup finely chopped fresh basil

½ cup thinly sliced green onion (tender tops included)

2 tablespoons minced chives

½ teaspoon salt

½ teaspoon freshly ground black pepper

In a medium bowl, mix together the cream cheese, yogurt, basil, green onion, chives, salt and pepper. The cream cheese can be used immediately or can be refrigerated, covered, for up to 3 days. Return to room temperature before using.

Gravlax with Sweet Mustard-Dill Sauce

In this traditional Scandinavian preparation, impeccably fresh salmon is cured with a mixture of salt, sugar and vodka. Seasoned with spices and fresh fennel (my choice) or dill, its texture altered by the two-day curing process into something silky and unique, gravlax is one of the world's greatest raw seafood dishes. Though I have seen it offered as a main course, like most raw fish it's rich and best enjoyed as a starter. Accompany it with a sweet mustard sauce and thinly sliced rye bread and pass finely chopped onions and capers as optional toppings. Sip frozen lemon vodka or caraway-flavored aquavit (set the bottle in the freezer until the liquor becomes syrupy, about 24 hours).

Serves 12

⅓ cup sugar
3 tablespoons salt, preferably coarse sea salt
1 tablespoon coarsely ground fresh white pepper
1 tablespoon roughly crushed fennel seeds
1 tablespoon roughly crushed coriander seeds
1 whole side of fresh salmon, about 2¾ pounds, with the skin on
2 tablespoons lemon vodka
Fronds from 1 head fennel, coarsely chopped (about 1¾ cups), or an equal amount of fresh dill
Sweet Mustard-Dill Sauce, recipe follows, for serving
Finely chopped onions, capers and thinly sliced rye bread, for serving

In a small bowl, mix together the sugar, salt, pepper, fennel and coriander.

With sterile tweezers or needle-nose pliers, pull out any bones remaining in the salmon (a typical side of salmon has about 30). Cut the salmon crosswise in half.

Lay one piece of the salmon, skin-side down, in a shallow, nonreactive dish. Drizzle with 1 tablespoon of the vodka. Sprinkle half the sugar mixture over the salmon. Layer the fennel fronds over the salmon. Drizzle the flesh side of the remaining salmon piece with the remaining vodka. Sprinkle the salmon piece with the remaining sugar mixture. Invert the salmon piece atop the fennel, creating a sandwich of salmon fillet pieces with a filling of fennel. Cover with plastic wrap. Set a small, flat-bottomed dish atop the salmon sandwich. Weight with 2 heavy cans or a small saucepan. Refrigerate for 24 hours.

Remove the weights, the dish and the plastic wrap. With a spatula, turn the salmon sandwich. Lift the salmon piece now on top and baste the fennel layer beneath with the accumulated pan juices. Set the salmon piece in place, cover again with plastic and weight with the dish and cans as before. Refrigerate for another 24 hours.

Remove the weights and plastic wrap. Scrape the fennel and the sugar mixture off the salmon pieces and pat dry. Let the salmon come almost to room temperature. Beginning with the tapered, tail-end piece of salmon, with a thin, sharp knife, cut the gravlax, across the grain and at an angle almost parallel to the work surface, into thin slices, releasing the slices from the skin as you do so. Cut out and discard the darker V-shaped portion of each slice if desired.

Arrange the salmon slices on plates as you go, overlapping them slightly. Repeat with the other piece of salmon, again beginning with the thinner end. Serve immediately, accompanied with the mustard sauce, onions, capers, bread and the peppermill.

Since the salmon has been cured, leftovers can be tightly wrapped in plastic and refrigerated for another day or even two.

Sweet Mustard-Dill Sauce

Makes about ¾ cup

⅔ cup store-bought hot honey mustard
2 tablespoons Dijon mustard
2 tablespoons finely chopped fresh dill

In a small bowl, stir together the honey mustard, Dijon mustard and dill. Cover and let stand at room temperature for 30 minutes before using. Leftover mustard sauce can be refrigerated for up to 1 week.

Because the cutting begins at the thinner end of the salmon, if you have unsliced leftovers, they will come from the thicker, head-end of the fish. These are delicious the next day, grilled as you would a piece of fresh salmon, just until pink at the center and beginning to flake, about 8 minutes total, depending upon thickness. The texture will be slightly firmer than fresh salmon, the fragrance and flavor of the fennel will be apparent, and, because it is not thinly sliced, the gravlax may be slightly salty. Serve it drizzled with any leftover mustard sauce, if desired.

Left to right: Zuppa di Primavera; Roasted Tomato Soup with Basil Oil; Squash, Apple and Ginger Soup

Soups

Comforting in winter, refreshing in summer, nourishing year-round, soups do indeed, as is often quoted, "breathe assurance." Restorative as they are to eat, they may be even more invigorating to make. I'm never happier than when at work on a pot of good, filling soup, knowing that soon loved ones and friends will be inhaling its fragrant vapors and spooning it up. Soups are satisfying without being calorie-dense, which means you can eat your fill without overdoing the fat, and if well planned, as the recipes in this chapter are, with their rich colors, pleasurable textures and—above all—hearty flavors, soups are simply among the most satisfying things I know of to cook and to eat. Hot or cold, for lunch, for supper, as the first course of a big feast or even as dessert, these are my all-time favorite soups. **Cold Red Pepper and Fennel Soup with Summer Herbs • Beautiful Borscht • Curried Vichyssoise • Cold Melon, Mango and Peach Soup • Roasted Tomato Soup with Basil Oil • Zuppa di Primavera • Creamless Corn Soup • Chicken, Corn and Noodle Soup with Saffron • Smoky Heirloom Bean Soup with Rosemary Oil • Duck, Barley and Mushroom Broth • Wild Mushroom Soup • Squash, Apple and Ginger Soup • Creamy Pink Shellfish Chowder • Savory Pumpkin Bisque with Fresh Sage • Chicken Stock • Vegetable Stock**

Cold Red Pepper and Fennel Soup
with Summer Herbs

Though I have lived in such hot places as Texas and Manhattan in the summer, nowhere is the heat more oppressive than in Provence when it sizzles. When a similar swelter befalls you, and until you can catch a fresh breeze from an ocean, lake or river, consider this smooth cooler. Packed with plenty of southern French flavors, it's also beautiful enough to have been photographed for the cover of Food & Wine. *If you have no chervil (an herb whose delicate anise flavor reinforces the fennel bulb, fennel seed and Pernod) increase the basil and parsley by 1 tablespoon each.*

Serves 8 as a first course, 4 as a main course

¼ cup olive oil
6 large sweet red peppers (about 2⅓ pounds), roasted, peeled and chopped
4 cups chopped fresh fennel
2 cups chopped yellow onion
2 cups chopped carrot
1½ cups chopped leek (2 medium leeks, white and pale green parts only)
2 tablespoons minced fresh thyme
3 garlic cloves, peeled and chopped
1 teaspoon fennel seeds
2 bay leaves
5 cups Chicken Stock (page 45) or reduced-sodium canned chicken broth
½ cup medium-dry white wine
2 tablespoons Pernod

Salt
Freshly ground black pepper
2 tablespoons roughly chopped fresh basil
2 tablespoons roughly chopped flat-leaf parsley
2 tablespoons roughly chopped chervil

In a medium-large pot over low heat warm the olive oil. Add the chopped peppers, chopped fennel, onion, carrot, leek, thyme, garlic, fennel seeds and bay leaves. Cover and cook, stirring occasionally, until the vegetables are almost tender, about 20 minutes. Add the chicken stock, wine, Pernod and 1 tablespoon salt. Bring to a simmer, partially cover, and cook, stirring occasionally, until the vegetables are very tender, about 30 minutes.

Cool the soup and remove the bay leaves. Puree the soup in batches in a food processor or blender or force it through

 Though the pepper soup was developed to be a simple picnic dish, the addition of a dollop of garlicky saffron-scented mayonnaise, afloat in the center of a bowl of the crimson soup, transforms it into something sophisticated and elaborate enough for an important summertime dinner party.

the medium blade of a food mill. Refrigerate until very cold, at least 5 hours or preferably overnight.

Adjust the salt and season the soup generously with fresh black pepper. Sprinkle the basil, parsley and chervil over the soup and serve cold.

Roasting peppers softens and partially cooks them, producing a tender texture and smoky sweetness that sautéing cannot impart. Roasting also loosens the indigestible skins, which can then be slipped off rather easily. Directly on the burner racks of a gas stove, under a preheated broiler or on a covered grill over medium-high heat, turn the peppers until the skins are lightly but evenly charred. (Under the broiler the pepper flesh will become more tender, while on a hot grill, which cooks the peppers less, it will remain crunchier.) In a closed paper bag or under an inverted bowl on the work surface, steam the peppers until cool. Rub off the burned peel—don't rinse the peppers or you'll lose crucial flavor—stem, seed and core the peppers and then proceed with the recipe as directed. The same method is used to roast and peel green chiles such as Anaheims or poblanos.

 FENNEL—Fennel here is bulb fennel, or Florence fennel, the delicately anise-flavored fresh vegetable, not the dried seeds (though I love them, too). The fist-sized bulbs, with their hollow, celerylike stalks topped by fragile green fronds, were once hard to locate, but now that Italian and Provençal food are in vogue, it seems that fennel is as well, and I find it in one market or another pretty much year-round. It can be eaten raw, shaved paper-thin into salads or dipped into oil or salt or even a flavored mayonnaise, like many other crudités, but then it can also be braised whole, served on its own as a vegetable, or sautéed and simmered into soups and stews, creating an aroma and flavor far too subtle to be described, though it often is, as "licorice-like." Few visitors to the south of France pass up a chance to enjoy loup au fenouil—bass baked on a bed of fennel stalks, with a splash of Pernod frequently added for emphasis. Buy firm, pale green-white bulbs (no brown spots!), and use within a few days. Don't discard the fronds: They can be minced and added to a dish that is made with fennel just before serving, providing a touch of color as well as a reinforcement of flavor.

Beautiful Borscht

Here is one of the most intensely flavored (not to mention vibrantly colored) cold soups I can think of. Sweet-tart and earthy, it will both fill you up and cool you off. The garnish of cucumber, sour cream and dill is classic, but the borscht can also be served with a drizzle of buttermilk, or with two or three piping-hot steamed new potatoes centered in each bowl. In either of these latter presentations, a generous sprinkle of dill remains a nice final touch.

Serves 12 as a first course, 6 to 8 as a main course

3 pounds (6 medium) beets, stems and roots trimmed to no more than ½ inch long

3 tablespoons canola oil

2 cups chopped yellow onion

3 garlic cloves, peeled and finely chopped

7 cups Chicken Stock (page 45) or reduced-sodium canned chicken broth

⅓ cup red wine vinegar

About ⅓ cup sugar

1¼ teaspoons salt

½ teaspoon freshly ground black pepper

2 cups finely diced hothouse or English cucumber

1 cup sour cream

½ cup finely chopped fresh dill

Position a rack in the middle of the oven and preheat to 400° F. Tightly wrap the beets in pairs in heavy-duty foil.

Bake the beets until they are just tender, about 1 hour and 15 minutes. Cool the beets in the foil to room temperature. The beets can be prepared to this point up to 3 days in advance. Refrigerate in the foil packets.

Peel the beets and with a box grater, grate them coarsely.

In a large, nonreactive pot over medium heat, warm the oil. Add the onion and garlic, cover and cook, stirring occasionally, for 10 minutes. Add the stock, the grated beets, vinegar, ¼ cup of the sugar, the salt and pepper. Bring to a simmer, then partially cover and cook, stirring often, until the beets are tender and the borscht is very thick, 30 to 35 minutes.

Remove from the heat and cool to room temperature. Cover and refrigerate until very cold, preferably overnight.

Adjust the seasoning, adding more sugar if necessary to taste. Ladle the borscht into bowls and garnish with cucumber, sour cream and dill. Serve cold.

Curried Vichyssoise

Potatoes and sour cream—what could be bad? Almost my first tingle of the sophisticated excitement of growing up (I was about twelve, lunching at the Neiman Marcus Zodiac Room) was the realization that some soups could be served cold. I dipped into that tiny cup of chilled vichyssoise with a sense of adventure that I'm not sure has ever quite been duplicated, at least not at the table. It was so different from the hot meal-in-a-bowl kind of soup I was used to, the kind that was eaten with a big spoon, accompanied by plenty of crackers, at the end of a Texas winter day. Vichyssoise still enchants me. I serve it often to catering clients and family alike, and sometimes, to recapture the adventure, I sweeten it as I have here with a little carrot and spice it with a touch of curry powder.

Serves 6 as a first course

3 tablespoons unsalted butter

3 medium leeks, white and pale green parts only, trimmed, finely chopped and rinsed (about 2 cups)

¾ cup chopped carrot

2 teaspoons curry powder

4 cups Chicken Stock (page 45) or reduced-sodium canned chicken broth

2 medium-large russet (baking) potatoes, about 1¼ pounds total, peeled and cut into ½-inch chunks

Salt

¼ teaspoon freshly ground white pepper

½ cup whipping cream

½ cup sour cream or plain yogurt

3 tablespoons thinly sliced chives

1 to 2 tablespoons fresh lemon juice

In a medium soup pot over moderate heat melt the butter. Add the leeks, carrot and curry powder, cover and cook, stirring once or twice, for 10 minutes. Add the chicken stock, potatoes, 1 teaspoon salt and the pepper and bring to a simmer. Partially cover the pan and cook, stirring once or twice, until the potatoes and carrots are tender, 20 to 25 minutes.

Cool the soup slightly, then puree it in batches in a food processor or force it through the medium blade of a food mill. Cool to room temperature. Whisk the cream and sour cream into the soup. Stir in the chives, cover and refrigerate until very cold, at least 5 hours.

Adjust the seasoning, adding salt and lemon juice if the soup seems too rich. Ladle it into chilled soup cups and serve immediately.

CURRY POWDER—Curry powders, like chili powders, are spice blends manufactured to someone else's taste. The trick is to find a brand that suits yours, and then stick with it (even more so than chili powders, curry powders vary widely, not only in heat but in the spices they emphasize). For this cool and creamy starter, a fiery hot curry powder would be completely out of place, and something as prosaic as a well-balanced, freshly opened supermarket brand may well be your best choice.

Cold Melon, Mango and Peach Soup

Served as a first course or as a dessert on a hot summer's day, this pretty golden soup always impresses guests. Asian five-spice powder adds an attractive, exotic note.

Serves 4 to 6

2 cups medium-dry white wine, such as
 Chardonnay
½ cup honey, preferably orange blossom honey
 Zest (colored part of peel) of 1 large orange,
 removed in wide strips with a vegetable peeler
½ teaspoon Asian five-spice powder
4 cups ¾-inch chunks ripe, juicy cantaloupe
2 cups ½-inch chunks ripe, juicy mango
2 cups ½-inch chunks ripe, juicy peach or
 nectarine
3 tablespoons fresh lime juice
¼ teaspoon salt
1 cup fresh blueberries or raspberries, picked over,
 rinsed only if necessary
 Sprigs of fresh mint, as garnish

In a small, nonreactive saucepan, combine the wine, honey, orange zest and five-spice powder. Set over medium heat and bring to a brisk simmer. Cook uncovered, stirring occasionally, until the liquid is reduced to 1½ cups, 10 to 15 minutes. Remove from the heat and cool to room temperature. Discard the orange zest.

Working in batches, in a food processor, puree the can-

 When serving this soup as dessert, ladle it into chilled wide bowls. Float a small scoop of sorbet (raspberry, orange, lemon, peach or mango) in the soup, then garnish it with berries and mint and serve immediately. Biscotti (page 205) or thin slices of toasted Very Lemony Pound Cake (page 214) are nice accompaniments.

taloupe, mango and peach. (For a completely smooth texture, the puree can be forced through a strainer.)

In a bowl, stir together the pureed fruit, reduced wine mixture, lime juice and salt. Cover and refrigerate until very cold, at least 5 hours or overnight for convenience.

Adjust the seasoning. Spoon the soup into wide bowls. Scatter the blueberries over the soup, garnish with a mint sprig and serve cold.

 ASIAN FIVE-SPICE POWDER—Like other seasoning blends (curry powder, chile powder, herbes de Provence), five-spice is a tremendously convenient way to add a boost of flavor to dishes ranging from soups to cookies. The five spices traditionally involved are star anise, cinnamon, cloves, fennel seed and pepper, usually white pepper. That is the order in which you want the ingredient list on the label to run, ensuring that star anise is the main ingredient. (Otherwise, the powerful cinnamon dominates and you might as well use straight cinnamon.) Finding this proportion of ingredients may require some shopping around, although the brand I use, Ka-Me, is widely available in supermarkets. As always with spices, store them away from heat and light and discard the unused portion after six months or so.

Roasted Tomato Soup with Basil Oil

Roasting concentrates the juices in already red-ripe tomatoes, and also caramelizes their natural sugars. The result is an intensified tomato soup experience unlike any other I can think of. The soup is good cold, on a scorching summer's day (it's my son Zach's absolute favorite), but it's also good hot, on a chilly night, made with the last of the tomatoes lingering in an Indian summer garden. Top wedges of focaccia with grated Parmesan cheese and bake until crusty to serve alongside.

Serves 6 to 8 as a first course, 4 as a main course

2½ pounds ripe plum tomatoes, trimmed and halved lengthwise
3 tablespoons olive oil
Salt
1 cup chopped yellow onion
1 bay leaf
2½ cups Chicken Stock (page 45) or

reduced-sodium canned chicken broth
3½ teaspoons Roasted Garlic Puree (page 162)
Freshly ground black pepper
3 to 4 tablespoons fresh lemon juice
2 teaspoons Basil Oil, recipe follows, or use a store-bought oil, such as Consorzio
Sprigs of fresh basil, as optional garnish

Position a rack in the middle of the oven and preheat to 450° F.

On a jelly-roll pan, toss the tomatoes with 1 tablespoon of the olive oil and ¼ teaspoon salt. Spread them in a single layer and roast them, turning once, until they are very soft and lightly browned, about 20 minutes. Cool and chop.

In a medium pan over moderate heat, warm the remaining 2 tablespoons olive oil. Add the onion and bay leaf, cover and cook, stirring occasionally, until the onion is becoming tender and is lightly browned, about 10 minutes. Add the tomatoes, stock, garlic puree, ½ teaspoon salt and a grinding of pepper. Bring to a simmer, partially cover and cook, stirring occasionally, until the tomatoes have almost dissolved into the broth, about 20 minutes.

Remove from the heat and cool. Discard the bay leaf. Force the soup through the medium blade of a food mill, or puree it in a food processor or blender. (The soup can be prepared to this point up to 3 days ahead. Cool completely, cover and refrigerate.)

To serve cold, stir in lemon juice to taste and adjust the seasoning.

To serve hot, in a saucepan over low heat, bring the soup to a simmer. Stir in lemon juice to taste and adjust the seasoning.

Ladle the soup into bowls. Drizzle each serving with ½ teaspoon Basil Oil, garnish with a sprig of basil and serve immediately.

Basil Oil

The oil can also be brushed onto bruschettas before they are grilled or broiled.

Makes about ⅔ cup

1¾ cups chopped fresh basil leaves
⅔ cup cold-pressed extra-virgin olive oil

In a food processor, combine the basil and 3 tablespoons of the oil. Process, scraping down the sides of the work bowl several times, until the basil is partially pureed. With the motor running, gradually add the remaining olive oil through the feed tube. Transfer to a container, cover and let the mixture stand at room temperature for 24 hours. Transfer to a fine strainer set over a bowl. Press on the puree with the back of a spoon to extract all the flavored oil. Cover and store in the refrigerator for up to 1 week, returning the oil to room temperature before using.

One cold soup can be a lunch or a supper, but two, three or four cold soups, along with an array of serve-yourself garnishes, is a cold soup "bar" and one of the nicest ways of staying cool while entertaining. I like to set the soups out in crockery bowls placed in larger bowls of ice. Two good choices would be Beautiful Borscht (page 29) and Curried Vichyssoise (page 30). Set out next to them smaller bowls of the vegetable salsa, plus sour cream or plain yogurt, cucumbers and dill. Supply plenty of small bowls and spoons, so guests can try each soup without reusing a bowl. As always, when soup is on the menu, good crusty bread, in several varieties, is the best accompaniment. Flavors' Apple Crisp (page213) would be a great summery dessert, or you could take the soup theme one step further, and serve Cold Melon, Mango and Peach Soup (page 31). Offer fresh berries for guests to spoon into the soup, and set out a plate of Extra-Spicy Gingersnaps (page 207).

Zuppa di Primavera

This is a light but still satisfying soup literally bursting with green springtime flavor, Italian-style. I first prepared it from an armload of irresistible farmer's market produce, lugged home on a day when I just couldn't say no to one perfect vegetable after another. It's free-form to some extent, so consider this recipe a guide, not a rigid plan, and be prepared to substitute other spring (and, later, summer) produce when necessity or invention require.

Serves 4 as a main course

2 tablespoons olive oil

2 medium leeks, white and pale green parts only, sliced into rounds, separated into rings, rinsed well and drained thoroughly

2 medium carrots, peeled and sliced into thin rounds

2 garlic cloves, peeled and thinly sliced

6 cups Chicken Stock (page 45) or reduced-sodium canned chicken broth

1 teaspoon salt

½ cup dried semolina soup pasta, such as tubetti

10 spears medium asparagus, trimmed and angle-cut into 1-inch pieces

1¼ cups fresh fava beans (from about 1 pound pods), briefly blanched (page 12)

½ pound sugar snap peas, trimmed and angle-cut into 1-inch pieces

¼ pound haricots verts, trimmed and halved crosswise

½ cup julienned fresh basil leaves

About ½ cup freshly grated Parmigiano-Reggiano cheese

In a medium pot over moderate heat, warm the olive oil. Add the leeks, carrots and garlic, cover and cook, stirring once or twice, until the vegetables are almost tender, about 10 minutes.

Add the stock and bring to a simmer. Partially cover the pan, lower the heat slightly and cook 15 minutes. (The soup base can be prepared up to 3 days ahead and will be the better for it. Cool, cover and refrigerate. Return the soup to a simmer before proceeding.)

Stir in the salt and the pasta; cook 5 minutes. Add the asparagus, fava beans, sugar snap peas and haricots verts and simmer another 5 to 7 minutes, or until the pasta and vegetables are just tender. Remove from the heat, stir in the basil, cover and let stand 1 minute.

Adjust the seasoning. Divide the soup among bowls and serve immediately, passing the cheese at the table.

Note: In a pinch, frozen baby limas can be substituted for the fava beans.

Creamless Corn Soup

Perfectly fresh and wonderful sweet corn has its own creamy quality, letting me transform it into a soup that seems elegantly enriched but which is, in fact, light, low-calorie and stock-free. The soup is also good cold. Just add a bit more salt to taste to compensate for the chilling.

Serves 6 as a first course, 4 as a main course

1 tablespoon canola oil

2 cups finely chopped leeks

2 cups coarsely chopped carrots

1½ cups coarsely chopped celery

1 cup coarsely chopped yellow onion

4 cups corn kernels and juices, cut and scraped from about 4 medium ears

½ medium seeded jalapeño, finely chopped

5 cups water

3¾ teaspoons salt

¼ teaspoon freshly ground black pepper

¼ cup thinly sliced chives

In a 5-quart pan over medium heat, warm the oil. Add the leeks, carrots, celery and onion. Partially cover and cook, stirring occasionally, until the vegetables are translucent, about 20 minutes. Add the corn and jalapeño and continue to cook partially covered, stirring occasionally, until the vegetables are lightly browned, another 10 minutes. Add the water, salt and pepper and bring to a simmer. Cook until just heated through, about 3 minutes.

Cool slightly, then strain the soup, pressing hard with the back of a spoon to extract all the juices. Discard the solids.

Return the soup to the pan and set over low heat, stirring often, just until hot. Adjust the seasoning and serve immediately, sprinkling each portion with some of the chives.

CORN—Perhaps the oldest cultivated crop, corn would barely exist without humankind's intervention. (The ancient ancestor plant produces ears only an inch or two long, with kernels so tiny they are hard to see. From this unlikely beginning, modified by humans, all modern corn is descended.) For corn lovers like me, the good news is that there is more delicious corn around than ever before. Improved hybrid types now stay sweet and tender longer, meaning I need not wait until the water boils before I pick the ears, meaning that even in the supermarket, even in months other than July and August, I can find corn that is so good it makes me want to laugh out loud. I still eat plenty of ears simply boiled (five minutes or less) and buttered (usually in the heat and humidity of summer), but I also scrape the kernels and sweet juices from the cobs and use them in all sorts of other ways—sautéed with a touch of onion, simmered in a little cream with a bit of fresh basil, baked into a velvety custard, stirred into corn bread, cooked up into a creamy but creamless soup, even churned into ice cream!

Chicken, Corn and Noodle Soup with Saffron

Saffron, one of my favorite spices, turns up often in the cooking of southern France, where its red-orange color and mysterious, slightly medicinal flavor make it as essential to good cooking there as cilantro is in Mexico. Other cooks around the world also use a lot of saffron, including, somewhat surprisingly, the Pennsylvania Dutch. One such usage is in Lancaster County's famed chicken, corn and noodle soup, from which this slightly lighter but still rib-sticking version is descended. I like it as the first course of a big feast, like Thanksgiving dinner, or as a one-pot main course on a chilly weekend night.

Serves 8 as a first course, 4 as a main course

8½ cups Chicken Stock (page 45) or reduced-sodium canned chicken broth

2 pounds assorted chicken parts, including both halves of a split breast, a thigh, a wing, the neck and giblets (except the liver)

3 tablespoons unsalted butter

2 cups chopped yellow onion

1½ cups finely diced carrot

¾ cup finely diced celery

3 garlic cloves, peeled and minced

¼ teaspoon dried thyme, crumbled

4 ounces dried wide egg noodles

¼ teaspoon roughly crumbled saffron threads

¾ teaspoon freshly ground black pepper

1½ cups canned or thawed corn kernels, drained

2 tablespoons minced flat-leaf parsley

2 tablespoons minced celery leaves

Salt

In a large pot, combine the stock and chicken pieces. Set over medium heat and bring to a simmer. Partially cover and cook, stirring occasionally and skimming as necessary, until the chicken is just cooked through while remaining juicy, 15 to 20 minutes. Remove from the heat. With a slotted spoon, transfer the chicken to a cutting board. Strain and degrease the broth and reserve it. When the chicken is cool enough to

SAFFRON—Saffron is the dried stigmas from a particular type of crocus (don't try to make your own; some varieties are poisonous). Cultivated as a seasoning since antiquity, the very labor-intensiveness of its harvesting make it extraordinarily expensive. (One source suggests it takes a quarter of a million blossoms to yield 1 pound of saffron!) Fortunately, a little goes a long way (a pound, even for a saffron lover like me, would be something like a lifetime supply). In fact, too heavy a hand with the saffron is a sure way to turn off diners experiencing it for the first time, since, at certain intensity levels, it tastes exactly the way I imagine iodine tastes. On the other hand, used with restraint, the red-orange threads (preferable to ground saffron, whose purity is somewhat suspect) add an ineffable color plus an undeniably attractive flavor to soups, sauces, stews, Spanish paella, the risotto that traditionally accompanies osso bucco alla Milanese and Mediterranean tomato and seafood dishes of all sorts. Expect saffron to be expensive. It should be a bright, rich red-gold, not a faded yellow; buy and use it as needed to ensure freshness.

handle, remove the skin, bones and cartilage; finely dice the meat.

In the same pot, over low heat, melt the butter. Add the onion, carrot, celery, garlic and thyme. Cover and cook, stirring occasionally, for 10 minutes. Add the broth and bring to a simmer. Partially cover and cook until the vegetables are almost tender, about 20 minutes.

Add the noodles, saffron and pepper and simmer for 5 minutes. Add the chicken and corn and simmer until heated through and the noodles are very tender, another 2 to 3 minutes. Remove from the heat and stir in the parsley and celery leaves. Adjust the seasoning. Serve hot.

(The soup can be prepared completely up to 3 days in advance. After the noodles have simmered for 3 minutes, remove the soup from the heat and cool to room temperature. Add the chicken and corn, cover and refrigerate. Bring the soup to a simmer over medium heat, stirring occasionally; do not overcook.)

Smoky Heirloom Bean Soup with Rosemary Oil

The heirloom beans known as Anasazi (named for the ancient cliff-dwelling residents of southern Colorado and New Mexico) simmer up with a sweet, meaty intensity unlike any others. Plenty of garlic, flavor from smoky ham hocks and a drizzle of pungent rosemary oil complete this hearty soup, which combined with a big green salad and corn bread, makes a great supper. Though the results will differ, other beans, heirloom or otherwise, can be successfully substituted.

Serves 6 to 8 as a main course

1 pound dried Anasazi (also called Jacob's cattle) beans, picked over
3 tablespoons olive oil
2 cups chopped yellow onion
1 cup chopped carrot
⅔ cup chopped celery
4 garlic cloves, peeled and chopped
1¼ teaspoons dried marjoram, crumbled
¾ teaspoon dried thyme, crumbled
¼ teaspoon crushed red pepper
1 bay leaf
4 cups Chicken Stock (page 45) or reduced-sodium canned chicken broth

4 cups water
2 small ham hocks weighing 1 pound total
    (or, if you're lucky enough to find one,
    1 large smoked turkey wing, about 1 pound,
    separated into segments)
⅓ cup finely chopped flat-leaf parsley
    Salt
    Freshly ground black pepper
    About 4 teaspoons Rosemary Oil, see Note, or
    use a store-bought oil, such as Consorzio

In a large bowl, cover the beans with cold water and let soak for at least 4 hours or overnight for convenience.

In a 5½-quart pot over low heat, warm the olive oil. Add the onion, carrot, celery, garlic, marjoram, thyme, crushed red pepper and bay leaf and cook, covered, stirring occasionally, for 10 minutes. Drain the beans and add them, the stock, water and ham hocks to the pot. Bring to a simmer, partially cover and cook, skimming occasionally, for 1½ hours. Transfer the ham hocks to a cutting board.

If necessary, continue to simmer the soup, partially covered, adding additional boiling water if the soup threatens to scorch, until the beans are very tender, another 30 minutes or so. Remove from the heat and cool slightly.

When the ham hocks are cool enough to handle, remove any meat from the bones and chop it.

Puree about half the soup in a food processor, or force it through the medium blade of a food mill. Return the puree to the remaining soup. Stir in the chopped ham. (The soup can be prepared to this point up to 3 days in advance. Cover tightly and refrigerate, returning the soup to a simmer over low heat before proceeding.)

Stir in the parsley. Adjust the seasoning. Ladle into bowls, drizzle each with about ½ teaspoon rosemary oil and serve immediately.

Note: Follow the recipe for Basil Oil on page 33, substituting 3 tablespoons minced fresh rosemary for the basil.

 HEIRLOOM BEANS—Of the nearly two thousand varieties of beans that exist, only a handful show up in tidy bags at the supermarket. Many of the rest, for whatever reason, have fallen out of commercial favor and have faded away or almost disappeared. Among these are beans that are delicious, colorful and/or have wonderful names like Rattlesnake, Esther's Brown and Oklahoma Cave. As beans have boomed in popularity, thanks to their many nutritional benefits as well as an increased interest in meatless eating, some of these varieties have been revived. Small growers often begin with literally a handful of beans (seed preservation organizations parcel them out sparingly to gardeners who will plant them, producing more beans for storage and keeping the supply vigorous) that can take years to "grow out" to viable commercial quantities. Such rescued bean varieties are called heirlooms, and they are increasingly available in specialty food shops and natural-food stores and catalogs. Many are pinto bean relatives, and I confess that once they are cooked, the colors nearly always fade and there is little to differentiate them from their supermarket cousins. Others, like the Anasazi, truly do taste different and, more important, they taste better. Bean lovers will surely want to seek them out.

Duck, Barley and Mushroom Broth

A leftover roast duck is something, I suppose, that could only happen to a caterer. Believe me, it does, and when that happy accident occurs, I immediately set a pot of this nourishing soup to simmering. (You, on the other hand, may want to head for Chinatown, where the already cooked ducks for sale often cost less than those you must prepare yourself.) Reminiscent of Scotch broth, which would be made with lamb, the carrot-and-barley-studded brew is wonderfully delicious and fortifying. Make it a day ahead, if you can, to let the deep flavors develop further.

Serves 6 to 8 as a main course

1 duck, about 5½ pounds, thawed if frozen, giblets reserved for another use, visible fat removed

1 ounce mixed dried wild mushrooms

About 9 cups Chicken Stock (page 45) or reduced-sodium canned chicken broth

3 tablespoons olive oil

2 cups chopped yellow onion

1 cup chopped carrot

1 cup chopped celery

6 garlic cloves, peeled and finely chopped

¾ teaspoon dried thyme, crumbled

1 bay leaf

⅓ cup red wine, such as Merlot

Salt

Freshly ground black pepper

⅓ cup medium-sized pearl barley

⅓ cup finely chopped flat-leaf parsley

Position a rack in the middle of the oven and preheat to 400° F. Set the duck on a rack in a shallow roasting pan. Set the pan in the oven and roast the duck, occasionally pouring off the rendered fat, until the duck is lightly browned and almost cooked through except near the thigh joints, about 1 hour. Remove from the oven and let stand on the rack until cool. (The duck can be roasted up to 1 day in advance. Wrap well and refrigerate.)

In a strainer under cold running water, rinse the mushrooms. In a small pan, bring 2 cups of the chicken stock to a boil. Add the mushrooms, remove from the heat, cover and let stand, stirring occasionally, until cool. With a slotted spoon, lift the mushrooms from the stock. Let the stock settle, then pour off and reserve the clear portion, discarding any sandy residue. Finely chop the mushrooms.

Remove and discard the duck skin. Remove the meat from the duck and cut it into ¼-inch dice.

In a medium nonreactive soup pot over moderate heat, warm the olive oil. Add the onion, mushrooms, carrot, celery, garlic, thyme and bay leaf. Cover and cook, stirring occasionally, for 10 minutes. Uncover, raise the heat to high and cook, stirring often, until the vegetables are lightly browned, another 5 to 7 minutes. Add enough of the remaining stock to the mushroom soaking liquid to equal 8 cups. Add this mixture, the duck meat, wine, 1 teaspoon salt and a generous grinding of pepper to the broth. Bring to a boil and add the barley. Partially cover and simmer, stirring once or twice, for 30 minutes. Uncover and cook, stirring often, until the soup has thickened and the barley is tender, another 10 to 15 minutes. Adjust the seasoning. Stir in the parsley, remove from the heat, cover and let stand 1 minute. Serve hot.

Wild Mushroom Soup

My appreciation for wild (and cultivated exotic) mushrooms really sprang up when I met John Gottfried nearly fifteen years ago. A specialty-mushroom dealer in New York City and a founder of The Gourmet Garage, he introduced me to porcini, morels, chanterelles and shiitakes, not to mention lobster mushrooms, chicken-of-the-woods and truffles, treating me to dishes featuring them in some of his best client restaurants. It was a real education, one that remains ongoing as more and more hand-harvested, truly wild mushrooms, plus a few new cultivated types, continue to turn up in the city's best produce shops. One of the most delicious ways to experience the woodsy harvest is in this intense mushroom soup, in which a mixture of dried mushrooms is supplemented by meaty fresh portobellos.

Serves 6 as a first course, 4 as a main course

1 ounce dried wild mushrooms
About 6 cups Chicken Stock (page 45) or reduced-sodium canned chicken broth
5 tablespoons unsalted butter
1¼ pounds (3 large) portobello mushrooms, stems discarded, caps chopped into ¼-inch pieces
Salt
1 cup finely chopped yellow onion
1 cup finely chopped carrot
1 cup finely chopped leek (white and pale-green parts only)
3 garlic cloves, peeled and chopped
½ teaspoon dried thyme, crumbled
1 bay leaf
2 tablespoons unbleached all-purpose flour
½ cup medium-dry (Sercial) Madeira wine
Freshly ground black pepper
⅓ cup whipping cream, optional
¼ cup finely chopped flat-leaf parsley

In a strainer under cold water, rinse the dried mushrooms. In a small saucepan, bring 2 cups of the chicken stock to a boil. Add the rinsed mushrooms, remove from the heat and let stand, stirring occasionally, until the liquid is cool and the mushrooms are reconstituted.

With a slotted spoon, remove the mushrooms from the liquid, pressing as much of the liquid out of them and back into the pan as possible; finely chop the mushrooms. Let the liquid settle, then pour off and reserve the clear portion; there should be about 1½ cups. Discard the sandy residue.

In a 5-quart pot over medium heat, melt the butter. Add the portobellos and 1 teaspoon salt. Cover and cook, stirring occasionally, until the mushrooms have rendered their juices, about 5 minutes. Add the chopped wild mushrooms, onion, carrot, leek, garlic, thyme and bay leaf. Lower the heat, cover and cook, stirring occasionally, until the vegetables are becoming tender, about 10 minutes more. Sprinkle the flour over the vegetables and cook, stirring often, for 2 minutes. Add the Madeira, raise the heat to high and cook, tossing and stirring often, until the liquid has evaporated, about 2 minutes.

Stir in the remaining 4 cups chicken stock, the reserved mushroom liquid and ½ teaspoon pepper. Bring to a simmer, partially cover and cook, stirring occasionally, until the

DRIED MUSHROOMS—Truly wild mushrooms are hand-gathered in the woods and are dried to preserve them for year-round use. (Some cultivated exotic mushrooms, such as shiitakes, can also be found dried.) Due to moisture loss—not to mention the labor involved—dried mushrooms are expensive, but an ounce (about 1 cup) will richly flavor a dish feeding at least six diners. Sometimes found in bulk, more increasingly sold in bags or even plastic jars, dried mushrooms of whatever variety should be free from dust or cobwebs, which indicate insect infestation. Store them away from heat and light (in the freezer in humid climates) and use them within a year or so. Dried mushrooms are rinsed to rid them of grit (hand-harvested in the wild, they have been subjected to minimal processing), then soaked in hot liquid, preferably one that can be incorporated into the dish, to reconstitute them. Less expensive fresh mushrooms are sometimes used in the dish to augment the bounty. The reconstituted mushrooms still need to be cooked to fully tenderize them and extract every drop of flavor.

vegetables are very tender and the soup has reduced to 6 cups, about 30 minutes.

Cool slightly, then transfer half the soup to a food processor and puree, or force it through the medium blade of a food mill. Return the puree to the soup pan and stir in the cream if you are using it. (The soup can be prepared to this point up to 3 days in advance. Cool completely, cover and refrigerate.)

In a medium pot over low heat, bring the soup to a simmer. Stir in the parsley and adjust the seasoning. Serve hot.

Squash, Apple and Ginger Soup

This easy, delicious soup—a favorite with catering clients—is wonderful proof of the theory that ingredients that come into season together are naturally complementary. Autumn, then, is the time to simmer up a pot of this golden potage (ginger really knows no season, but it does add a lively kick to an otherwise sweet and mellow dish). Try the soup as the starter in a menu with pork or duck as the main course, or serve it as lunch or a light supper.

Serves 8 as a first course, 4 as a main course

2 small butternut squash (2½ pounds total)
3 tablespoons unsalted butter
3 small Granny Smith apples (about 1¼ pounds total), cored, peeled and chopped
1½ cups finely chopped yellow onion
3 tablespoons minced peeled fresh ginger

2 garlic cloves, peeled and chopped
6 cups Vegetable Stock (page 46) or canned vegetable broth
1 teaspoon salt
½ teaspoon freshly ground black pepper
½ cup whipping cream, optional

Position a rack in the middle of the oven and preheat to 450° F. Line a jelly-roll pan with foil.

Halve the squash lengthwise and with a sharp metal spoon scrape out and discard all the seeds and fibers. Lay the squash halves, cut sides down, on the jelly-roll pan and bake them until they are very tender when pierced with a fork, about 40 minutes. Remove the jelly-roll pan from the oven and when the squash is just cool enough to handle, scoop the flesh, including any well-browned edges, out of the peels. Chop and reserve the flesh.

In a large pot over moderate heat melt the butter. Add the apple, onion, ginger and garlic and cook uncovered, stirring once or twice, until lightly browned, 15 to 20 minutes. Add the stock, reserved squash, salt and pepper and bring to a simmer. Partially cover the pan and cook the soup, stirring occasionally, until the apples are very tender, 30 to 35 minutes. Remove from the heat and cool slightly.

Puree the soup in batches in a food processor or blender, or force it through a food mill fitted with the medium blade.

The soup can be prepared up to 3 days in advance, and will taste the better for it. Cool, cover and refrigerate.

Return the soup to the pan. Add the cream if you are using it, and heat, stirring often, until steaming, about 5 minutes. Adjust the seasoning. Ladle the soup into bowls and serve hot.

Note: A spoonful of sweetly caramelized apples and a dollop of ginger cream will transform this simple country soup into a dazzling starter. Or, sprinkle it with crumbled Gorgonzola (about 1 cup), diced raw red apple (about $^3/_4$ cup) and chopped pistachios or toasted pumpkin seeds (about $^1/_2$ cup).

Caramelized Apples

In a medium skillet over moderate heat, melt 3 tablespoons unsalted butter. Add 2 medium-large cored, peeled and diced Granny Smith apples and cook, stirring often, until lightly browned, about 5 minutes. Add 1 tablespoon packed golden brown sugar, a big pinch of salt and a generous grinding of black pepper and cook, stirring, until the apples are well browned and glazed, another 5 minutes. Use hot.

Ginger Cream

In a small bowl, whisk ⅓ cup chilled whipping cream into soft peaks. Stir in 1 tablespoon fresh ginger juice (made by finely shredding the ginger on a grater and pressing it through a sieve set over a small bowl).

Creamy Pink Shellfish Chowder

This rich, pretty dish makes a perfectly elegant main course on a chilly fall or winter night. Serve it with the Frisée, Roquefort and Pear Salad with Pistachios on page 146, plus Corn Bread (page 177), and offer baked apples (page 187) for dessert.

Serves 6 as a main course

2 medium-sized red-skinned potatoes, about 1⅓ pounds total, peeled and cut into ½-inch dice
Salt
4 tablespoons (½ stick) unsalted butter
2 cups chopped yellow onion
¾ cup finely chopped celery
1 large carrot, peeled and finely chopped
1 tablespoon Hungarian sweet paprika
1 teaspoon dried thyme, crumbled
¼ teaspoon fennel seeds
1 cup bottled clam juice
1 cup medium-dry white wine, such as Chardonnay
1 (14-ounce) can Italian plum tomatoes, crushed, with their juices
2 cups half-and-half
1 tablespoon tomato paste
Freshly ground black pepper
¾ pound (about 28) medium shrimp, shelled and deveined
¾ pound bay scallops
½ cup finely chopped flat-leaf parsley
⅓ cup medium-dry (Amontillado) sherry

Bring a small saucepan of water to a boil over high heat. Add the potatoes and 1 teaspoon salt and cook, stirring once or twice, until almost tender, about 6 minutes. Drain.

In a medium soup pot over moderate heat, melt the butter. Add the onion, celery, carrot, paprika, thyme and fennel seeds. Cover and cook, stirring often, for 10 minutes. Add the clam juice, white wine, tomatoes and their juices and the half-and-half. Stir in the tomato paste, ¾ teaspoon salt and a generous grinding of pepper. Bring to a simmer, partially cover and lower the heat. Simmer, stirring occasionally, for 20 minutes. Add the potatoes and simmer for 10 minutes. The soup can be prepared to this point up to 1 day in advance. Cool, cover and refrigerate. Rewarm over low heat.

Add the shrimp, scallops, parsley and sherry. Simmer until the shrimp are curled and pink and the scallops are opaque, 3 to 5 minutes. Adjust the seasoning and serve immediately.

Savory Pumpkin Bisque with Fresh Sage

Here is another fine soup for starting off an autumn feast. It's always a pleasant surprise to taste a non-sweet pumpkin dish, and people may at first not quite know what they're eating—but they'll certainly clean their bowls.

Serves 8 as a first course, 6 as a main course

3 tablespoons unsalted butter

1½ cups chopped leek (white and pale green parts only)

1½ cups chopped carrot

½ cup chopped yellow onion

4 garlic cloves, peeled and chopped

½ teaspoon dried thyme, crumbled

1 bay leaf

6½ cups Chicken Stock (page 45) or reduced-sodium canned chicken broth

1 (29-ounce) can solid-pack pumpkin (not pie filling)

2 tablespoons packed dark brown sugar

Salt

Freshly ground black pepper

¼ teaspoon freshly grated nutmeg

⅓ cup whipping cream, optional

2 tablespoons minced fresh sage leaves

In a large, heavy pot over low heat, melt the butter. When it foams, add the leek, carrot, onion, garlic, thyme and bay leaf. Cover and cook, stirring once or twice, for 10 minutes. Add the chicken stock, pumpkin, brown sugar, 1 teaspoon salt, ½ teaspoon pepper and the nutmeg. Bring to a simmer, then partially cover, lower the heat and cook, stirring occasionally, for 30 minutes. Remove from the heat.

Cool slightly, then puree the soup in batches in a food processor or blender or force it through the medium blade of a food mill. The recipe can be prepared to this point up to 3 days in advance. Cool completely, then cover and refrigerate.

In a large pan over low heat, bring the soup to a simmer. Stir in the cream, if you are using it, and the sage. Adjust the seasoning. Simmer, stirring often, for 5 minutes. Serve hot.

 Scoop out mini-pumpkins. Set them on a baking sheet and bake at 350° F. until heated through (they do not actually need to cook) or steam them in a vegetable steamer. Set the pumpkins on plates, ladle the soup into them and sprinkle with chopped hulled pumpkin seeds, also known as pepitas (available in health-food stores), and a bit more minced fresh sage, if desired. Serve immediately.

Chicken Stock

Making chicken stock takes only time and a big pot—fine kitchen skills are not required. Although canned broths have improved (they are leaner and less salty than they used to be), there's still nothing like the deep sweet flavor and incomparably silky texture of a soup or sauce based upon homemade stock. Here is our recipe tester Rhonda Stieglitz's excellent version.

Makes about 2 quarts

    2 tablespoons olive oil
    4 pounds chicken wings, backs and necks
    3 cups thinly sliced leek (white and pale-green
        parts only)
    3 cups coarsely chopped carrot
    1 cup chopped yellow onion
    1 celery rib, coarsely chopped
   14 cups water
    2 cups white wine, such as Chardonnay
    8 sprigs flat-leaf parsley
   10 whole peppercorns
    2 bay leaves
    ¼ teaspoon dried thyme
    1 teaspoon salt

In an 8-quart pot over high heat warm the oil. Pat the chicken pieces dry. Add them to the oil and cook uncovered, stirring occasionally, until evenly browned, about 30 minutes. Transfer the chicken pieces to a bowl. To the fat remaining in the pan, add the leek, carrot, onion and celery. Cook uncovered, stirring occasionally, until browned, about 10 minutes. Return the chicken pieces to the pot. Add 6 cups of the water, 1 cup of the wine, the parsley, peppercorns, bay leaves and thyme. Bring to a boil, scraping to dissolve the browned deposits from the bottom of the pot.

Lower the heat and simmer uncovered, stirring occasionally, until reduced by half, about 1 hour. Add 4 cups of the water, the remaining 1 cup wine and the salt. Simmer uncovered, stirring occasionally, until reduced by half, about 40 minutes. Add the remaining 4 cups water and simmer uncovered, stirring often, until the stock is richly flavored and reduced by about one-third, 25 to 35 minutes.

Strain, discarding the solids. Refrigerate until cold, preferably overnight. Remove any solidified fat. The stock can be refrigerated for up to 2 days or frozen for up to 1 month.

Vegetable Stock

Though canned vegetable stock is available these days (and it works just fine in our meatless soups), when I really want to do the job right I simmer up a batch of this. It is, hands-down, the best vegetable stock I have ever tasted (almost good enough to eat as is, perhaps with a handful of soup pasta and a dice of small mixed vegetables simmered in). Make it on a hanging-around-the-house kind of day, and freeze it for future batches of soup.

Makes 2 quarts

3 tablespoons olive oil
3 medium-large yellow onions, about 1½ pounds total, unpeeled, sliced
2 large unpeeled carrots, scrubbed and coarsely chopped
2 large ribs celery, coarsely chopped
1 cup finely chopped mushroom stems
4 garlic cloves, unpeeled, chopped
4 quarts water
2 large unpeeled parsnips, scrubbed and coarsely chopped
2 leeks, green parts only, cleaned and coarsely chopped
1 cup coarsely chopped flat-leaf parsley stems
1 medium baking potato, peeled and chopped
1 (6-ounce) can tomato paste
⅓ cup soy sauce, preferably tamari
1½ tablespoons dried thyme, crumbled
3 large bay leaves
2 teaspoons salt
1 teaspoon freshly ground black pepper

In a stockpot, heat the oil. Add the onions, carrots, celery, mushroom stems and garlic. Cook over high heat, stirring often, until well browned, 15 to 20 minutes.

Add the water, parsnips, leeks, parsley stems, potato, tomato paste, soy sauce, thyme, bay leaves, salt and pepper. Bring to a rapid boil. Lower the heat and simmer uncovered, stirring occasionally, until reduced by half, 1½ to 2 hours.

Cool slightly, then pour the stock through a strainer set over a large bowl. Press hard on the solids with the back of a spoon to extract all the liquid. Discard the solids. Refrigerate the stock to mellow the flavors for at least 1 day. The stock can be refrigerated for up to 3 days or frozen for up to 1 month.

Sandwiches

Grilled Portobello Hero
Loaf with Smoky Tomatoes,
Ricotta and Arugula

In the rush of daily life (not just a New York City problem), grabbing a sandwich can be a crucial time-saver. At home, sandwiches take on a more serious air, the very best sort of casual lunch and supper party fare for family and guests. The challenge in either case is to make sure the sandwich is lively, complex and interesting, an artful whole combining bread, filling and condiments. Here are the absolute favorites from Flavors' huge repertoire. **Santa Fe–Style Bacon-and-Egg-Salad Tortilla Sandwiches • Grilled Portobello Hero Loaf with Smoky Tomatoes, Ricotta and Arugula • Low-Fat Tuna and Fennel Salad Pitas • BBQ Chicken Breast Sandwiches with Mustardy Slaw • Grilled Caesar Chicken Sandwiches with Fennel • Chris's Turkey Salad Sandwiches • Black Forest Ham Sandwiches with Dijon-Brie Spread • Smoked Turkey and Avocado Sandwiches with Tangy Corn Relish • Roast Leg of Lamb Sandwiches with Smoky White Bean Spread • Salami and Provolone Panini with Pesto Mayonnaise**

Santa Fe–Style Bacon-and-Egg-Salad Tortilla Sandwiches

In Santa Fe, breakfast may well be the liveliest meal of the day, with many of the most interesting restaurants in town already closed by two in the afternoon. Among morning favorites is the breakfast burrito, a scrambled egg–filled tortilla, usually including meat, cheese and fiery red or green chile. We don't do eggs to order at Flavors, but this breakfast (lunch, or supper) sandwich, in which a green chile–spiked bacon-and-egg salad is folded into a tortilla, is every bit as satisfying as the Santa Fe sort. These are wonderfully portable and make good car snacks or lunch-box fare.

Serves 4

1 medium-sized red-skinned potato, about 8 ounces
1 medium poblano chile or 2 long green (Anaheim, New Mexico or pasilla) chiles, roasted (page 28), peeled and chopped
⅓ cup mayonnaise
1 teaspoon fresh lime juice
6 hard-cooked eggs, shelled and coarsely chopped
4 strips thick-sliced preservative-free bacon, cooked crisp and coarsely chopped
4 10-inch flour tortillas
Salsa, as optional accompaniment

In a medium saucepan, cover the potato with cold water. Set over medium heat and bring to a simmer. Partially cover and cook, stirring once or twice, until the potato is tender, about 30 minutes. Drain and cool. Coarsely chop the potato.

Position a rack in the middle of the oven and preheat to 200° F.

In a medium bowl, whisk together the chopped chile, mayonnaise and lime juice. Add the eggs, potato and bacon and stir well.

Heat the tortillas in the oven just until warm and flexible, about 2 minutes. Lay 1 tortilla on a plate. Spoon one-fourth of the egg mixture down the center of the tortilla. Fold up the bottom, then fold in the sides, creating a burrito shape. Repeat with the remaining egg mixture and tortillas. With a serrated knife, angle-cut each sandwich in half. Serve immediately, accompanied by salsa if desired.

Grilled Portobello Hero Loaf with Smoky Tomatoes, Ricotta and Arugula

I developed this sandwich for a Food & Wine *magazine picnic piece featuring the fashion designer Betsey Johnson. Since she is a vegetarian, it is meatless, but because of the hearty, smoky quality of the grilled mushrooms, it's very satisfying. On the other hand, it is also perfectly delicious (don't tell Betsey) with a few strips of crisp-cooked, preservative-free bacon tucked in next to the mushrooms.*

Makes 4 sandwiches

6 **tablespoons olive oil**

4 **tablespoons balsamic vinegar**

2 **tablespoons soy sauce, preferably tamari**

1 **garlic clove, peeled and crushed through a press**

Freshly ground black pepper

4 **medium portobello mushrooms (1¼ pounds total), stemmed**

5 **large, ripe plum tomatoes, halved lengthwise, interiors scooped out**

Salt

2 **cups wood chips, preferably hickory**

1 **baguette-type crusty bread (21 inches long, 3 inches wide)**

½ **cup ricotta cheese**

About 16 arugula leaves

In a shallow, nonreactive dish, whisk together 3 tablespoons of the olive oil, 3 tablespoons of the vinegar, the soy sauce, garlic and a generous grinding of pepper. Add the mushroom caps, turning to coat well, cover, and marinate, basting occasionally, for 1 hour.

Drizzle the tomatoes on both sides with 1 tablespoon of the remaining olive oil. Season lightly with salt and pepper.

Prepare a hot charcoal fire or preheat a gas grill (medium-high). When the fire is hot, distribute the wood chips if you are using them. Position the grill rack about 6 inches above the heat.

When the grill is hot, lay the mushroom caps on the rack. Cover and grill until lightly marked, about 3 minutes. Baste with any unabsorbed marinade (use it all), turn the caps, and grill another 2 to 3 minutes, or until well browned, tender and smoky. Transfer to a cutting board. Cut the mushrooms in half.

Lay the tomatoes cut sides down on the rack, cover and grill until lightly marked, about 2½ minutes. Turn, cover and grill until lightly browned and fairly tender, another 2 to 2½ minutes. Transfer to a plate and let cool, cut sides down.

With a serrated knife, cut the loaf of bread in half horizontally. Brush the cut sides lightly with 1 tablespoon of the remaining olive oil. Toast the bread on the grill, cut sides down, until lightly marked, about 1 minute.

Evenly spread the cut side of the bottom half of the loaf with the ricotta; season with salt and pepper. Lay the tomato halves over the ricotta. Lay the arugula leaves over the tomatoes. Drizzle evenly with the remaining 1 tablespoon olive oil and the remaining 1 tablespoon balsamic vinegar. Lay the mushroom pieces over the arugula. Season with salt and fresh pepper to taste. Set the top half of the bread loaf in place and press gently. With a serrated knife, cut the loaf crosswise into 4 sandwiches. Serve within an hour or two of completion.

PORTOBELLO MUSHROOMS—These huge brown mushrooms (sometimes called portobellas) are merely fully grown cremini mushrooms (sometimes called Roman). And cremini are merely a slightly heartier-tasting variety of the common white mushroom (sometimes called button). If you've followed all this, you've probably realized that portobellos are just big brown button mushrooms (although they cost several times as much per pound). In a final irony, only a few years ago they were consigned to the compost heap by mushroom growers who considered them too big and too old to sell. Why the new popularity and price tag? Their size is wonderfully dramatic, for one, and recalls the thick slabs of porcini (often grilled) that are enjoyed in Italy. Second, as they mature and their caps open away from the stems, the portobellos begin to dehydrate. Since mushrooms are mostly water, this concentrates their flavor, and while they do not approach the woodsy intensity of a real wild mushroom, they do taste significantly stronger than their cultivated, closed-up cousins. Buy firm, whole specimens and use them soon—remember, they're almost compost.

Low-Fat Tuna and Fennel Salad Pitas

The light anise taste of fennel is nicely complementary to fish of all kinds, even canned tuna. The mayo-free sandwich filling can also be served plated, atop dressed, mixed salad greens, with wedges or slices of tomato alongside.

Makes 3 sandwiches

3½ teaspoons cold-pressed extra-virgin olive oil
2½ teaspoons red wine vinegar
1 tablespoon whole-grain mustard
2 teaspoons fresh lemon juice
½ teaspoon Worcestershire sauce
½ teaspoon freshly ground black pepper
⅛ teaspoon salt
1 (12-ounce) can water-packed chunk light or white tuna, drained
½ cup finely chopped fennel bulb
⅓ cup thinly sliced green onion (tender tops included)
3 tablespoons finely chopped fresh basil leaves
1 tablespoon finely chopped fennel fronds

3 6-inch white or whole-wheat pita breads, trimmed to open the pockets
6 slices ripe, juicy tomato
Leaves of Boston lettuce and sprigs of watercress

In a large bowl, whisk together the oil, vinegar, mustard, lemon juice, Worcestershire, pepper and salt.

Add the tuna, fennel bulb, green onion, basil and fennel fronds. Mix well and adjust the seasoning.

Spoon the tuna salad into the pitas, dividing it evenly and using it all. Tuck the tomato slices, lettuce and watercress into the pockets and serve more or less immediately.

BBQ Chicken Breast Sandwiches with Mustardy Slaw

These hearty barbecue sandwiches are in the Carolina style, featuring big buns stacked with warm meat topped by cool, mustardy slaw. That the meat is chicken, rather than the more traditional pork favored by Tarheels, matters not at all. To enjoy the sandwiches at their best, serve them while the chicken is still warm and accompany them with sweet potato chips and plenty of cold beer.

Makes 4 sandwiches

1 cup store-bought barbecue sauce

2 teaspoons soy sauce, preferably tamari

2 teaspoons Tabasco Pepper Sauce

2 teaspoons Worcestershire sauce

2 teaspoons unsulphured molasses

2 large, thick whole boneless, skinless chicken breasts (about 1½ pounds total), trimmed and separated

2 cups wood chips, preferably hickory, optional

4 large seeded sandwich buns, such as sesame Kaiser rolls, split horizontally

Salt

Freshly ground black pepper

2 cups Mustardy Purple Cabbage and Carrot Slaw (page 149)

In a shallow, nonreactive dish just large enough to hold the chicken breasts, whisk together the barbecue sauce, soy sauce, Tabasco, Worcestershire and molasses. Add the chicken breasts, cover, and let stand at room temperature, turning occasionally, for 1 hour.

Prepare a hot charcoal fire or preheat a gas grill (medium-high). When the fire is hot, distribute the wood chips if you are using them. Position the grill rack about 6 inches above the heat.

When the wood chips are smoking, lift the chicken breasts from the marinade, reserving the marinade, and lay them on the rack. Cover and grill, turning the breasts once and basting them with the reserved marinade, until the marinade is used up and the chicken breasts are just cooked through while remaining juicy, about 10 minutes. Transfer to a cutting board and cool slightly.

If desired, toast the cut sides of the rolls on the grill until they are lightly browned and crisp, 1 to 2 minutes.

Cut the chicken breasts across the grain and at a slight angle into thin slices. Divide the slices over the bottom sections of the rolls. Season lightly with salt and pepper. Divide the slaw over the chicken breasts, using it all. Set the tops of the rolls in place. Cut the sandwiches in half on the diagonal and serve immediately.

Grilled Caesar Chicken Sandwiches with Fennel

By now you know my fondness for fennel. Here it shows up, fragrant and crunchy, dressed with pungent Caesar dressing, atop a Caesar-marinated grilled chicken breast sandwich—double the garlic and anchovy for double the fun. Like so many of our sandwiches, I think this one is special enough to serve to company, for a wonderful, summertime lunch.

Makes 4 sandwiches

2 large, thick whole boneless, skinless chicken breasts (about 1½ pounds total), trimmed and separated

¾ cup Caesar Dressing (page 144)

1 cup coarsely chopped fresh fennel bulb

2 tablespoons minced fennel fronds
Freshly ground black pepper

2 cups wood chips, preferably mesquite, optional

4 5-by-3-inch pieces rosemary focaccia, at least 2 inches thick, split horizontally

1 large, ripe tomato, thinly sliced

Brush both sides of the chicken breasts evenly with ¼ cup of the Caesar dressing. Let stand at room temperature for 1 hour.

In a small bowl, stir together the remaining ½ cup Caesar dressing, the chopped fennel and minced fennel fronds.

Season generously with fresh pepper. Let stand for 1 hour.

Prepare a hot charcoal fire or preheat a gas grill (medium-high). When the fire is hot, distribute the wood chips if you are using them. Position the grill rack about 6 inches above the heat.

When the wood chips are smoking, lay the chicken breasts on the rack. Cover and grill, turning them once, until they are just cooked through while remaining juicy, 8 to 10 minutes. Transfer to a cutting board and cool slightly.

Cut the chicken breasts across the grain and at a slight angle into thin slices. Divide the chicken slices over the bottom focaccia sections. Season the chicken to taste with fresh pepper. Divide the fennel mixture over the chicken, using it all. Top the fennel with the tomato slices. Set the top focaccia sections in place. Cut the sandwiches in half on the diagonal and serve immediately.

Chris's Turkey Salad Sandwiches

This terrific recipe, from Flavors' chef Chris Siversen, includes instructions for cooking the turkey, but, of course, if you have leftovers on hand (turkey or chicken), use them for even speedier results.

Makes 4 sandwiches

2 boneless, skinless turkey breast fillets (about 1¾ pounds total)
   Salt
¾ cup Sunberry Jam (page 185), chutney or other tart fruit relish, such as cranberry-orange
¾ cup mayonnaise
2½ tablespoons balsamic vinegar
1½ teaspoons cumin, preferably from toasted seeds (page 4)
½ cup diced red onion
¼ cup golden raisins
   Freshly ground black pepper
8 slices marbled rye bread
   Leaves of oak leaf lettuce

In a large skillet that will just hold the fillets in a single layer, cover the turkey with cold water. Add 1 teaspoon salt and set over medium heat. While bringing the water to a simmer, turn the turkey once or twice. Simmer until just cooked through while remaining juicy, about 5 minutes. Cool the turkey to room temperature in the cooking water. Drain and pat dry. Separate and trim the breasts and cut the meat into ¼-inch cubes.

In a medium bowl, whisk together the jam, mayonnaise, vinegar and cumin. Add the turkey, onion and raisins and stir well. Season generously with pepper and stir again.

Divide the turkey mixture evenly among 4 bread slices and spread it to the edges. Set a leaf or two of lettuce atop each sandwich. Set the remaining 4 bread slices in place. With a serrated knife, cut the sandwiches in half. Serve more or less immediately.

Black Forest Ham Sandwiches with Dijon-Brie Spread

This classic Flavors sandwich is a subtle twist on ham-and-cheese (still the most popular sandwich in America, according to a recent poll). For so few ingredients, these sandwiches are hugely flavorful, but be sure to buy only the best ham and Brie, and put them on good gutsy bread, or the results will be ordinary.

Makes 4 sandwiches

1 **pound ripe Brie, chilled**
¼ **cup Dijon mustard**
¾ **teaspoon Tabasco Pepper Sauce**
1 **large green onion, thinly sliced (tender top included)**
1 **21-inch-long crusty baguette, split horizontally**
1 **pound thinly sliced Black Forest ham, at room temperature**

Trim the rind off the chilled Brie. Let the cheese come to room temperature. In a food processor, combine the Brie, mustard and Tabasco. Process, stopping once or twice to scrape down the sides of the work bowl, until smooth. Transfer to a container and stir in the green onion. The spread can be used immediately or prepared several days in advance. Cover tightly and refrigerate. Return to room temperature if chilled.

Spread the cut sides of the baguette with the Brie mixture, dividing it evenly and using it all. Ruffle the ham onto the baguette bottom. Set the top section in place. Cut the baguette crosswise diagonally into 4 equal sections. Serve within an hour or two.

Smoked Turkey and Avocado Sandwiches with Tangy Corn Relish

The smokiness of the turkey is perfectly complemented by the sweet-hot relish and the buttery avocado in this Flavors classic, which we make with apple wood–smoked, preservative-free turkey (see Note). If you think a turkey sandwich has to be swimming in mayonnaise to be good, this one will change your mind.

Makes 2 sandwiches

1 small, ripe black-skinned California avocado
4 5-inch slices multigrain sandwich bread
  Salt
½ pound thinly sliced smoked turkey breast, preferably preservative-free
½ cup Tangy Corn Relish
½ cup coarsely chopped watercress

Halve and pit the avocado and scoop the flesh into a small bowl. With a fork, roughly mash the avocado.

Evenly spread 1 side of each of the bread slices with the mashed avocado, using it all. Season to taste with salt. Ruffle the sliced turkey over 2 of the bread slices, using it all. Divide the corn relish evenly over the turkey, using it all. Top the corn relish with the watercress. Set the other 2 slices of bread in place, avocado side down.

Cut the sandwiches in half diagonally and serve more or less immediately.

Note: Mail-order Jugtown smoked turkey breast from D'Artagnan, Inc., 280 Wilson Avenue, Newark, NJ 07105 (call them at 800-327-8246). Each turkey breast weighs approximately 6 to 8 pounds and costs $7.10 per pound.

Tangy Corn Relish

This is a quick version of the sort of colorful corn relish good Texas cooks put up each year there's a bumper crop in the garden. It turns smoked turkey (also ham) sandwiches into real treats. For a zestier relish, leave some—or all—of the ribs and seeds in the jalapeño.

Makes about 2 cups

1 tablespoon olive oil
¼ cup finely diced sweet red pepper
¼ cup finely diced sweet green pepper
1 medium jalapeño chile, stemmed, seeds and ribs removed
1 large green onion, tender top included, trimmed and thinly sliced
3 garlic cloves, peeled and finely chopped
2½ cups very sweet fresh corn kernels and juices, cut and scraped from about 3 medium ears
3 tablespoons seasoned rice wine vinegar
2 tablespoons fresh lime juice
2 tablespoons minced cilantro

In a small, heavy, nonreactive saucepan over medium heat, warm the olive oil. Add the sweet red and green pepper, the jalapeño, green onion and garlic. Cover and cook, stirring once or twice, for 5 minutes. Add the corn and juices, cover and cook, stirring often, until the mixture has thickened and the corn is tender and just cooked through, 8 to 10 minutes.

Remove from the heat and transfer to a bowl. Stir in the vinegar and lime juice. Cool completely, then cover and refrigerate for at least 24 hours and up to 3 days.

Return the relish to room temperature and stir in the cilantro just before using.

Roast Leg of Lamb Sandwiches with Smoky White Bean Spread

Leftover lamb is a truly valuable resource, one I covet for using in all sorts of creative meals when the party's over. Not the least of these is this sandwich, celebrating the classic Provençal duo of lamb and white beans. It's less work if the spread is already on hand, but making it's so easy and the sandwich so good I think it's worth whipping up a batch on purpose.

Makes 4 sandwiches

1 21-inch-long crusty loaf (wider than a baguette), split horizontally
1⅓ cups Smoky White Bean Spread (page 3)
1 pound leftover leg of lamb (page 72) thinly sliced and well trimmed, at room temperature
   Salt
   Freshly ground black pepper
2 medium tomatoes, preferably yellow, trimmed and sliced
24 large arugula leaves

Pull the excess crumb out of the upper half of the bread loaf. Spread the bean mixture evenly over the cut sides of the upper and lower bread halves, using it all. Arrange the lamb slices over the bottom bread half. Season to taste with salt and pepper. Top the lamb with the tomato slices. Top the tomato slices with the arugula. Set the top half of the bread loaf in place. Cut crosswise with a serrated knife. Serve more or less immediately.

Salami and Provolone Panini with Pesto Mayonnaise

Panini are merely Italian sandwiches. Sometimes on the small side, to encourage the nibbling of an assortment, they may also be, as they are at Flavors, more of a meal, though still considerably less overstuffed and intimidating than a New York deli triple-decker. Once you understand the basic plan, other meats and cheeses can be substituted, and additions like hot pickled peppers or sun-dried tomatoes can also be enjoyed.

Makes 4 sandwiches

4 medium, crusty sandwich rolls, or
    4 3½-by-5-inch sections of soft, crusty bread
    such as ciabatta, split horizontally
    Pesto Mayonnaise
6 ounces thinly sliced Genoa salami
6 ounces thinly sliced smoked provolone

Spread the cut sides of the rolls with the mayonnaise, dividing it evenly and using it all. Ruffle the salami over the mayonnaise on the sandwich bottoms, dividing it evenly and using it all. Ruffle the provolone over the salami, dividing it evenly and using it all. Set the sandwich tops in place. Serve immediately.

Pesto Mayonnaise

Don't make pesto on purpose for this mayonnaise, but do use homemade if you already have some on hand. Otherwise, any good store-bought product, preferably a fresh, refrigerated one, can be used successfully.

Makes about ½ cup

½ cup mayonnaise
4 teaspoons store-bought pesto
1 teaspoon fresh lemon juice
    Tabasco Pepper Sauce, to taste

In a bowl, stir together the mayonnaise, pesto, lemon juice and Tabasco. Use immediately or cover and refrigerate for up to 3 days. Return to room temperature if chilled.

The Main Dish

Thai Red Seafood Curry; Grilled Duck Breast
with Indian Spices and Apricot-Tomato Relish

This is the meat, not to mention the turkey, chicken and fish, of the book. Appetizers may challenge my creativity, while desserts, for some guests at least, may be the only part of the meal that truly matters, but without a terrific main dish at the heart of the matter, I know I haven't really done my job as host. Here are my personal favorites, culled from Flavors as well as from my own tattered home recipe file. They fall into two general categories: Carving Board Meats and Fishes and Other Main Dishes. Carving board meats and fishes are lightly sauced (if at all) and some are as good warm or cool as they are hot. "Other" favorites range from quick last-minute pasta suppers to slow, oven braises to meatless main courses. Many are the sort that reheat well and along with, perhaps, some good bread and a salad, can stand alone as a meal. Collectively this is hearty food that is unfussy to prepare, casual to serve and packed with bold, intriguing flavors.

Grilled Duck Breast with Indian Spices and Apricot-Tomato Relish • Smoky Chicken with Herbed Goat Cheese Stuffing • Red Chile–Rubbed Roast Young Turkey • Spice-Rubbed Grilled Quail with Ginger-Honey Glaze • Provençal-Marinated Leg of Lamb with Pan Vegetables • Hot and Smoky West Texas Barbecue Meat Loaf • Grilled Steaks with Peppery Lemon-Herb Marinade • Party Fillet of Beef with Rosemary-Fig Chutney • Roast Pork Loin with Savory Spinach Stuffing • Salmon Brûlée with Tarragon-Mustard Cream • Seared Loin of Tuna with Wasabi Mayonnaise • Bourbon- and Mustard-Glazed Country Ham Crisp Unfried Chicken • Caraway Sausage, Cabbage and Apple Skillet Supper • Chunky Turkey and Red Bean Chili • Thai Red Seafood Curry • Salmon and Wild Rice Cakes • Cumin-Grilled Sea Bass with Preserved-Lemon Sauce • Veal Meatballs and Baby Carrots in Creamy Dill Sauce • Spice-Braised Lamb Shanks with Figs • Herb's Pot-Roasted Brisket • Herbed Lamb and White Bean Ragout • Easy Stuffed Veal Chops • Fusilli with Greens, Pine Nuts and Raisins • Pantry Linguine with Tuna, Green Olives, Sun-Dried Tomatoes and Capers • Three-Cheese Pasta Gratin with Mushrooms and Radicchio • Polenta-Crusted Deep-Dish Cheese and Roasted Vegetable Tart

Grilled Duck Breast with Indian Spices and Apricot-Tomato Relish

Here is a dish in which my goal was multiple layers of flavor, which I accomplished by combining three elements: a zesty marinade, a spicy rub and the smoke of the grill. I then tamed all three with a tart fruit relish. Some foods might not stand up to all that intensity, but duck does just fine. Though I have made this with quartered regular ducks (not force-fed and oversize), it's much more satisfying to eat (and much less work to prepare) when big boneless duck breast steaks (magrets) are used.

Serves 6

3 tablespoons soy sauce, preferably tamari

3 tablespoons fresh orange juice

1 tablespoon minced orange zest (colored part of peel, removed with a zester and minced)

1½ tablespoons Garam Masala (an Indian spice blend available in specialty shops, or see my easy recipe, which follows)

½ teaspoon salt

½ teaspoon freshly ground black pepper

⅛ teaspoon cayenne pepper

2 boneless duck breasts (magrets), about 3 pounds total

2 cups hickory or apple wood chips, optional

Sprigs of fresh cilantro, as garnish

Apricot-Tomato Relish, recipe follows, as accompaniment

In a small, nonreactive saucepan, combine the soy sauce, orange juice and orange zest. Cover tightly, set over low heat and bring to a simmer. Cook gently for 5 minutes; cool to room temperature.

In a small bowl, stir together the garam masala, salt, black pepper and cayenne. In a shallow, nonreactive dish, rub the spice mixture firmly into the duck breasts on all sides. Drizzle the soy mixture evenly over all sides of the duck breasts. Cover and let stand, turning occasionally, at room temperature for 2 hours or in the refrigerator overnight. Return to room temperature if chilled.

Prepare a hot charcoal fire or preheat a gas grill (medium-high). When the fire is hot, distribute the wood chips if you are using them. Position the grill rack about 6 inches above the heat.

When the grill is hot, lay the duck breasts on the rack. Cover and grill, basting the breasts with any marinade remaining in the dish and turning them once, until the marinade is used up and they are done to your liking, about 10 minutes total for medium-rare. Transfer to a cutting board and let rest for 5 minutes.

Carve the duck breasts across the grain and at an angle into thin slices. Arrange the breast slices on a platter. Garnish with cilantro and serve warm or at room temperature, accompanied by the relish.

Garam Masala

I make this powerful spice mixture a little differently each time, and I encourage you, too, to experiment. It makes a fine rub on grilled meats, especially duck, chicken, pork and lamb, or can supplement or be substituted for ordinary curry powder in dishes where a bigger, hotter flavor is desired.

Makes about 1½ tablespoons

¾ teaspoon ground ginger
¾ teaspoon ground cardamom
¾ teaspoon ground cumin, preferably
    from toasted seeds (page 4)
¾ teaspoon curry powder
¾ teaspoon cinnamon
¾ teaspoon freshly ground white pepper

Combine the ginger, cardamom, cumin, curry powder, cinnamon and pepper. Store the garam masala in an airtight container at room temperature for up to 1 month.

 TAMARI—Japanese soy sauce—is made from a higher proportion of fermented soybeans than Chinese soy sauce and so has a deeper, richer flavor. You will find it in better supermarkets, in specialty shops and surely in health-food stores. Ordinary soy sauce can be substituted. Kikkoman, the common supermarket brand, is quite good.

Apricot-Tomato Relish

This chutneylike relish will keep for at least a week in the refrigerator and is good alongside a traditional curry of lamb or chicken, a pork roast or a smoky country ham.

Makes about 4 cups

2 pounds ripe plum tomatoes, seeded and chopped
1 pound fresh apricots, pitted and chopped
2 cups chopped yellow onion
½ cup white wine vinegar
½ cup sugar
⅓ cup 1-inch julienne of peeled fresh ginger
2 garlic cloves, peeled and finely chopped
1 teaspoon salt
¾ teaspoon crushed red pepper
½ teaspoon freshly grated nutmeg
½ cup finely chopped cilantro

In a large, heavy, nonreactive pan, combine the tomatoes, apricots, onion, vinegar, sugar, ginger, garlic, salt, red pepper and nutmeg. Cover, set over medium heat and bring to a simmer. Uncover and cook, stirring often, until the relish has thickened and is reduced to 4 cups, 30 to 40 minutes. Remove from the heat and cool. The relish can be prepared up to 1 week ahead. Return it to room temperature.

Stir the cilantro into the relish and adjust the seasoning just before serving.

MAGRETS—Magrets are the boneless, skinless breast fillets of special oversize ducks, raised to produce the delicious fattened livers known as foie gras. Impressively thick and meaty, magrets look rather like small flank steaks but taste like the best duck ever. They are at their finest grilled or pan-seared and served thinly sliced and ideally quite rare. There is only one source for magrets in the United States. They are available by mail from D'Artagnan, Inc., 280 Wilson Avenue, Newark, NJ 07105 (call them at 800-327-8246).

Smoky Chicken with Herbed Goat Cheese Stuffing

This chicken—one of my all-time favorite dishes—is the direct result of the first cooking class I ever took. Held in the kitchen of a tiny (now defunct) bistro in Greenwich Village, it was an eye-opener and my first real lesson in how exciting the food business could be. There, next to the ancient stove and beneath the dangling, battered saucepans, we stuffed an herb and garlic butter under the skins of chickens and roasted them to crackly, juicy perfection. Sometime later it occurred to me to replace that butter mixture with one of seasoned goat cheese, and to finish the roasting of the bird on the grill, over plenty of smoky wood chips. The result is this boldly fragrant dish—perfectly assertive summer eating, and equally good hot, warm or at room temperature.

Serves 6

⅔ cup (about 6 ounces) soft, fresh goat cheese, at room temperature

½ cup finely chopped flat-leaf parsley

2 tablespoons unsalted butted, softened

1 shallot, peeled and finely chopped

3½ tablespoons Roasted Garlic Puree (page 162)

2 teaspoons finely chopped fresh rosemary

2 teaspoons finely chopped fresh thyme

1 teaspoon herbes de Provence, crumbled (page 9)

Salt

Freshly ground black pepper

1 large roasting chicken, about 6 pounds, giblets reserved for another use

1 cup Chicken Stock (page 45) or reduced-sodium canned chicken broth

½ cup dry white wine

4 large, whole, unpeeled garlic cloves

2 cups wood chips, preferably hickory, optional

Sprigs of fresh rosemary, thyme and other herbs, as optional garnish

Position a rack in the middle of the oven and preheat to 400° F.

In a medium bowl, thoroughly stir together the goat cheese, parsley, butter, shallot, garlic puree, 1½ teaspoons each of the rosemary and thyme, and ½ teaspoon each of the herbes de Provence, salt and pepper.

Pat the chicken dry. Remove all visible fat. Loosen the skin over the breast meat, thighs and as far down the legs as possible by gently sliding your fingers between the skin and the meat; avoid tearing the skin. Stuff the cheese mixture under the skin of the breasts, thighs and legs, using it all. Rub the remaining ½ teaspoon each of rosemary, thyme and herbes de Provence into the skin of the chicken. Set it on a rack in a shallow disposable foil roasting pan just large enough to hold it comfortably. Add the stock, wine and whole garlic to the pan.

Roast the chicken for 20 minutes, then begin basting every 10 minutes with the liquid from the pan, until the chicken has baked for a total of 1 hour. The chicken will not be fully cooked, but will finish cooking as it smokes on the grill.

Meanwhile, prepare a hot charcoal fire or preheat a gas grill (medium-high). When the fire is hot, distribute the wood chips if you are using them. Position the grill rack about 6 inches above the heat.

Pour off and reserve the pan juices and whole garlic. Immediately transfer the chicken in its pan to the grill rack (do not allow it to sit out of the oven, or the temperature will drop and bacterial contamination may occur). Cover the grill and hot-smoke the chicken until the skin is browned and the meat is just cooked through while remaining juicy,

20 to 30 minutes. (A thigh, pricked at its thickest, will yield pinkish-yellow juices.) Remove from the grill and let rest for at least 20 minutes.

Degrease the pan juices. Force the softened garlic from the peels through a sieve into the juices; adjust the seasoning.

Carve the chicken and arrange it on a platter; garnish with herbs if desired. Serve the chicken warm or at room temperature, accompanied by the pan juices.

Note: Though the smoky flavor makes the chicken special, the bird can also be cooked completely through in the oven and then served, omitting the grill step altogether. Extend the oven time by 20 to 30 minutes, using the cues given above to judge doneness.

Red Chile–Rubbed Roast Young Turkey

This turkey is easy, beautiful and delicious. The garlicky chile butter that goes under the skin adds color and flavor but is in no way spicy-hot. Serve the turkey as part of a buffet spread at any time of the year, or team it with Tangy Corn Relish (page 59), Roasted Garlic Mashed Potatoes (page 162), Corn Bread, Mushroom and Toasted Pecan Dressing (page 176) and Succotash (page 167) for a big-flavor Thanksgiving feast.

Serves 12

6 tablespoons unsalted butter, softened

3 tablespoons genuine maple syrup

3 tablespoons orange zest (colored part of peel, removed with a zester and minced)

2 tablespoons pure, unblended medium-hot powdered red chile or Hungarian sweet paprika

2 tablespoons Roasted Garlic Puree (page 162)

1 turkey, preferably fresh, about 13 pounds, brought just to room temperature, giblets reserved for another use

Salt

1 cup Chicken Stock (page 45) or reduced-sodium canned chicken broth

½ cup white wine, such as Chardonnay

½ cup fresh orange juice

In a small bowl, stir together the butter, maple syrup, orange zest, chile powder and garlic puree. The butter can be prepared up to 3 days ahead and refrigerated, or frozen for up to 1 month. Soften to room temperature before using.

Position a rack in the lower third of the oven and preheat to 325° F.

Set the turkey on a rack in a shallow roasting pan just large enough to hold it comfortably. Working from the vent end of the turkey, carefully slide your fingers between the skin and the meat of the breast and thighs. Spread about three-fourths of the butter mixture under the skin of the breast and thigh meat. Rub the remaining butter mixture over the turkey skin. Season lightly with salt.

Set the turkey in the oven and roast undisturbed for 1 hour. Add the stock, wine and orange juice to the pan. Tilt the turkey to combine any melted butter mixture from the cavity with the pan juices. Roast the turkey, basting it every 10 minutes with the pan juices, adding a cup or so of water to the pan if the juices eventually evaporate, until the skin is richly browned and the dark meat is just cooked through while the white meat remains juicy, another 1 hour and 30 minutes. An instant-read thermometer, inserted into the thickest part of the thigh, should register 165° to 170° F. Transfer the turkey to a cutting board.

Tent the turkey with foil and let it rest for at least 15 minutes before carving. Serve hot, warm or at room temperature.

CHILI POWDER VS. POWDERED CHILES—Chili (not chile) powder is the prefabricated spice blend used to make the great Texas dish, chili con carne. Containing cumin, oregano, garlic powder and other seasonings, it's a quick way to get your bowl of red to taste just right. Powdered chiles, however, plain and unblended, are just the chiles themselves, no other seasonings. Rather than resort to the blends, I prefer to combine my own seasonings in a pot of chili con carne and in dishes like the Red Chile–Rubbed Roast Young Turkey (page 69), where the sweet-hot flavor of the pure chiles is what I desire. Specialty-food shops and mail-order catalogs are the best sources for unblended ground chiles. The best come from New Mexico (look for those grown near the little mountain towns of Chimayo and Dixon) and Arizona. The flavor fades, so if you're not a fast chile user, store the powder airtight in the freezer. Hungarian sweet paprika mixed with a bit of hot paprika can be substituted. Mail-order sources: Coyote Café General Store, 132 West Water Street, Santa Fe, NM 87501, (505) 982-2454; and Old Southwest Trading Company, P.O. Box 7545, Albuquerque, NM 87194, (505) 836-0168.

Spice-Rubbed Grilled Quail with Ginger-Honey Glaze

Perfumed with sweet spices and the smoke from wood chips and brushed with a sweet and tangy glaze, these little birds are vaguely Moroccan, utterly delicious. Serve them hot or warm, accompanied with Saffron Couscous Pilaf with Roasted Vegetables (page 174). Guests may be inclined to pick the quail up and eat them with their fingers, a sticky, spicy practice I completely endorse.

Makes 8 quail, serving 4

1½ teaspoons freshly ground star anise
¾ teaspoon ground cardamom
½ teaspoon ground cinnamon
½ teaspoon freshly ground nutmeg
½ teaspoon ground cloves
8 butterflied quail, patted dry
¼ cup finely chopped fresh ginger
¼ cup honey
2 tablespoons soy sauce, preferably tamari
2 tablespoons Dijon mustard
2 teaspoons red wine vinegar
2 garlic cloves, peeled and chopped
2 cups wood chips, preferably fruitwood such as apple, optional

In a small bowl, mix together the star anise, cardamom, cinnamon, nutmeg and cloves. Sprinkle the spice mixture evenly over the skin sides of the quail, using it all and patting firmly to encourage it to adhere. Arrange the quail on a platter, cover and let stand at room temperature for 1 hour.

In a blender or small food processor, combine the ginger, honey, soy sauce, mustard, vinegar and garlic. Blend until fairly smooth. Transfer to a small bowl.

Meanwhile, prepare a hot charcoal fire or preheat a gas grill (medium).

When the fire is hot, distribute the wood chips if you are using them. Position the rack about 6 inches above the heat source. Lay the quail on the rack and grill, turning occasionally and basting with the ginger mixture, until the mixture is used up and the quail are just cooked through while remaining juicy, 8 to 10 minutes total. Remove from the heat and serve hot or warm.

Provençal-Marinated Leg of Lamb with Pan Vegetables

Deeply marinated, then roasted to a rosy-pink turn, this leg of lamb, with its citrusy herbal sauce, is a perfect (and pefectly easy) main course for a dinner party at any time of year. Accompany it with Vegetables Glazed with Balsamic Vinegar (page 169) and Rosemary-Pancetta Potato Sauté (page 161). Plan on using any leftover lamb in the delicious sandwiches on page 60.

Serves 6 to 8

5 tablespoons olive oil

4 garlic cloves, crushed through a press, plus 4 garlic cloves, thinly sliced

3 tablespoons minced shallot

1 cup medium-dry red wine

¼ cup fresh orange juice

3 tablespoons Dijon mustard

1 tablespoon minced fresh rosemary

1 tablespoon orange zest (colored part of peel, removed with a zester and minced)

1 tablespoon balsamic vinegar

5 teaspoons herbes de Provence (page 9)

1 boneless leg of lamb
  Salt
  Freshly ground black pepper

3 cups yellow onion cut into 1-inch chunks

6 carrots, peeled and cut into ½-inch chunks

1¾ cups Chicken Stock (page 45) or reduced-sodium canned chicken broth

1 tablespoon cornstarch

3 tablespoons mint jelly

1 tablespoon finely chopped fresh mint, optional

In a small saucepan over medium-low heat, warm 2 tablespoons of the olive oil. Add the crushed garlic and shallot and cook uncovered, stirring often, until fragrant but not brown, about 3 minutes. Add the wine, orange juice, mustard, rosemary, orange zest, vinegar and 2 teaspoons of the herbes de Provence. Raise the heat slightly, bring to a simmer, and cook, stirring once or twice, for 3 minutes. Remove from the heat and cool.

With the tip of a small knife, make slits in the lamb. Insert the garlic slices in the slits. Transfer the lamb to a nonreactive dish just large enough to hold it, pour over the marinade and cover. Let stand at room temperature for 2 hours or in the refrigerator overnight, turning occasionally.

Return the lamb to room temperature if chilled. Position a rack in the lower third of the oven and preheat to 450° F.

Remove the lamb from the marinade, reserving the marinade, and set on a rack in a shallow roasting pan. Season with salt and pepper.

Set the pan in the oven and roast the lamb for 15 minutes. Lower the oven temperature to 350° F. and bake the lamb for another 30 minutes.

In a large bowl, toss the onion and carrot with the remaining 3 tablespoons oil, the remaining 3 teaspoons herbes de Provence, ½ teaspoon salt and a generous grinding of pepper. Pour off any drippings from the roasting pan. Add the vegetables and continue to roast, stirring the vegetables once or twice, until the lamb is done to your liking and the vegetables are tender, another 40 to 50 minutes for rare lamb. (An instant-read thermometer inserted into the thickest part of the leg should register 130° F.) Transfer the lamb to a cutting board and tent with foil. With a slotted spoon, transfer the vegetables to a serving platter and keep warm.

Strain the reserved marinade into a small, nonreactive saucepan. In a small bowl, stir 2 tablespoons of the chicken stock into the cornstarch. Add the remaining chicken stock to the saucepan, set over medium-high heat and bring to a boil. Boil, uncovered, for 8 minutes. Lower the heat and whisk the cornstarch mixture and the mint jelly into the simmering liquid. Cook, stirring often, for 5 minutes, or until the sauce has thickened slightly. Stir in the mint. Adjust the seasoning.

Carve the lamb, arranging it on the platter with the vegetables. Serve, accompanied with the sauce.

Hot and Smoky West Texas Barbecue Meat Loaf

With this recipe my roots are showing—my Texas roots, that is. Updating traditional dishes is one of my favorite parts of cooking these days, especially when the result tastes as Texas good as this. Plus, several kitchen tricks substantially reduce the fat and calories in this otherwise moist and very satisfying loaf. Don't forget to save a big slice or two for sandwiches the next day!

Serves 8

2 cups finely chopped yellow onion

1 cup Chicken Stock (page 45) or reduced-sodium canned chicken broth

4 garlic cloves, peeled and finely chopped

2 teaspoons olive oil

½ teaspoon ground cumin, preferably from toasted seeds (page 4)

½ teaspoon dried oregano, crumbled

½ teaspoon dried thyme, crumbled

½ cup plus ⅓ cup store-bought thick, hot, smoky tomato-based barbecue sauce

½ cup evaporated milk, preferably skim

2 large eggs

4 teaspoons soy sauce, preferably tamari

4 teaspoons Worcestershire sauce

2 canned chipotles en adobo

¾ cup old-fashioned rolled oats

2 pounds lean, freshly ground beef, brought just to room temperature

In a medium skillet over medium heat combine the onion, chicken stock, garlic, olive oil, cumin, oregano and thyme. Cover and bring to a simmer. Cook, stirring once or twice, for 10 minutes. Uncover, raise the heat slightly and continue to cook, stirring often, until all of the liquid has evaporated and the vegetables are lightly browned, 8 to 10 minutes. Remove from the heat. Add ½ cup of the barbecue sauce and the evaporated milk and stir, scraping any browned deposits from the bottom of the skillet. Cool to room temperature.

Position a rack in the middle of the oven and preheat to 350° F.

In a small bowl whisk together the eggs, soy sauce, Worcestershire sauce and chipotles. In a large bowl combine the oats, the cooled mixture from the skillet, the beef and the beaten egg mixture. Stir together lightly but thoroughly. Spoon into a 9-by-5-by-3-inch loaf pan, mounding the meat mixture slightly. Spread the remaining ⅓ cup barbecue sauce evenly over the top of the loaf.

Bake the meat loaf until the top is lightly browned, the juices are bubbling, and an instant-read thermometer inserted into the center of the loaf registers 130° F., about 1 hour.

Let the loaf rest in the pan on a rack for 10 minutes (it will reabsorb rendered juices and become firm enough to cut). Slice the meat loaf and serve immediately.

> **Meat that is freshly ground will be juicier and more flavorful; meat that is at room temperature will combine more readily with the other ingredients without overhandling, which can result in a tough, dense loaf. Don't let the meat sit around for any real length of time, however, or you risk bacterial contamination.**

Grilled Steaks with Peppery Lemon-Herb Marinade

Descended from steak au poivre and perked up with some herbal Provençal touches, this recipe produces a mightily peppered hunk of meat (without the traditional creamy sauce) that is easy to make and wonderfully satisfying to eat. The days when people (me included) could get themselves around an entire rib-eye steak are pretty much over, but when the protein tastes as good as this, no one will feel deprived at a smaller than cave man–sized portion.

Serves 6 to 8

4　1½-inch-thick boneless sirloin or rib-eye steaks, preferably grade prime
½　cup plus 3 tablespoons fresh lemon juice
2　tablespoons olive oil
2　tablespoons minced fresh rosemary
2　tablespoons minced fresh thyme
6　teaspoons whole black peppercorns
1　tablespoon lemon zest (colored part of peel, removed with a zester and minced)
　　Salt
2　cups mesquite or hickory wood chips, optional

Lay the steaks in a large, shallow nonreactive dish just large enough to hold them comfortably. Pour ½ cup of the lemon juice over them.

In a small food processor, combine the remaining 3 tablespoons lemon juice, the olive oil, rosemary, thyme, peppercorns, lemon zest and ¾ teaspoon salt and process until a paste forms (bits of peppercorn should remain visible). Spread the paste over the steaks, cover them, and marinate at room temperature for 2 hours (or overnight in the refrigerator), turning occasionally. Return the steaks to room temperature if chilled.

Prepare a hot charcoal fire or preheat a gas grill (medium-high). When the fire is hot, distribute the wood chips if you are using them. Position the grill rack about 6 inches above the heat.

When the chips are smoking, remove the steaks from the marinade, reserving the marinade, and lay them on the rack. Cover and grill, basting occasionally with the marinade and turning the steaks once, for 10 minutes for rare meat, or until they are done to your liking.

Transfer to a cutting board and let rest for 10 minutes. Cut the steaks across the grain and at a slight angle to the board into thin slices. Season lightly with salt. Serve warm or cool.

 Thinly sliced leftover steak (you never know) makes a fine sandwich. Try it on Tuscan-style sourdough bread with tomato, red onion, Black Olive Aioli (page 18) or mustard, and arugula.

Party Fillet of Beef with Rosemary-Fig Chutney

As a big glazed ham sets an automatically festive party note, so, too, does fillet of beef. Cold or hot, as an hors d'oeuvre or entrée, tender, versatile fillet is a classic on the catering circuit. It's not the most flavorful cut of beef, however, and needs to be seasoned and served imaginatively. Here is our flavor-packed method, in which the beef is marinated in a mustardy peppercorn mixture, partially cooked on a smoky grill, then finished in the oven and served with an herbal fruit chutney.

Serves 8

½ cup olive oil
¼ cup Dijon mustard
¼ cup whole-grain mustard
3 tablespoons balsamic vinegar
2 tablespoons coarsely crushed black peppercorns
2½ tablespoons drained, brine-packed green peppercorns, mashed (page 77)
2 tablespoons soy sauce, preferably tamari
6 garlic cloves, peeled and crushed through a press
2 tablespoons minced fresh rosemary
1 oven-ready center-cut prime fillet of beef, about 2½ pounds
2 cups wood chips, preferably hickory, optional
Rosemary-Fig Chutney, recipe follows

In a large, nonreactive bowl, whisk together the olive oil, Dijon and whole-grain mustards, vinegar, 1 tablespoon of the black peppercorns, the green peppercorns and the soy sauce. Rub the garlic, rosemary and remaining 1 tablespoon black peppercorns firmly into the fillet. Add the fillet to the mustard mixture in the bowl and turn to coat it. Cover and refrigerate overnight, turning occasionally. Return the fillet to room temperature.

Prepare a hot charcoal fire or preheat a gas grill (medium-high). When the fire is hot, distribute the wood chips if you are using them. Position the grill rack about 6 inches above the heat.

Meanwhile, position a rack in the middle of the oven and preheat to 450° F.

When the fire is hot, set the fillet on the rack, reserving the mustard mixture. Grill, turning once, until richly browned, about 25 minutes. Immediately transfer the fillet to a rack set in a shallow roasting pan. Spread the fillet with the reserved mustard mixture. Set the rack in the oven and roast the fillet until an instant-read thermometer inserted into the thickest part of the roast registers 130° F. for rare, about 20 minutes, or until the meat is done to your liking.

Transfer to a cutting board, tent with foil, and let rest at least 10 minutes before carving. Serve hot, warm or at room temperature, with Rosemary-Fig Chutney.

Rosemary-Fig Chutney

This is one of several herbal fruit relishes that we use to garnish meats. The tangy, complex flavors wake up the palate, and wake up guests as well. No one dozes when I'm cooking this chutney and certainly not when it is on the plate! It's also good with pork, lamb and chicken.

Makes about 6 cups

4 cups fresh orange juice
1½ pounds dried Calimyrna figs, tough stems
     removed, figs coarsely chopped, see Note
1 cup golden raisins
½ cup apricot preserves or orange marmalade
½ cup sugar
¼ cup apple cider vinegar
½ teaspoon salt
½ teaspoon crushed red pepper
3 tablespoons minced fresh rosemary

In a large, heavy, nonreactive pan, combine the orange juice, figs, raisins, apricot preserves, sugar, vinegar, salt and crushed red pepper. Set over medium heat and bring to a simmer, skimming any foam that may form. Stir in the rosemary, then cook partially covered, stirring occasionally, until the figs are tender and the chutney has thickened and is shiny, 20 to 30 minutes. Remove from the heat and cool to room temperature. Cover and refrigerate at least overnight. Return to room temperature before serving. The chutney will keep for 1 month.

Note: Golden Calimyrnas make a prettier chutney than darker Mission figs, although the latter can be substituted if necessary.

GREEN PEPPERCORNS—Softly waxy and pungent, green peppercorns are those that have not been sun-dried (which turns them familiarly hard and black). They can also be found freeze-dried (they keep their color that way) but most commonly come packed in jars in a salty brine. Roughly mashed or pureed into sauces, they are especially compatible with beef and lamb. As if the flavor weren't reason enough to enjoy pepper in all its forms, it's worth noting that one component of peppercorns, an alkaloid called piperine, stimulates the flow of saliva and gastric juices and thus is an aid to digestion. Store any unused green peppercorns in their jar in the original brine (topped off with a little vinegar if necessary) in the refrigerator. They will keep indefinitely.

Roast Pork Loin with Savory Spinach Stuffing

This moist, tender pork loin, with its Mediterranean-inspired stuffing, makes a nice change from the very popular fruit-stuffed version. It's good hot, paired with Roasted Garlic Mashed Potatoes (page 162) and terrific cold, accompanied with Tuscan White Bean Salad (page 128) and Grilled Asparagus with Lemon Mayonnaise (page 171).

Serves 6 to 8

3 tablespoons olive oil

½ cup finely chopped yellow onion

3 garlic cloves, peeled and finely chopped, plus 6 whole, peeled garlic cloves

¼ teaspoon crushed red pepper

1 (10-ounce) package frozen chopped spinach, thawed and squeezed dry

½ cup fine fresh bread crumbs

½ cup shredded Italian Fontina cheese

½ cup finely chopped fresh basil

¼ cup finely chopped pitted Greek black olives (Kalamatas)

¼ cup finely chopped drained oil-packed sun-dried tomatoes

3 tablespoons freshly grated Parmigiano-Reggiano cheese

3 tablespoons toasted pine nuts (page 114)
Freshly ground black pepper

1 4-pound boneless, center-cut pork loin roast, with a pocket prepared for stuffing, rolled and tied
Salt

1½ cups dry Marsala wine

MARSALA—This fortified wine from Sicily comes in varying degrees from quite sweet to very dry. Softly flavored, with a trace of almond-like bitterness, sweet Marsala is not much drunk these days, though it is nice with a slice of not-too-sweet nut cake or a few biscotti and essential to the frothy dessert custard zabaglione. The dry version, on the other hand, is endlessly versatile, not only as an aperitif (try it with a few slices of fine prosciutto or a bowl of good olives) but in the kitchen, where its nutty bouquet enriches marinades and sauces for veal, chicken, pork and game.

Position a rack in the middle of the oven and preheat to 350° F.

In a medium skillet over moderate heat, warm 2 tablespoons of the oil. Add the onion, chopped garlic and crushed red pepper and cook uncovered, stirring occasionally, until tender and lightly browned, about 7 minutes. Add the spinach and stir well. Remove from the heat and cool to room temperature.

In a medium bowl, mix together the spinach mixture, bread crumbs, Fontina, basil, olives, tomatoes, Parmesan, pine nuts and a generous grinding of black pepper. Stuff the spinach mixture into the pocket in the pork loin. Set the loin, fat side up, on a rack in a shallow roasting pan just large enough to hold it. Season the loin lightly with salt and pepper. Scatter the whole garlic cloves around the pork loin. Drizzle the cloves with the remaining 1 tablespoon olive oil.

Roast for 30 minutes, stirring the garlic once or twice. Add the Marsala to the pan. Continue to roast the pork, basting every 10 minutes with the Marsala, until the roast is crisply browned and just cooked through while remaining juicy (an instant-read thermometer inserted into the thickest part of the roast, but not the stuffing, should register between 160° and 170° F.), another 50 to 60 minutes.

Transfer the roast to a cutting board, tent with foil and let rest for at least 10 minutes. Serve hot, warm or at room temperature.

Salmon Brûlée with Tarragon-Mustard Cream

This grand party dish is the creation of one of my first chefs, Lorena Stearns. For it, a whole side of salmon (festive, indeed) is broiled, then topped with a sweet and herbal sauce that hardens into a crunchy glaze. Mustard-and-tarragon-spiked whipped cream is the opulent garnish. Serve the salmon hot, warm or at room temperature.

Serves 8

1½ cups packed golden-brown sugar
½ cup finely chopped fresh tarragon,
    plus sprigs of tarragon, as optional garnish
¼ cup unsulphured molasses
¼ cup water
2 tablespoons finely chopped shallots
1 side of fresh salmon, about 3 pounds,
    pinbones removed (page 80), patted dry
    Salt
    Freshly ground black pepper
    Tarragon-Mustard Cream,
        recipe follows

In a small, deep, nonreactive saucepan, combine the sugar, chopped tarragon, molasses, water and shallots. Set over medium heat and bring to a simmer. Lower the heat and cook uncovered, stirring occasionally, until thick, about 15 minutes (the mixture will register 260° F. on a candy thermometer). Let stand at room temperature while preparing the salmon.

Position a rack about 6 inches from the heat source and preheat the broiler.

Set the salmon, skin side up, on a broiler-proof serving plate. Season lightly and evenly with salt and pepper. Broil the salmon until it is just cooked though while remaining moist, 12 to 15 minutes. Transfer to a rack.

Coat the hot salmon evenly with the brown-sugar mixture, using it all. Garnish with sprigs of tarragon, if desired, and serve, accompanied with the Tarragon-Mustard Cream.

Tarragon-Mustard Cream

For the liveliest sauce, choose a good, strong, hot mustard. Your chances are better if it is imported from Dijon, France, and is from a freshly opened jar.

Makes about 4 cups

2 cups chilled whipping cream
½ cup finely chopped fresh tarragon
¼ cup strong, hot prepared mustard, preferably imported from Dijon
½ teaspoon salt
Freshly ground black pepper

In a medium bowl, whip the cream to stiff peaks. Fold in the tarragon, mustard, salt and a generous grinding of pepper. Taste and adjust the seasoning. The cream can be prepared up to 1 hour before using. Cover and refrigerate, letting it stand at room temperature for about 10 minutes before serving.

Though the side of salmon will come "boneless" there will still be plenty of bones to remove. As with Gravlax (page 22), a large pair of tweezers is the best implement for pulling the long bones out of the salmon. It's not a requirement, but it does make the fish more pleasant to eat. Some cookware shops and professional equipment catalogs offer wide-tipped stainless-steel tweezers designed expressly for this purpose.

Seared Loin of Tuna with Wasabi Mayonnaise

Marinated in Asian flavors, then pan-seared, this sensational tuna remains meaty, medium-rare and moist within. Thinly sliced and served at room temperature, it is drizzled with a potent mayonnaise flavored with powdered wasabi—the same green, horseradish-like root that is a principal condiment of sushi. If you would like to serve this as an appetizer, it will feed eight; accompany the tuna and mayonnaise on the plate with a small salad of mesclun, tossed with olive oil, balsamic vinegar and toasted sesame seeds.

Serves 4 to 6

3 tablespoons soy sauce, preferably tamari
3 tablespoons fresh ginger juice (from about ¾ cup finely chopped ginger, pureed and then pressed through a sieve)
2 garlic cloves, peeled and crushed through a press
Freshly ground black pepper
2 pounds sashimi-quality fresh tuna loin, a single piece about 6 inches in diameter
2 tablespoons dark sesame oil
Wasabi Mayonnaise

In a medium, shallow dish, stir together the soy sauce, ginger juice, garlic and a generous grinding of pepper.

Cut the tuna lengthwise into 3 equal pieces (viewed end-on, the cuts will resemble the classic peace symbol).

Lay the tuna pieces in the dish, cover and marinate at room temperature, turning once or twice, for 2 hours.

In a heavy skillet over medium-high heat, warm the oil. Add the tuna and cook, turning occasionally, until well-browned on all sides, about 15 minutes for medium rare.

Transfer to a cutting board. Slice thin and serve, drizzled with the mayonnaise.

Wasabi Mayonnaise

Makes about ⅔ cup

½ cup mayonnaise
1 green onion, chopped
2 tablespoons Dijon mustard
1 tablespoon finely chopped fresh ginger
1½ teaspoons wasabi powder
1 teaspoon soy sauce
Pinch of salt

In a small food processor, combine the mayonnaise, green onion, mustard, ginger, wasabi powder, soy sauce and salt. Process until smooth. Transfer to a bowl, cover and refrigerate for up to 2 days, returning the mayonnaise just to room temperature before using.

Bourbon- and Mustard-Glazed Country Ham

Anytime the main dish is also a magnificent centerpiece, the cook's job is that much easier. Guests who see a big, smoky ham glistening under a shiny and flavorful crust of bourbon, mustard and brown sugar know automatically that they're in for a good time. And don't forget the old adage that defines eternity as "two people and a ham": You'll have lots of leftovers to enjoy in the days to come.

Serves 12 with leftovers

1 good-quality smoky ham (not an actual Smithfield country ham, but a brine-cured "city" ham), about 15 pounds, brought to room temperature
½ cup whole-grain mustard
½ cup packed golden-brown sugar
⅓ cup honey
1 teaspoon Tabasco Pepper Sauce
1½ cups bourbon

Position a rack in the lower third of the oven and preheat to 325° F.

If the ham has a rind, pull it away with your fingers. With a thin, sharp knife, slice away all but ¼ inch of any fat on the upper surface. Score a diamond pattern about ⅛ inch deep into the upper surface of the ham. Set the ham, scored side up, on a rack in a shallow roasting pan just large enough to hold it. Add 3 cups water to the pan. Set the pan in the oven and bake the ham for 1½ hours.

Meanwhile, in a small bowl, stir together the mustard, brown sugar, honey and Tabasco.

Pour off the water from the pan. Spread the mustard mixture evenly over the upper surface of the ham, using it all. Add the bourbon to the pan. Bake the ham, basting every 10 minutes with the bourbon and the accumulated pan juices, until the ham is richly browned and thoroughly heated through, another 30 to 40 minutes. Transfer to a cutting board.

Let the ham rest for at least 15 minutes before carving. Serve hot, warm or at room temperature.

Crisp Unfried Chicken

No picnic of my Texas youth was complete without a big platter of genuine fried chicken. Marinated in Tabasco-spiked buttermilk and fried up in big black cast-iron skillets of hot oil, it was mahogany-brown and almost noisily crisp outside, moist and deeply flavored within. We knew nothing about free-range chickens then (though that's what they all were), and we knew nothing about fat and cholesterol either, which is just as well. Here's my modern picnic chicken, every bit as satisfyingly moist and flavorful (thanks to a tangy marinade and a crunchy crumb coating) as the old-fashioned kind, but head and shoulders better for you.

Serves 6 to 8

Zest (colored part of peel) from 6 lemons
   (removed with a zester and minced)
1 cup fresh lemon juice (from about 6 lemons)
8 garlic cloves, peeled and chopped
⅓ cup chopped fresh rosemary
¼ cup olive oil
2 chickens (about 7 pounds total), each in
   8 serving pieces, all visible fat removed
2 cups fine dry bread crumbs
¼ cup grated Parmigiano-Reggiano cheese
   Salt
   Freshly ground black pepper

In a food processor, combine the lemon zest and juice, garlic, rosemary and olive oil. Process until fairly smooth.

In a shallow, nonreactive dish combine the lemon mixture and the chicken. Cover and refrigerate overnight, turning once or twice. Return the chicken just to room temperature.

Position a rack in the middle of the oven and preheat to 425° F.

In a wide, shallow bowl, stir together the bread crumbs and cheese. Remove the chicken pieces from the marinade and season lightly with salt and pepper. One at a time, dredge the chicken pieces in the bread-crumb mixture, coating thoroughly. Transfer the chicken to a jelly-roll pan. Bake the chicken until it is crisp, golden-brown and just cooked through while remaining juicy, about 40 minutes.

Serve hot or warm.

Note: If desired, substitute boneless chicken breasts or thighs; just shorten the baking time by about half.

Caraway Sausage, Cabbage and Apple Skillet Supper

The expression "skillet supper" can conjure up hamburger, helped out by something from a box, or it can instead mean a casual but delicious one-pan meal like this, adapted from one by our chef, Chris Siversen. It goes together almost as easily as a boxed meal, but it's good and interesting and sophisticated enough to serve to company. Great, as is, with just some good pumpernickel or rye bread for mopping up the juices, it's even better accompanied with Roasted Garlic Mashed Potatoes (page 162). Either way, drink champagne (not too expensive, not too dry) or the best beer you can find.

Serves 4

2 slices thick-cut preservative-free bacon, chopped

1½ pounds (about 6 links) fully cooked, smoked sausage, such as Aidells' smoked-chicken-with-apple, see Note

2 medium McIntosh apples, cored, peeled and sliced

1 medium-sized yellow onion, about 6 ounces, peeled, halved and thinly sliced

4 carrots, peeled and thinly sliced

3 garlic cloves, peeled and chopped

1¼ teaspoons caraway seeds

6 cups thinly sliced green cabbage (about half a 2½-pound head)

¾ teaspoon salt
Freshly ground black pepper

1 cup Chicken Stock (page 45) or reduced-sodium canned chicken broth

⅓ cup white wine, such as Chardonnay

⅓ cup finely chopped flat-leaf parsley

In a large, deep skillet over medium-low heat, cook the bacon, stirring often, until almost crisp, 8 to 10 minutes.

With a slotted spoon, transfer the bacon to a small bowl and reserve.

Add the sausages to the skillet and cook, turning them once or twice, until they are well browned, 8 to 10 minutes. Transfer to a cutting board. When cool, quarter the sausages crosswise on the diagonal.

Meanwhile, add the apples, onion, carrots, garlic and caraway seeds to the skillet. Cover, lower the heat slightly and cook, stirring once or twice, for 10 minutes. Add the cabbage, reserved bacon and the salt. Season with pepper to taste. Add the stock and wine, cover and bring to a simmer. Cook undisturbed for 10 minutes. Stir the cabbage and vegetables together well. Scatter the sausage pieces over the cabbage. Cover and cook, stirring once or twice, until the sausages are heated through and the cabbage is almost tender, another 7 to 10 minutes. Uncover, raise the heat to high, and cook, stirring often, until the cooking juices have evaporated, 6 to 8 minutes. Adjust the seasoning, sprinkle the parsley over all and serve hot.

Note: Supermarket-sausage substitutions include kielbasa, knockwurst and bratwurst.

Chunky Turkey and Red Bean Chili

Ground turkey was not even a concept during my Texas years, much less chili made from it. So, I'm pleased to report that as long as the flavorings are kept authentic, the substitution of turkey for beef in no way prevents this from being just about the most delicious pot of Texas Red you'll ever taste. Make it a day or two ahead, to allow the flavors to develop, and serve it with an array of toppings, letting guests help themselves.

Serves 10

3 tablespoons plus 1 teaspoon olive oil

1¼ pounds Italian-style hot turkey sausage links

2½ pounds ground turkey

5 cups chopped yellow onion

1 large sweet pepper, preferably red, stemmed, cored and diced

2 to 4 medium-sized fresh jalapeño chiles, stemmed and finely chopped

8 garlic cloves, peeled and chopped

⅓ cup pure medium-hot powdered red chiles or Hungarian sweet paprika

2½ tablespoons ground cumin, preferably from toasted seeds (page 4)

2 tablespoons dried oregano, crumbled

1 tablespoon unsweetened cocoa powder

1 tablespoon freshly ground black pepper

1 teaspoon ground cinnamon

4½ cups Chicken Stock (page 45) or reduced-sodium canned chicken broth

1 (15-ounce) can crushed tomatoes with added puree

1 cup flat amber beer, such as Dos Equis

2 (15-ounce) cans dark red kidney beans, drained and rinsed

2 teaspoons salt

2 tablespoons yellow cornmeal

About ¾ cup each of any or all of these toppings: grated sharp cheddar or Monterey Jack cheese; pickled jalapeño slices; sour cream; chopped black olives; chopped red or green onion; diced tomatoes; diced avocado; salsa or finely chopped cilantro

In a large, heavy nonreactive pan, such as a Dutch oven, over medium heat, warm 1 teaspoon of the oil. Add the sausage links. Cook uncovered, turning once, until well browned, about 10 minutes (the sausages will not be cooked through). Transfer to a cutting board and cool. Quarter the sausages lengthwise, then cut them crosswise into ½-inch pieces.

Set the pan over medium heat. Add the ground turkey and cook, breaking up any lumps, until just cooked through, about 10 minutes. With a slotted spoon, transfer the turkey to a bowl. Pour off the drippings. Return the pan to medium heat and add the remaining 3 tablespoons oil. Stir in the onion, sweet pepper, jalapeños, garlic, powdered chile, cumin, oregano, cocoa, black pepper and cinnamon. Cover, lower the heat and cook, stirring often to prevent sticking, for 15 minutes. Stir in the sausage pieces, chicken stock, tomatoes, beer, beans and salt. Bring to a simmer, partially cover and cook, stirring occasionally, for 35 minutes. Stir in the ground turkey, partially cover and cook another 10 minutes.

In a small bowl, stir together ¼ cup of the hot chili liquid and the cornmeal. Stir this paste back into the chili and simmer until thick, 5 to 10 minutes. Adjust the seasoning.

Note: The chili can be prepared (without the cornmeal) up to 3 days in advance, which will give the flavors a chance to develop. Reheat the chili, without thinning, until hot, then thicken with the cornmeal as directed.

Thai Red Seafood Curry

Here is a very nearly ideal main course for a dinner party—assuming your guests like spicy food. Though the curry base for this wonderfully fiery and creamy pink stew has a long ingredient list, it goes together quickly and can be prepared hours or even a day in advance. Completing it then requires only a few minutes for poaching the seafood in the base while the accompanying white rice finishes cooking. The seafood can be varied according to what is best in the market (mussels with their dramatic black shells look nice in the pink sauce), or pieces of boneless dark-meat chicken can be substituted for the fish and shrimp, and green chile paste—slightly hotter and with a different flavor—can replace the red.

Serves 6 to 8

3 tablespoons olive oil

½ small yellow onion, peeled and thinly sliced

2 tablespoons thinly sliced fresh lemongrass bulb

6 garlic cloves, peeled and finely chopped

4 teaspoons finely chopped fresh ginger

1 serrano chile, stemmed and sliced into thin rounds, optional

½ pound cremini (brown) mushrooms, trimmed and thinly sliced

1 large sweet pepper, preferably red, cored, seeded and cut into 2-inch-long julienne strips

1 medium-large zucchini, about ½ pound, scrubbed, trimmed and cut into ½-inch chunks

2 (14-ounce) cans Thai coconut milk, well stirred

¾ cup Chicken Stock (page 45) or reduced-sodium canned chicken broth

⅔ cup white wine

¼ cup nam plah (Thai fish sauce, page 122)

2 tablespoons Thai red chile paste

2 tablespoons packed golden-brown sugar

1¼ pounds boneless halibut, in 1 thick piece, skin removed, cut into 1-inch chunks

1 pound (about 20) large shrimp, shelled and deveined

1 tablespoon lime zest (colored part of peel, removed with a zester and minced)

½ cup finely chopped cilantro

¼ cup finely chopped basil

¼ cup finely chopped mint, plus sprigs of mint, as optional garnish

3 green onions, trimmed and thinly sliced (tender tops included)

2 tablespoons fresh lime juice
    Hot jasmine rice, as recommended accompaniment

In a wide, deep skillet over medium heat, warm the oil. Add the onion, lemongrass, garlic, ginger and serrano. Cover and cook, stirring occasionally, for 5 minutes. Add the mushrooms, sweet pepper and zucchini, raise the heat slightly, and cook uncovered, tossing and stirring often, until the vegetables are almost tender, 8 to 10 minutes. Stir in the coconut milk, chicken stock, wine, fish sauce, chile paste and brown sugar. (The dish can be prepared to this point up to 1 day in advance. Cool, cover and refrigerate.)

Set the skillet over medium heat and bring to a simmer. Add the halibut, shrimp and lime zest and cook, stirring once or twice, until the fish is just cooked though while remaining moist and the shrimp are curled and pink, 7 to 10 minutes. Stir in the cilantro, basil, mint, green onions and lime juice. Remove from the heat, cover and let stand for 1 minute.

Mound rice in the center of 6 to 8 wide, shallow bowls. Spoon the curry around the rice, dividing it evenly. Garnish with mint if desired and serve immediately.

LEMONGRASS—Fresh lemongrass looks like bamboo crossbred with a green onion and has a delicate lemony scent and flavor. It can be found in very good supermarkets, specialty produce shops and the occasional health-food store, usually among the herbs or in the exotic Asian produce section. If you can't locate it, don't despair, just omit it. (Or you may add additional lime or lemon zest by way of compensation.) Only the tender bulbs are used in Thai cooking. Discard the woody stalks and mince the lemongrass more or less right before adding it to the curry. Unused fresh lemongrass can be frozen. While dried lemongrass can be ground and used in beverages like Chai (page 198), it is not suitable in this dish.

THAI RED CURRY PASTE AND COCONUT MILK—Thai cookbooks are full of recipes for curry pastes to make from scratch, and indeed, if you have the patience, you should make your own, grinding together the chiles, onions, garlic and aromatics shortly before use. That said, there are brands of prepared chile paste out there that can save hours of eye-tingling kitchen time (I find Thai Kitchen line to be good and fairly widely available). Don't buy curry "sauce," an entirely different and rather nasty product, and do store leftover paste in the refrigerator—one small jar will flavor at least three batches of curry.

Thai coconut milk, an essential flavoring element in this seafood curry, is readily available canned. What is called for in the recipe is technically coconut "cream"—the thoroughly stirred up contents of the entire can—though the label will indeed read "milk." Richly flavored (and just plain <u>rich</u>), there is really no substitute, not even "lite" coconut milk, which will make a weak and watery curry. Coconut milk is not a good keeper. Once opened, it should be refrigerated and used up within a day or two.

Salmon and Wild Rice Cakes

Even the best-laid plans of caterers sometimes go awry, leading to unscheduled leftovers that require—at least if the bottom line is to be respected—a creative metamorphosis into a second, equally delicious entrée. Since salmon is so often on our party menus, a dish using cold poached salmon is essential. Here is a delicious budget saver that turns up often both at work and at home. (If you already have about 2 cups flaked, boneless cooked salmon, you can omit the poaching step.) Serve the cakes hot from the skillet, accompanied with a dollop of Lemon Mayonnaise (page 171) if you're splurging or lemon wedges if not.

Makes 8 cakes (serves 4)

1 salmon steak, about ¾ pound
2 tablespoons red wine vinegar
　Salt
⅓ cup uncooked wild rice (or 1 cup cooked,
　　cooled leftover rice)
3 large eggs
⅓ cup unbleached all-purpose flour
½ cup freshly grated Parmigiano-Reggiano cheese
2 tablespoons milk
½ teaspoon baking powder
½ teaspoon freshly ground black pepper
½ cup thinly sliced green onion (most tender 2
　　inches of green tops included)
1 tablespoon olive oil

In a deep skillet, cover the salmon steak with cold water. Stir in the vinegar and 1 teaspoon salt and set over medium heat. Bring to a simmer, then cook, turning once at the halfway point, until almost cooked through while remaining moist, about 8 minutes. Remove the skillet from the heat and cool the salmon in the poaching water to room temperature. Drain and pat dry. Remove the skin and bones.

Bring a medium saucepan of water to a boil. Add the wild rice and ½ teaspoon salt. Partially cover, lower the heat and simmer, stirring occasionally, until the rice is tender, about 55 minutes (wild rice cooking times vary widely). Drain and cool.

In a large bowl, whisk the eggs. Whisk in the flour, cheese, milk, baking powder, ¾ teaspoon salt and the pepper. Add the salmon, rice and green onion and mix well. The batter can be prepared several hours in advance. Cover and refrigerate, returning it to room temperature before proceeding.

Divide the batter equally into 8 thick cakes. Set a large skillet over medium heat. Add the oil and when it is hot, working in batches if necessary, add the cakes. Cover the skillet and cook until lightly browned, about 4 minutes. Turn the cakes, cover and cook until lightly browned and just cooked through while remaining moist, another 3 to 4 minutes. Remove from the skillet and serve immediately.

Cumin-Grilled Sea Bass with Preserved-Lemon Sauce

Preserved lemons add their subtle bite to the spice-scented tomato sauce that naps these fillets of sea bass. The firm, meaty fish holds up well to the heat of the grill and the pungent flavor of cumin—great Moroccan-inspired eating for a sultry summer's night. Tuna or swordfish can be substituted; shorten the cooking time accordingly.

Serves 8

4 tablespoons olive oil
3 shallots, peeled and finely chopped
4 garlic cloves, peeled and finely chopped
¼ teaspoon ground cinnamon
¼ teaspoon ground cardamom
¼ teaspoon crushed red pepper
4 cups chopped fresh plum tomatoes
Salt
⅓ cup finely chopped preserved lemon, recipe follows, see Note
⅓ cup halved pitted black Greek olives (Kalamatas)
2 cups wood chips, preferably mesquite, optional
About 4 pounds sea bass, in 8 thick pieces
4 teaspoons ground cumin, preferably from toasted seeds (page 4)

In a medium nonreactive saucepan over low heat warm 2 tablespoons of the oil. Add the shallots, garlic, cinnamon, cardamom and crushed red pepper. Cover and cook, stirring once or twice, for 5 minutes. Add the tomatoes and ¾ teaspoon of the salt and bring to a simmer. Cook uncovered, stirring occasionally, until slightly reduced and no longer watery but still fresh-looking, about 15 minutes. Stir in the preserved lemon and the olives. The sauce can be used hot or at room temperature, and can be prepared up to 3 days in advance, if desired.

Prepare a medium-hot charcoal fire or preheat a gas grill (medium). When the fire is hot, distribute the wood chips if you are using them. Position the rack about 6 inches above the heat source.

Rub the flesh sides of the bass fillets with the remaining 2 tablespoons oil. Season lightly with salt to taste. Sprinkle the flesh sides with the cumin, using it all and patting it to encourage it to adhere.

Lay the fillets on the rack. Cover and cook, carefully turning once, until the fish is just cooked though but still moist and barely flaking, 12 to 15 minutes.

Transfer to plates. Spoon the sauce around the fish, using it all. Serve immediately.

Note: The softened flesh of the lemons should be scraped off the peel and discarded and the peels rinsed of their brine before chopping. For a sharper lemon taste, chop the preserved peel coarsely, rather than finely.

Quick Preserved Lemons

Preserved lemons are one of the world's great flavor experiences. Most commonly found in Morocco, they are preserved in one of several ways, my favorite (and the easiest) being this quick, salt-brine method, adapted from a recipe of Paula Wolfert's. Following a simmer and a 5-day marination, the peel (the flesh is scraped off and discarded) becomes silky, with a powerful lemony essence. They're no trouble to make (and the jar of lemons and spices looks wonderful in the refrigerator), but they can be purchased in some gourmet shops, if you prefer.

Makes 4 preserved lemons

- 4 medium lemons
- ½ cup salt
- 2 cinnamon sticks
- ¼ teaspoon crushed red pepper
- ⅛ teaspoon cardamom seeds
- 6 cloves
- 6 coriander seeds
- 6 whole white peppercorns
- 2 bay leaves

With a razor blade or a very sharp knife, make 8 thin, evenly spaced vertical cuts in the peel of each lemon (do not cut deeper than the membrane that protects the pulp).

In a nonreactive saucepan, combine the lemons, salt, cinnamon sticks, red pepper, cardamom, cloves, coriander, peppercorns and bay leaves with water just to cover. Set over medium heat and bring to a simmer. Cook uncovered, stirring occasionally, until the peels are very soft, about 30 minutes. (Avoid inhaling the vapors, which are spicy.)

Transfer the lemons to a clean, heatproof jar. Pour the cooking liquid over them. Transfer any spices and the bay leaves remaining in the pan to the jar. Cover and let stand at room temperature for 5 days before using.

Refrigerate the unused lemons for up to 1 month.

 For a simple (and simply marvelous) modern tartar sauce for grilled fish or shrimp, stir finely chopped preserved lemon peel along with some finely chopped, pitted Kalamata olives if desired, into mayonnaise. Great on sandwiches too!

Veal Meatballs and Baby Carrots in Creamy Dill Sauce

Even in a rich and sophisticated sauce like this—an unusually caloric one for Flavors—meatballs are really just kid food: great fun to eat, even for grown-ups. And so addictively delicious is this dish that Rhonda Stieglitz, our recipe tester, has requested it as her last meal. This easy, do-ahead recipe makes fine dinner-party fare, served with Noodles with Browned Caraway Butter (page 175).

Serves 6

7 tablespoons unsalted butter
⅔ cup minced yellow onion
2 pounds ground veal, brought just to room temperature
¾ cup fine fresh white bread crumbs
2 large eggs, beaten
2¼ cups whole milk
Salt
Freshly ground black pepper
¾ teaspoon freshly grated nutmeg
½ teaspoon ground coriander
2 tablespoons vegetable oil
1 pound peeled baby carrots
¼ cup unbleached all-purpose flour
1 cup Chicken Stock (page 45) or reduced-sodium canned chicken broth
1 cup whipping cream
2 tablespoons Dijon mustard
3 tablespoons finely chopped fresh dill, plus sprigs of fresh dill as optional garnish

In a small skillet over medium-high heat, melt 3 tablespoons of the butter. Add the onion and cook uncovered, stirring occasionally, until lightly browned, about 7 minutes. Remove from the heat and cool.

In a large bowl, mix together the veal, bread crumbs, eggs, ¼ cup of the milk, 1 teaspoon salt, a generous grinding of pepper, the nutmeg, coriander and sautéed onions until well blended. Form the mixture into 30 meatballs (about 3 tablespoons of the veal mixture each).

In a large, heavy skillet over medium-high heat, warm the vegetable oil. Working in batches to avoid crowding the skillet, cook the meatballs, turning them often, until well browned on all sides, about 8 minutes. With a slotted spoon transfer the meatballs to paper towels to drain.

Bring a medium pot of water to a boil. Add 2 teaspoons salt and the carrots and cook, stirring occasionally, until almost tender, about 6 minutes. Drain; rinse under cold water. Drain thoroughly.

In a large, heavy pot over medium-low heat, melt the remaining 4 tablespoons butter. Whisk in the flour; cook, stirring often without allowing the flour to brown, for 3 minutes. Gradually whisk in the remaining 2 cups milk and the stock. Bring to a simmer, whisking constantly. Simmer uncovered, whisking often, until the mixture is thick, about 8 minutes. Whisk in the cream and mustard. Bring to a simmer. Adjust the seasoning. Add the meatballs and carrots. (The dish can be prepared to this point 1 day ahead. Cool, cover and refrigerate. Return to medium heat before proceeding.) Simmer partially covered, stirring often, until the meatballs are just cooked through, about 5 minutes.

Stir in the chopped dill. Remove from the heat, cover and let stand for 1 minute. Serve hot, garnished with dill sprigs, if desired.

Spice-Braised Lamb Shanks with Figs

As a child I liked the rich taste of lamb, and for years, for catered events and at home, I prepared a wildly popular Moroccan lamb stew, containing dried fruit and turnips, from James Beard. Here is a descendant of that dish, one that is, if anything, even tastier than the original. The shanks take a long, slow, moist braising to become tender, and then they are among the most succulent and satisfying morsels imaginable. Serve the lamb over Saffron Couscous Pilaf with Roasted Vegetables (page 174).

Serves 6 to 8

¼ cup olive oil
6 large lamb shanks, sawed crosswise by the butcher into thirds
2 cups chopped yellow onion
1½ cups chopped carrot
8 garlic cloves, peeled and finely chopped
1 tablespoon ground cumin, preferably from toasted seeds (page 4)
10 green cardamom pods, lightly crushed, with any seeds that come free
1 3-inch piece cinnamon stick
¾ teaspoon dried thyme, crumbled
½ teaspoon ground ginger
½ teaspoon ground coriander
½ teaspoon freshly ground black pepper
½ teaspoon cayenne pepper

¼ teaspoon Hungarian hot paprika
1 bay leaf
2½ cups plus 1 tablespoon Chicken Stock (page 45) or reduced-sodium canned chicken broth
¾ cup red wine, such as Merlot
¾ cup canned crushed tomatoes with added puree
Salt
8 ounces dried figs (Black Mission or Calimyrna), stemmed and quartered lengthwise
1 tablespoon cornstarch
1 tablespoon red wine vinegar

Position a rack in the middle of the oven and preheat to 350° F.

Set a large, heavy 5½-quart ovenproof pan (such as a Dutch oven or a covered flameproof casserole) over medium-

With a slotted spoon, transfer the lamb to a heat-proof dish (discard any bones that may have come free) and keep warm.

Set the pan over medium heat and bring to a simmer. Boil, skimming any fat, for 5 minutes. In a small bowl, stir together the remaining 1 tablespoon stock and the cornstarch. Stir the cornstarch mixture and the vinegar into the simmering sauce and cook just until thick, about 30 seconds. Discard the cinnamon stick and bay leaf. Adjust the seasoning.

Pour the sauce over the lamb shanks and serve immediately, preferably on heated plates.

high heat. Add 1½ tablespoons of the oil. When it is hot, working in 3 or 4 batches, cook the lamb shank pieces, turning them occasionally, until they are lightly and evenly browned, about 10 minutes per batch. With a slotted spoon, transfer the browned shanks to a bowl. Add an additional ½ tablespoon oil to the pan if needed to prevent sticking.

Pour off the oil from the pan but do not clean it. Add the remaining 2 tablespoons oil and set the pan over low heat. Stir in the onion, carrot, garlic, cumin, cardamom, cinnamon stick, thyme, ginger, coriander, black pepper, cayenne, paprika and bay leaf. Cover and cook, stirring once or twice and scraping the bottom of the pan, for 10 minutes. Return the lamb to the pan. Add the 2½ cups stock, wine, tomatoes and ½ teaspoon salt. Bring to a simmer, stirring once or twice. Cover the pan, set it in the oven and bake for 1 hour, stirring occasionally. Uncover the pan, stir in the figs, and continue to cook, stirring once or twice, until the lamb is tender and beginning to fall from the bones, about 1 hour more.

Herb's Pot-Roasted Brisket

Herb Maxwell, Zach's grandfather, is the brisket maven in the family, and when I wanted the quintessential recipe for what may well be the most delectable cut of beef, I didn't hesitate to call him. It's a must once a year at Passover, but Herb happily makes it for Zach anytime they need a bonding moment; family and guests who taste it will be similarly attached to you for life.

Serves 8

1 flat-cut brisket of beef, preferably grade prime, about 5 pounds, patted dry

2 medium yellow onions, about 1 pound total, peeled and thinly sliced

6 garlic cloves, peeled and finely chopped

2 (28-ounce) cans crushed tomatoes with added puree

3 cups dry red wine

1¾ cups Chicken Stock (page 45), canned beef broth or reduced-sodium canned chicken broth

2 teaspoons dried thyme, crumbled

2 bay leaves

Salt

Freshly ground black pepper

2 pounds (about 8 medium) all-purpose, red-skinned potatoes, quartered

1 pound medium carrots, peeled and angle-cut into 1-inch pieces

½ cup chopped flat-leaf parsley

Position a rack in the middle of the oven and preheat to 325° F.

Select a large, heavy nonreactive ovenproof pot with a tight-fitting lid (such as a Dutch oven) that will just hold the brisket comfortably. Set it over medium-high heat. When the pot is hot, add the brisket, fat-side down. Cook until lightly browned, about 8 minutes. Turn the meat and cook until browned, another 8 minutes. Scatter the onions and garlic over the beef. Add the tomatoes, wine, stock, thyme, bay leaves, 2 teaspoons salt and 1 teaspoon pepper and stir to mix. Cover the pot and bring to a simmer. Set the pot in the oven and bake for 2 hours, stirring the cooking liquid once or twice. Add the potatoes and carrots, submerging them as much as possible in the cooking liquid. Cook until the meat, potatoes and carrots are tender, about 1 hour more.

Transfer the brisket to a cutting board and tent with foil. With a slotted spoon, transfer the potatoes and carrots to a dish and keep warm in the turned-off oven.

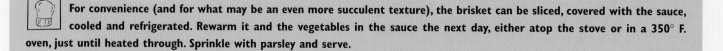

For convenience (and for what may be an even more succulent texture), the brisket can be sliced, covered with the sauce, cooled and refrigerated. Rewarm it and the vegetables in the sauce the next day, either atop the stove or in a 350° F. oven, just until heated through. Sprinkle with parsley and serve.

Degrease the sauce. If desired, transfer it to a medium nonreactive saucepan and set over moderate heat. Bring to a brisk simmer and cook uncovered, stirring once or twice, for 30 minutes. Remove from the heat. Adjust the seasoning. For a smooth, gravy-like sauce, puree it in a food processor or force it through the medium blade of a food mill. Rewarm the sauce if necessary. Stir in ⅓ cup of the parsley.

Across the grain and at an angle, thinly slice the brisket. Arrange the slices, overlapping, on a platter. Surround the brisket with the vegetables. Spoon some of the sauce over the brisket. Sprinkle the remaining parsley over all. Serve immediately, passing the remaining sauce at the table

Herbed Lamb and White Bean Ragout

Lamb with garlic and strong herbs is the very essence of Provençal cooking. Comforting, because of the meltingly tender texture of the meat and beans and the rich gravy, yet stimulating, thanks to the vivid herbal flavors, the ragout comes very close to being a perfect dish of food.

Serves 6 to 8

1½ cups (about 10 ounces) dried small beans, such as flageolets, cannellini or baby limas, picked over
3 pounds lamb, preferably shoulder, cut into well-trimmed 1-inch cubes
1 cup dry red wine
⅓ cup red wine vinegar
8 garlic cloves, peeled and finely chopped
6 tablespoons olive oil
1½ tablespoons herbes de Provence, crumbled (page 9)
2 bay leaves
Freshly ground black pepper
2½ cups diced (½-inch) carrot (about 5 medium)
2 cups chopped yellow onion

3 tablespoons unbleached all-purpose flour
1 (28-ounce) can plum tomatoes, crushed, with their juices
2½ cups Chicken Stock (page 45) or canned beef broth, plus extra stock for thinning
⅓ cup canned crushed tomatoes with added puree
2 teaspoons salt
¾ cup drained Niçoise olives
½ cup finely chopped flat-leaf parsley
3 tablespoons minced mixed fresh herbs, such as rosemary, thyme and oregano

In a medium bowl, cover the beans with cold water. Let soak for at least 4 hours or overnight for convenience.

In a large, nonreactive bowl, combine the lamb, wine, vinegar, garlic, 2 tablespoons of the olive oil, the herbes de

Provence, bay leaves and a generous grinding of pepper. Cover and marinate at room temperature, stirring once or twice, for 2 hours or overnight in the refrigerator. Return to room temperature if chilled.

Meanwhile, drain the beans. In a medium pan, cover them with fresh cold water. Set over medium heat and bring to a boil. Tightly cover and lower the heat until the beans simmer gently. Cook until just tender, 40 to 50 minutes (bean cooking times vary widely; add boiling water as needed and continue to simmer until tender). Drain.

Position a rack in the lower third of the oven and preheat to 350° F.

With a slotted spoon, lift the lamb from the marinade, reserving the marinade. Pat the lamb dry with paper towels. Set a large, heavy 5½-quart ovenproof pan (such as a Dutch oven or a covered flameproof casserole) over medium-high heat. Add 2 tablespoons of the oil, and when it is hot, working in 4 or 5 batches to avoid crowding the pan, brown the lamb well on all sides, about 7 minutes per batch. Transfer the browned lamb to a bowl. Add additional olive oil to the pan by tablespoons as necessary to prevent sticking.

Add the remaining olive oil to the pan. Stir in the carrot and onion. Lower the heat, cover the pan and cook, stirring occasionally and scraping the browned bits from the bottom, for 7 minutes. Sprinkle the flour over the vegetables and cook uncovered without browning the flour, stirring once or twice, for 3 minutes. Add the browned lamb, reserved marinade, plum tomatoes, stock, crushed tomatoes, salt and ¾ teaspoon pepper. Cover and bring to a simmer.

Set the pan in the oven and bake, stirring occasionally and regulating the oven temperature if necessary to maintain the stew at a moderate simmer, for 45 minutes. Uncover and bake for another 45 minutes. Stir in the beans and bake until the stew is thick and the meat and beans are tender, another 10 to 15 minutes. Remove from the oven. (The stew can be prepared to this point up to 2 days in advance. Cool completely, cover and refrigerate. Rewarm over low heat, stirring occasionally, until steaming. Thin the stew with additional stock only after it is hot.) Stir in the olives, parsley and mixed herbs. Cover and let stand 1 minute. Adjust the seasoning. Serve hot, on heated plates.

Easy Stuffed Veal Chops

This quick and easy dish, one I have been making for workday suppers for years, is, with the right accompaniments, dressy enough for a dinner party as well. Fine choices would be Rosemary-Pancetta Potato Sauté (page 161) or Roasted Garlic Mashed Potatoes (page 162) and Vegetables Glazed with Balsamic Vinegar (page 169).

Serves 4

¾ cup coarse fresh bread crumbs

¼ cup freshly grated Parmigiano-Reggiano cheese

¼ cup finely chopped flat-leaf parsley

4 tablespoons olive oil

4 garlic cloves, peeled and finely chopped

1 tablespoon finely chopped fresh rosemary

¼ teaspoon lemon zest (colored part of peel, removed with a zester and minced)

4 1-inch-thick loin veal chops, each with a pocket prepared for stuffing

Salt

Freshly ground black pepper

½ cup Chicken Stock (page 45) or reduced-sodium canned chicken broth

¼ cup dry white wine

1 tablespoon fresh lemon juice

Position a rack in the middle of the oven and preheat to 425° F.

In a medium bowl, lightly toss together with a fork the bread crumbs, cheese, parsley, 2 tablespoons of the oil, the garlic, rosemary and lemon zest. Divide the stuffing evenly among the pockets in the chops, using it all. Pat the chops dry and season with salt and pepper to taste.

In a large skillet over medium-high heat, warm the remaining 2 tablespoons oil. When it is hot but not smoking, add the chops. Cook, turning once, until browned, about 6 minutes total. Transfer the chops to a shallow baking dish, set in the oven and bake until the chops are done to your liking, 15 to 20 minutes for pale pink and juicy.

Meanwhile, discard the oil but do not clean the skillet. Set it over high heat, add the stock, wine and lemon juice and bring to a boil. Boil, scraping the browned bits from the bottom of the skillet, until the sauce has thickened slightly and is syrupy, 3 to 5 minutes.

Set the chops on plates, drizzle with the sauce and serve immediately.

Fusilli with Greens, Pine Nuts and Raisins

This startlingly delicious pasta takes advantage of the nutrition and other good things packed into dark, leafy greens. Flavor is not the least of these, and here slightly bitter broccoli raab and beet-sweet chard unite to show greens off at their very best. This pasta is good as either a first course or a main course.

Serves 4 to 6

BROCCOLI RAAB AND RED CHARD—Broccoli raab (sometimes spelled rabe, sometimes called rapini) is a non-heading broccoli related to turnips. The flavor is quite bitter (one writer calls it "ferocious"), but it tames a bit when cooked or when combined with sweetening and mellowing ingredients as it is in this pasta. Aside from the Chinese (who like bitter flavors), raab is enjoyed most by the Italians, who braise it for a rather long time, seasoned with garlic and crushed red pepper. It then makes a fine accompaniment to grilled sausages. Discard the tough bottom stems, but chop and cook everything else.

Swiss chard, and the sweeter, red-stalked ruby or rhubarb chard, is a beet that has been encouraged to produce long crunchy stems instead of bulbous roots. The leaves look like rather thick spinach (they taste like spinach, too, and are cooked similarly as well), while the stalks are chopped and sautéed al dente or very tender, depending on your taste. For a beet lover like me, red chard, with its distinct beetlike flavor, is the best choice, but regular green chard can be used in the pasta with good results.

¼ cup olive oil
    Stems from 1 bunch red chard, trimmed and diced (about 2 cups)
1 sweet yellow pepper, stemmed, cored and cut into long, ¼-inch-wide strips
6 garlic cloves, peeled and finely chopped

¼ teaspoon crushed red pepper
1 cup Chicken Stock (page 45) or reduced-sodium canned chicken broth
½ cup golden raisins
    Leaves from 1 bunch red chard, thinly sliced crosswise (about 6 cups)
1 bunch broccoli raab, tough stems removed, tops (leaves, tender stems and buds) thinly sliced crosswise (about 2¼ cups)
    Salt
12 ounces dried short fusilli semolina pasta, preferably imported
⅓ cup (about 2 ounces) pine nuts, toasted (page 114)
1 tablespoon fresh lemon juice
    Freshly grated Parmigiano-Reggiano cheese, for serving

In a large skillet over medium heat, warm the olive oil. Add the chard stems, sweet pepper, garlic and crushed red pepper. Cover and cook, stirring once or twice, for 5 minutes. Add the stock and raisins and simmer, covered, stirring once or twice, for 5 minutes. Add the chard leaves and broccoli raab, season with ½ teaspoon salt and cook, covered, tossing and stirring often, until the greens are wilted and fairly tender and the cooking juices have reduced by half, about 5 minutes.

Meanwhile, bring a large pot of water to a boil. Add the pasta and 1 tablespoon salt. Bring to a boil, partially cover and cook according to the package directions, stirring occasionally, until the pasta is just tender, 12 to 15 minutes. Drain immediately.

Return the pasta to the pot. Add the contents of the skillet, the pine nuts and lemon juice. Set the pot over medium heat and cook, tossing and stirring often, until everything is heated through and the pasta has absorbed some of the juices from the greens, 1 to 2 minutes.

Divide the pasta among heated plates and serve immediately, accompanied with the cheese at the table.

Pantry Linguine with Tuna, Green Olives, Sun-Dried Tomatoes and Capers

Like a lot of modern kids, my son, Zach, would rather have pasta for dinner than almost anything, and this quick linguine dish, with its sauce of pantry staples, is a new favorite. It's also good at room temperature, rather like a pasta salad.

Serves 4

12 ounces dried semolina linguine pasta, preferably imported
2 teaspoons salt
¼ cup olive oil
5 garlic cloves, peeled and finely chopped
¼ teaspoon crushed red pepper
1 cup Chicken Stock (page 45) or reduced-sodium canned chicken broth
½ cup white wine, such as Chardonnay
½ cup coarsely chopped drained pimiento-stuffed green olives
½ cup coarsely chopped drained oil-packed sun-dried tomatoes
2 tablespoons drained small (nonpareil) capers
1 (6-ounce) can chunk light tuna in oil, drained
⅓ cup finely chopped flat-leaf parsley
Freshly grated Parmigiano-Reggiano cheese

Bring a large pan of water to a boil. Add the linguine and salt, partially cover and cook according to the package directions, stirring often, until just tender, about 11 minutes.

Meanwhile, in a large, deep skillet over low heat, warm the olive oil. Add the garlic and crushed red pepper, cover and cook without browning the garlic, stirring once or twice, for 5 minutes. Add the stock, wine, olives, tomatoes and capers and bring to a simmer. Cook 1 minute.

Drain the pasta. Immediately add it to the skillet. Scatter the tuna over the linguine. Raise the heat slightly and cook the pasta, tossing and stirring it often, until it has absorbed about half the liquid and everything is hot, 1 to 2 minutes. Stir in the parsley.

Divide the pasta among 4 bowls or plates and serve immediately, passing the grated cheese at the table.

Three-Cheese Pasta Gratin with Mushrooms and Radicchio

This, I guess, is my macaroni and cheese. Extra-flavorful, thanks to the multicheese sauce, and combined with Italian vegetables, the pasta bakes up crusty, brown and very satisfying—great for a sort of dressed-up supper main dish, but also nice, in place of mashed potatoes or such, alongside roast chicken or pork. The radicchio loses its bright burgundy color when cooked, but acquires a wonderful bittersweet flavor.

Serves 6

3 tablespoons unsalted butter, plus butter
   for the baking dish
4 garlic cloves, peeled and finely chopped
½ teaspoon crushed red pepper
1 pound (3 large) portobello mushrooms,
   stem ends trimmed, cut into ½-inch chunks
   Salt
1 (10-ounce) head radicchio, cored and thinly
   sliced vertically (as for coleslaw)
   Freshly ground black pepper
12 ounces curly pigtail semolina pasta
   (cavatapi or tortiglioni), preferably imported
   Three-Cheese Sauce, recipe follows

In a large, deep skillet over low heat, melt the butter. Add the garlic and crushed red pepper. Cover and cook without browning, stirring occasionally, for 5 minutes. Raise the heat to medium, add the mushrooms, season with ½ teaspoon salt and cook, covered, stirring once or twice, for 5 minutes. Raise the heat to high, add the radicchio, season generously with black pepper and cook, tossing and stirring often, until the vegetables are lightly browned, 4 to 6 minutes. Remove from the heat and cool.

Bring a large pot of water to a boil. Add the pasta and 2 teaspoons salt. Partially cover and cook according to the package directions until just tender, about 12 minutes. Drain.

Position a rack in the middle of the oven and preheat to 375° F. Lightly butter a shallow 3-quart baking dish. In a large bowl, stir together the pasta, the mushroom mixture and the sauce. Spoon into the prepared dish and spread evenly. Bake until the sauce is bubbling and the top is lightly browned, 30 to 40 minutes. Let stand in the pan on a rack for 5 minutes before serving.

Three-Cheese Sauce

This cheese sauce, made with creamy Bel Paese, earthy goat cheese and genuine Italian Parmesan, is at least three times as good as any other you've ever tasted.

Makes about 4½ cups

3 tablespoons unsalted butter
3 tablespoons unbleached all-purpose flour
3 cups milk
½ teaspoon salt
½ teaspoon freshly ground black pepper
¼ teaspoon freshly grated nutmeg
10 ounces shredded Bel Paese cheese
4 ounces rindless goat cheese, such as Montrachet
1 cup (about 2½ ounces) freshly grated
    Parmigiano-Reggiano cheese

In a medium, heavy saucepan over low heat, melt the butter. Whisk in the flour and cook, stirring often without allowing the flour to brown, for 4 minutes. Remove the pan from the heat and gradually whisk in the milk. Set the pan over medium heat. Whisk in the salt, pepper and nutmeg. Bring to a simmer, then lower the heat, partially cover and cook, stirring often, until thick, about 15 minutes. Remove from the heat. Add the Bel Paese, goat cheese and Parmigiano-Reggiano and stir until smooth. The sauce can be prepared up to 3 days in advance. Cool, cover and refrigerate, returning it to room temperature before using.

 Since portobellos are fully opened, their gills are completely exposed, and some chefs find their inky-brown color unattractive. This is especially true if the mushrooms are to be used in something like a creamy sauce, which can actually be discolored by the gills. This is less important when the mushrooms are grilled, but if you want to remove the gills, first trim the stems even with the caps. Lay the portobellos, gills-up, on the work surface. With a paring knife held parallel to the work surface, slice just below the gills, shaving them away from the firm, light-brown caps, and discard.

Polenta-Crusted Deep-Dish Cheese and Roasted Vegetable Tart

This beautiful tart is a real production number and a fine lunch or brunch main dish (served with a green salad on the same plate) or, in smaller portions, first course. The tart can be completely baked up to 1 day in advance, if desired, and reheated just before serving. It's also good at room temperature, and sturdy enough to travel along on a picnic.

Serves 6 as a main course, 8 to 10 as a first course

1 medium eggplant, about 1 pound,
    cut lengthwise into ¾-inch-thick slices

2 large portobello mushroom caps,
    about ¾ pound total

3 fresh plum tomatoes, halved lengthwise and
    seeded

6 tablespoons olive oil
    Salt
    Freshly ground black pepper

3 cups water

1 cup plus 1 tablespoon instant polenta,
    see Note

5 teaspoons finely chopped fresh rosemary

1¼ cups shredded Gruyère cheese

1¼ cups shredded Monterey Jack cheese

2 tablespoons hot chile oil, see Note
    Caramelized Onions (see page 8)

Position a rack in the middle of the oven and preheat to 450° F.

On two jelly-roll pans, brush the eggplant slices, porto-bellos and tomato halves with 5 tablespoons of the olive oil. Season with salt. Working in batches if necessary, roast the vegetables in the oven, turning them once or twice, until lightly browned and tender, about 15 minutes. Cool to room temperature.

Lower the oven temperature to 350° F.

Cut the eggplant slices and mushroom caps into ½-inch strips. Chop the tomatoes. Season the eggplant, mushrooms and tomatoes lightly with salt and generously with black pepper.

In a small, heavy saucepan over high heat, bring the water to a boil. Stir in 1½ teaspoons salt. Gradually whisk in the polenta. Stir in 3 teaspoons of the rosemary. Lower the heat and cook gently, uncovered, stirring often, until very thick, 3 to 5 minutes. Remove from the heat. In a bowl, mix together the Gruyère and Monterey Jack cheeses. Add ½ cup of the mixed cheeses and a generous grinding of pepper to the hot polenta. Stir well. With the remaining 1 tablespoon oil, lightly coat the inside of a 10-inch diameter, 2-inch-deep fluted quiche pan with a removable bottom. Spoon the hot polenta into the prepared pan. With a spatula, spread it over the bottom and up the sides to form a shell about ½ inch thick. Brush the inside of the shell with the chile oil.

Set the quiche pan on a baking sheet and set it in the oven. Bake until the shell has firmed and is lightly browned, 10 to 15 minutes. Transfer to a work surface. Scatter ½ cup of the mixed cheeses over the bottom of the shell. Spread the caramelized onions over the cheese. Scatter another ½ cup cheese over the onions. Spoke fashion, arrange the eggplant and mushroom strips, alternating them, in 2 layers over the onions. Scatter the remaining 1 cup cheese over the vegetables. Stir the remaining 2 teaspoons rosemary into the tomatoes. Dollop the tomatoes atop the cheese in a decorative pattern (for instance, 1 dollop in the center and 6 around the edge of the tart). Return the tart to the oven and bake until the cheeses are just melted, 15 to 20 minutes.

Cool completely on a rack. With a small knife, carefully release the sides of quiche pan. Remove the sides. Cut the tart into wedges. Serve at room temperature or rewarm the tart in a 300° F. oven if desired.

Note: Most instant polenta comes boxed, as a preportioned mix. To make this recipe, measure out the required amount of polenta meal, reserving the remainder for another use. Some Italian chile pastes separate and the oil that rises to the top can be used here. Or, prepared chile-flavored olive oil is available in bottles in gourmet shops and some supermarkets. Asian hot oils, with added seasonings, are not appropriate for this.

Big Salads

My Tuna Salad Niçoise

Tart and cool, full of contrasting textures and light but satisfying, main course salads—big salads—are my favorite foods to eat. Served at room temperature, lively with vinegar or citrus juice, the various ingredients are at their most succulent and respective bests, their colors bright and sharp, the flavors clear and distinct. A minimal amount of luscious oil—most often olive oil—ties everything together. Even better, perhaps, than how good big salads taste and look, is how they simplify the cook's life. Composed of precooked ingredients, most often dressed just before serving, they are foods that go together with little last-minute fussing and wait patiently until guests are ready to enjoy them. Pretty and casual, big salads are a caterer's buffet mainstay—and they're every bit as wonderful to make and serve at home as well. **Southwestern Chicken Salad • Mediterranean Chicken and Beefsteak Tomato Salad • Chinese Chicken and Noodle Salad with Peanut Dressing • Chopped Salad with Cranberry-Orange Vinaigrette • Broiled Szechuan Tofu Salad • Shrimp, Sausage and Saffron Paella Salad • My Tuna Salad Niçoise • Grilled Shrimp, Fennel and White Bean Salad with Sage Vinaigrette • Sizzling Thai Beef Salad**

Southwestern Chicken Salad

Big, bold food is a Flavors signature, one never more evident than in this smoky, slightly fiery and tangy dish. It's a long way from the chicken salads of my youth, liberally dressed with mayonnaise from a jar, embellished with a few bits of celery and spooned into a hollow tomato or spread between slices of squishy white bread. This salad is what I serve to customers and company when I want them to sit up and take notice. As with almost all of my grill recipes, the wood chips are optional, but for me, it just isn't summer without the fragrance of mesquite wafting through the yard.

Serves 4 to 6

3 large, thick, whole boneless, skinless chicken
  breasts (about 2½ pounds total), trimmed
  and separated
    Tequila–Green Onion Marinade,
    recipe follows
2 cups wood chips, preferably mesquite, optional
1 large ear tender, sweet corn, shucked
1 teaspoon olive oil
2 large sweet red peppers, roasted, peeled and cut
    into ¼-inch strips (page 28)
½ cup diced red onion
¼ cup finely chopped cilantro, plus sprigs of
    cilantro as optional garnish
2 tablespoons finely chopped flat-leaf parsley
1 tablespoon lime zest (colored part of peel,
    removed with a zester and minced)
¾ teaspoon freshly ground black pepper
⅓ cup fresh lime juice

¼ cup cold-pressed extra-virgin olive oil
1½ teaspoons salt
½ teaspoon ground cumin,
    preferably from toasted seeds (page 4)
½ teaspoon Tabasco Pepper Sauce
1 buttery ripe, black-skinned California avocado
1 medium-large ripe, juicy tomato, trimmed and
    chunked

In a shallow, nonreactive dish, combine the chicken breasts with the marinade. Cover and let stand at room temperature, turning occasionally, for 1 hour.

Prepare a hot charcoal fire or preheat a gas grill (medium-high). When the fire is hot, distribute the wood chips if you are using them. Position the grill rack about 6 inches above the heat.

Brush the corn with the 1 teaspoon olive oil. When the chips are smoking, lift the chicken breasts from their mari-

> We choose extra-thick chicken breasts for grilling for two reasons: Their thickness makes them less prone to overcooking (and dry chicken breasts are a bore) and the extra time it takes to just cook them through allows them to pick up the maximum smoky flavor from the fire. Naturally, thinner breasts can be used, but shorten the grill time by about one-third and expect them to be less intensely flavored.

nade, reserving the marinade, and lay them and the corn on the rack. Cover and grill, basting the chicken breasts with the reserved marinade and turning them once, until the marinade is used up and they are lightly browned and just cooked through while remaining juicy, and the corn is lightly browned, 10 to 12 minutes total. Transfer the chicken and corn to a cutting board.

Cut the chicken breasts with the grain into long, thin strips; cut the strips crosswise into 2-inch pieces. With a serrated knife, cut the corn kernels off the cob; with the back edge of the knife, scrape any corn pulp and juices off the ear.

In a large bowl, toss together the chicken pieces, pepper strips, corn kernels, pulp and juices, onion, cilantro, parsley, lime zest and black pepper. In a small bowl, whisk together the lime juice, the extra-virgin olive oil, salt, cumin and Tabasco. Pour the dressing over the ingredients in the bowl and toss well.

The salad can be prepared to this point up to 1 hour in advance, if desired. Cover and hold at room temperature. Toss again and transfer to plates or a large platter. Halve and pit the avocado and with the dull side of a table knife score the flesh down to the peel into ½-inch chunks. With a spoon, scoop the avocado chunks out of the peels and over the salad. Scatter the tomato chunks over the salad. Garnish with cilantro sprigs, if desired, and serve immediately.

Tequila-Green Onion Marinade

This zesty marinade is also good on other foods headed for the grill, especially shrimp, swordfish, and beef skirt steak.

Makes about 1 cup

3 green onions, trimmed and chopped (tops included)
¼ cup fresh lime juice
¼ cup olive oil
3 tablespoons gold tequila
6 garlic cloves, peeled and chopped
1 tablespoon packed golden-brown sugar
1 tablespoon soy sauce

In a food processor or blender, combine the green onions, lime juice, olive oil, tequila, garlic, sugar and soy sauce. Process until fairly smooth.

For a roll-your-own fajita party, warm 3 or 4 6-inch flour tortillas per person on the grill (it takes only seconds) and serve them along with the salad. Encourage guests to spoon chicken, avocado and tomato into the tortillas (along with sprigs of peppery watercress if desired), roll and eat them out of hand. Pass salsa at the table for those who like a hotter flavor.

Mediterranean Chicken and Beefsteak Tomato Salad

Tart and colorful, this grilled chicken salad is a staple at Flavors and recalls (without actually duplicating) the sunny, lemony, smoky foods I associate with the Mediterranean. It makes a colorful, satisfying, mayonnaise-free summertime main dish, especially when the chicken is served over a bed of juicy-ripe red and yellow beefsteak tomato slices. The rest of the menu should be classic Mediterranean rustic too—good bread, cool white wine, seasonal fresh fruit.

Serves 4 to 6

⅓ cup dry white wine

¼ cup olive oil

3 tablespoons fresh lemon juice

2 tablespoons lemon zest (colored part of peel, removed with a zester and minced)

2 tablespoons Roasted Garlic Puree (page 162) or minced fresh garlic

1 tablespoon finely chopped fresh rosemary

1 tablespoon finely chopped fresh thyme
  Salt
  Freshly ground black pepper

3 large, thick, whole boneless, skinless chicken breasts (about 2½ pounds total), halved and trimmed

2 cups wood chips, preferably mesquite, optional

⅓ cup coarsely chopped pitted drained Greek black olives (Kalamatas)

⅓ cup finely chopped flat-leaf parsley

¼ cup small (nonpareil) capers, drained

⅓ cup cold-pressed extra-virgin olive oil

½ teaspoon Tabasco Pepper Sauce

2 large, ripe beefsteak tomatoes, about 1½ pounds total, preferably 1 each of red and yellow, trimmed and sliced ½ inch thick

In a food processor, combine the white wine, the ¼ cup olive oil, 1 tablespoon of the lemon juice, 1 tablespoon of the lemon zest, 1 tablespoon of the garlic puree, the rosemary, thyme and ½ teaspoon each of the salt and pepper. Process, stopping to scrape down the sides of the work bowl once or twice, until fairly smooth. In a shallow, nonreactive dish, pour the marinade over the chicken breasts. Cover and let stand at room temperature, turning occasionally, for 1 hour.

Prepare a hot charcoal fire or preheat a gas grill (medium-high). When the fire is hot, distribute the wood chips if you are using them. Position the grill rack about 6 inches above the heat.

When the chips are smoking, lift the chicken breasts from their marinade, reserving the marinade, and lay them on the rack. Cover and grill, basting the chicken breasts with the reserved marinade and turning them once, until the marinade is used up and they are lightly browned and just cooked through while remaining juicy, about 10 minutes total. Transfer to a cutting board and cool.

Cut the chicken breasts with the grain into thin strips. Cut the strips crosswise into 2-inch pieces. In a large bowl, combine the chicken strips, olives, parsley and capers. In a small bowl, whisk together the extra-virgin olive oil, the remaining 2 tablespoons lemon juice, the remaining 1 tablespoon lemon zest, the remaining 1 tablespoon garlic puree, the Tabasco and ¼ teaspoon salt. Pour the dressing over the salad and toss well. Adjust the seasoning. The salad can be prepared up to 1 hour ahead. Cover and hold at room temperature.

Arrange the tomato slices in an overlapping layer on a platter or individual plates. Spoon the salad over the tomatoes. Serve immediately.

 CAPERS AND CAPER BERRIES—Capers are the tightly furled buds of a common Mediterranean plant, often seen sprawling over tumbled stone walls. Capers are preserved by pickling in a salty vinegar brine or are dried and packed in salt, to be reconstituted by the cook at home. Nonpareil capers are the smallest, the hardest to pick and thus the most expensive, but we think they are worth their price and call for them specifically in all recipes. (They are also easier to find in this country than the salt-dried, and frankly somewhat easier to like.) Tart and with a strong wild flavor, capers are good complements to cold meats, vegetables and seafood; combine well with garlic, lemon and anchovy; and are essential in tangy sauces such as tartar and rémoulade. Any unused capers can be covered with vinegar if necessary, and refrigerated in their jar, though to a caper lover like me, the concept of leftovers is foreign. Says Tom Stobart, in The Cook's Encyclopedia, "Addicts eat them on bread and butter when nobody is looking." Hear, hear. (Less common caper berries, one of my favorite edible garnishes, are the grown-up fruit of the caper plant. Picked in small clusters on the stem and pickled, they are delicious and visually dramatic, and for caper fans, the ultimate experience. They are increasingly available in jars and gourmet shops.)

Chinese Chicken and Noodle Salad with Peanut Dressing

Back when I first started catering, lunches for photo shoots at Vogue *were among my steadiest jobs. Often this incredibly appealing salad, with its universal "Asian" dressing, was on the menu. How the chicken is cooked (poached, roasted, grilled, even rotisseried at the supermarket) and what it is tossed with (bean sprouts, baby corn, sugar snap peas, mushrooms) matters far less than the seductively spicy peanut dressing. Even those skinny models at* Vogue *cleaned their plates, so you know your friends, with their normal measurements, are going to love this too.*

Serves 6

2 large, whole boneless, skinless chicken breasts
   (about 1½ pounds total)
  Salt
4 cups broccoli florets
3 cups angle-cut 2-inch pieces of asparagus
9 ounces narrow fresh egg noodles, such as
   Contadina Linguine
1 tablespoon Asian dark sesame oil,
   from toasted seeds
  Peanut Dressing, recipe follows
1 large sweet red pepper, stemmed, cored and
   angle-cut into ½-inch pieces
⅔ cup sliced green onion (tender tops included)
  About 5 cups finely shredded Napa cabbage
¾ cup roasted peanuts
⅓ cup finely chopped cilantro

In a medium skillet just large enough to hold them in a single layer, cover the chicken breasts with cold water. Add 1 teaspoon salt, set over medium heat and bring to a simmer. Turn the chicken breasts and simmer until just cooked through while remaining juicy, about 5 minutes. Remove from the water and cool to room temperature. Trim off any fat and the central cartilage and cut the chicken breasts into ½-inch cubes.

Bring a large pot of water to a boil. Add the broccoli and 2 teaspoons salt and cook uncovered, stirring once or twice, until crisp-tender, about 4 minutes (the water need not return to a boil). With a slotted spoon, transfer the broccoli immediately to a bowl of iced water. Add the asparagus to the water and cook, stirring once or twice, until crisp-tender, 3 to 4 minutes. With a slotted spoon, transfer the asparagus to the bowl with the broccoli. When cool, drain the vegetables immediately and pat dry.

Bring a second pot of water to a boil. Add the linguine and 2 teaspoons salt and cook according to the package directions, stirring occasionally, until just tender, about 3 minutes. Drain well, rinse under cold water and drain again. Transfer to a large bowl and toss with the sesame oil. The salad can be prepared to this point several hours in advance. Cover the ingredients and hold at room temperature.

Just before serving, add the dressing, broccoli, asparagus, sweet pepper and green onion to the bowl with the noodles and toss well. The salad can be prepared to this point up to 1 hour ahead. Cover and hold at room temperature.

Spread the cabbage in a layer on a single large platter or on serving plates. Divide the salad over the cabbage. Sprinkle with the peanuts and cilantro and serve immediately.

ASIAN DARK SESAME OIL—Usually—but not always—the label for dark sesame oil will say that it is made from toasted seeds. In any case, you will know it by its rich orange-brown color. It is a seasoning oil, powerfully flavored, and while a little can make magic, too much can overwhelm a delicate dish. Pale, cold-pressed sesame oils (I see them most often in health-food stores) are not acceptable substitutes.

Peanut Dressing

The dressing can be prepared several days in advance, letting the flavor of the ginger and garlic become even more pronounced. I'm a sensible woman, but I really do believe I could eat this with a spoon.

Makes about 1¾ cups

½ cup supermarket-type peanut butter, smooth or chunky
½ cup reduced-sodium canned chicken broth
⅓ cup soy sauce, preferably tamari
¼ cup Asian dark sesame oil, from toasted seeds
5 teaspoons red wine vinegar
5 teaspoons sugar
4 teaspoons minced fresh ginger
3 garlic cloves, peeled and minced
1 tablespoon Tabasco Pepper Sauce

In a food processor, combine the peanut butter, broth, soy sauce, oil, vinegar, sugar, ginger, garlic and Tabasco. Process, stopping several times to scrape down the sides of the work bowl, until smooth. The dressing can be used immediately or may be refrigerated, tightly covered, for up to 3 days. Return to room temperature if chilled before using.

Chopped Salad with Cranberry-Orange Vinaigrette

Chopped salad—also called Cobb salad—is one of the great American culinary inventions, ranking right up there with cheeseburgers and chocolate chip cookies as a delicious symbol of the casual way in which we think about food. A classic, Cobb salad nevertheless lends itself to improvisation. Here is my version, using a tangy cranberry-orange dressing. Perfect as the repository of the last of the Thanksgiving turkey, it is also terrific in summer, made with freshly poached meat. The salad is presented in a large wooden salad bowl or on a big platter and then dressed and tossed at the table.

Serves 6

2 boneless, skinless turkey breast fillets, about 1½ pounds total, or 1 pound cooked or smoked turkey breast, trimmed and cut into ¼-inch cubes
Salt

1 large head romaine lettuce, trimmed and finely chopped

8 strips (¾ pound) thick-sliced preservative-free bacon, crisply cooked and finely chopped

¼ pound Roquefort cheese, preferably imported, crumbled

2 large plum tomatoes, about ⅔ pound total, trimmed and finely diced

4 hard-cooked eggs, shelled and finely chopped

1 large black-skinned California avocado, pitted, peeled and diced

1 medium-sized red onion, peeled and chopped

½ cup chopped toasted walnuts

Cranberry-Orange Vinaigrette, recipe follows
Freshly ground black pepper

In a medium skillet, cover the uncooked turkey fillets with cold water. Add 1 teaspoon salt and set over medium heat. Bring to a simmer, turning once or twice. Simmer 5 minutes, turn and simmer until just cooked through while remaining juicy, another 5 minutes.

Cool the turkey to room temperature in the cooking water. Drain and pat dry. Trim the breasts and cut the meat into ¼-inch cubes.

In a large bowl, toss together the lettuce, bacon and Roquefort cheese. Mound the lettuce mixture in the center of a large wooden salad bowl or a big platter. Around the lettuce arrange mounds of turkey, tomato, egg, avocado and red onion. Scatter the walnuts over all. Present the salad at the table, then drizzle it with dressing, season generously with pepper and toss. Plate the salad or let guests serve themselves.

Cranberry-Orange Vinaigrette

Though commercial cranberry relish seems widely available, don't hesitate to use leftover homemade or even canned cranberry sauce in this tangy dressing.

Makes about 1 cup

⅔ cup walnut oil
¼ cup raspberry vinegar
2 tablespoons Cranberry-Orange Relish, available in some supermarkets
2 teaspoons Dijon mustard
Pinch of salt
Freshly ground black pepper

In a small bowl, whisk together the oil, vinegar, relish, mustard, salt and a generous grinding of pepper. The dressing can be prepared several hours in advance. Cover tightly and hold at room temperature.

COBB SALAD—Created by Robert Cobb, owner of the legendary Hollywood eatery The Brown Derby, this chopped salad was supposedly invented to use up kitchen leftovers. In its traditional form, the ingredients (turkey, tomato, bacon, avocado, hard-cooked eggs, Roquefort cheese, all very finely chopped) were presented in separate mounds in a salad bowl, then dressed, tossed and plated at the table. Though it evokes the same naive West Coast glamour that Caesar salad does, the Cobb has not undergone quite the same renaissance. Still, good versions are increasingly available in the hipper restaurants, and few main-course salads, whether classically presented or skillfully updated, are as satisfying.

 To toast walnuts (and all other nuts for that matter) position a rack in the middle of the oven and preheat to 375° F. Spread the walnuts in a single layer in a metal pan (such as a cake tin) and toast, stirring once or twice, until crisp and fragrant, 8 to 10 minutes. Do not overcook or the nuts will be bitter. Transfer immediately to a bowl and cool to room temperature before using. Store the toasted nuts airtight at room temperature for up to 3 days if desired.

Broiled Szechuan Tofu Salad

For those wanting to skip meat altogether, this hearty tofu dish will serve nicely at the center of the plate. The rest of us can enjoy it, too, served in smaller portions as part of an Asian appetizer spread or as a side dish. Broiling the tofu enhances the texture and flavor (come summer it can also be grilled); the pungent dressing is addictive.

Serves 4 to 6

3 pieces firm tofu, about 2½ pounds total, drained, patted dry and sliced ½ inch thick

4 tablespoons peanut oil
Shredded Napa cabbage and sprigs of watercress

5 teaspoons hoisin sauce

5 teaspoons Asian chile-garlic paste

4 teaspoons seasoned rice wine vinegar

4 teaspoons soy sauce, preferably tamari

1 tablespoon Asian dark sesame oil, from toasted seeds

1 tablespoon sugar

1 teaspoon Asian hot chile oil

⅓ cup thinly sliced green onion, tender tops included

Position a rack about 3 inches from the broiler and preheat.

Cover the broiler pan with foil. Lay the tofu slices on the foil-covered pan and brush them on both sides with 1 tablespoon of the peanut oil. Broil, carefully turning the tofu slices once with a wide spatula, until they are lightly browned on both sides, about 8 minutes total.

Toss the cabbage and watercress together on a platter. Cool the tofu slices to room temperature, then arrange them, overlapping them slightly, over the cabbage mixture.

In a medium bowl, whisk together the remaining 3 tablespoons peanut oil, the hoisin sauce, chile-garlic paste, vinegar, soy sauce, sesame oil, sugar and hot chile oil. Adjust the seasoning. Drizzle the dressing over the tofu, using it all. Scatter the green onion over all and serve at room temperature.

HOISIN SAUCE, SEASONED RICE WINE VINEGAR, ASIAN HOT CHILE OIL, CHILE-GARLIC PASTE—Increasingly, these convenient Asian ingredients are turning up in good supermarkets, saving a trip to an esoteric specialty shop—a boon to cooks like me, who use them often for their flavor-boosting qualities, and not just in Asian dishes. Hoisin sauce is made from ground fermented beans and other seasonings. Slightly sweet, garlicky and maybe a bit picante, depending on the brand, it is used in dipping sauces and in glazes for roasted meats. Japanese seasoned rice wine vinegar is delicate, and flavored with a touch of salt and sugar. I use it primarily in vegetable salads, where I want the flavors of the main ingredients to shine through. Hot oil is usually flavored with chiles and garlic, plus sesame, ginger, even onion. A seasoning oil, it is used sparingly in marinades and dressings. There are Vietnamese and Chinese chile-garlic pastes. Brands vary (and the Chinese ones can be saltier), but the thick, tart, red, very garlicky and thoroughly incendiary paste keeps indefinitely in the refrigerator and can be added, a spoonful at a time, to soups, glazes, sauces, stews, dips and almost any other dish that needs a boost of heat or garlic.

Shrimp, Sausage and Saffron Paella Salad

Here is one of the first buffet dishes I ever developed for Flavors Catering, many years ago. Inspired by the classic Spanish saffron rice dish paella, it was prepared for Dr. Nathan Kase of The Mount Sinai Medical School on the occasion of his wife Judy's birthday. A good omen it proved to be, for the Kases are now dear friends. The salad is a bit of an operation, which is why I've built in plenty of do-ahead steps. Like the best of such salads, it requires little more by way of accompaniment than bread, possibly a green salad and plenty of good wine, so despite the kitchen time, it ultimately makes feeding a crowd an easy pleasure.

Serves 8 to 10

Shrimp, Peppers and Sausage

¾ cup dry white wine

3 plum tomatoes, cored, seeded and finely chopped

2 tablespoons olive oil

2 garlic cloves, peeled and crushed through a press

1 lightly packed teaspoon crushed saffron threads
Salt
Freshly ground black pepper

1½ pounds (about 24) large shrimp, shelled and deveined

2 cups mesquite or hickory wood chips, optional

2 large sweet peppers, preferably 1 red and 1 yellow, stemmed, seeded and quartered lengthwise

1 tablespoon olive oil

1 pound smoked sausage, such as andouille, hot links or kielbasa

Rice

3 tablespoons olive oil

1½ cups chopped yellow onion

4 garlic cloves, peeled and finely chopped

1 bay leaf

5 cups Chicken Stock (page 45) or reduced-sodium canned chicken broth

3 cups converted rice

1 lightly packed teaspoon crumbled saffron threads

1 (10-ounce) box frozen tiny peas, thawed and drained

3 tablespoons finely chopped flat-leaf parsley

To make the shrimp, peppers and sausage: In a small, nonreactive saucepan, combine the wine, tomatoes, olive oil, garlic, saffron, 1 teaspoon salt and a generous grinding of pepper. Set over medium heat and bring just to a simmer. Remove from the heat and cool. In a nonreactive dish just large enough to hold the shrimp comfortably, combine them with the tomato mixture. Cover and let stand at room temperature for 2 hours.

 On their own, these saffron-marinated shrimp make a delicious grilled appetizer or entrée. Serve them with Chipotle Rémoulade (page 17), Black Olive Aiolo (page 18) or Pesto Mayonaise (page 61).

Lift the shrimp from their marinade, reserving the marinade, and divide the shrimp among 4 or 5 flat metal skewers. Transfer the marinade to a small, nonreactive saucepan and set it over medium heat. Bring to a brisk simmer and cook uncovered for 1 minute. Remove from the heat and cool.

Prepare a hot charcoal fire or preheat a gas grill (medium-high). When the fire is hot, distribute the wood chips if you are using them. Position the grill rack about 6 inches above the heat.

Brush the pepper sections with the 1 tablespoon olive oil. When the fire is hot, working in batches if necessary, lay the skewered shrimp, pepper sections and sausage on the grill. Cover and cook, turning once, until the shrimp are just cooked through while remaining moist, about 5 minutes total, and the peppers and sausage are lightly charred by the fire, about 6 minutes total. Return the shrimp to the cooled marinade. Cool the sausage and peppers.

To make the rice: In a medium-sized heavy saucepan over moderate heat, warm the 3 tablespoons olive oil. Add the onion, garlic and bay leaf, cover and cook, stirring occasionally, until tender and lightly colored, 8 to 10 minutes. Add the stock and bring to a simmer. Stir in the rice and saffron, cover, lower the heat, and cook until the rice is tender and all the liquid is absorbed, about 20 minutes. Let stand off the heat, covered, for 5 minutes, then transfer to a bowl. Cool the rice to room temperature, fluffing it occasionally with a fork. Season to taste with salt and pepper. The shrimp, sausage, peppers and rice can be prepared to this

 Reserving a few "beauty shrimp" for show atop the salad is a caterer's trick that home cooks can make use of as well. In fact, when serving this on jobs, we frequently include 6 or 8 really jumbo shrimp in the cooking process specifically to serve as garnish (and as an indication of the shrimpy abundance to be found within). For a really grand show, you might even cook and shell a small lobster, slice the body meat into rounds and arrange the rounds and the claw meat over the rice in place of, or along with, the beauty shrimp.

point 1 day ahead. Cover or wrap tightly and refrigerate. Return to room temperature before proceeding.

Cut the pepper wedges into thin strips. Slice the sausage at an angle crosswise into 1-inch pieces. Reserve 6 of the shrimp. Add the remaining shrimp, their marinade, the sausage and the peas to the bowl with the rice and toss well. Transfer to a large platter. Mound the peppers atop the salad. Arrange the reserved shrimp over the peppers. Sprinkle the parsley over all. Serve immediately.

Note: The main ingredients need not be grilled. The shrimp and sausages can be broiled and the peppers can be roasted in your usual preferred way. Ingredient substitutions can also be made. For example, if I have some cold roast chicken, I remove it from the bones, discard the skin, tear the meat into bite-sized pieces, then toss it with the rice along with the other ingredients.

My Tuna Salad Niçoise

Canned tuna is the traditional—and tasty—star of salade Niçoise, but black olive–crusted grilled tuna steaks are a contemporary twist that really remodels the classic. People go crazy when I serve this, one of my favorite summer lunches when weekending in the Hamptons. The terrific flavors and colors aside, what I think people like most about my admittedly personal interpretation of this composed salad is the presentation. Arranged on a big platter, with the various ingredients lightly dressed and separately arrayed, it lets people pick and choose which foods they want to eat and combine—a salad "bar" of the very finest kind. As with several of my big salads, there are a number of steps, but the actual techniques involved are minimal, much of the work can be accomplished in advance, and the final assembling and serving are cool and leisurely.

Serves 6 to 8

1½ pounds (3 medium) beets, top stems and roots trimmed to not less than ½ inch

1½ pounds (about 10) small red-skinned potatoes, scrubbed, larger potatoes quartered, smaller potatoes halved

4 teaspoons olive oil
Salt
Freshly ground black pepper

8 baby artichokes, tops trimmed, tough outer leaves removed

½ pound haricots verts, trimmed

2 cups wood chips, preferably mesquite, optional

1½ pounds 1½-inch-thick tuna steak

3 tablespoons store-bought black olive tapenade or puree (from a jar, not the recipe on page 6)
Balsamic Vinaigrette (page 120)

½ cup diced (½-inch) red onion

1 pound cherry tomatoes, trimmed and halved

½ pound mesclun (mixed baby salad greens)

3 hard-cooked eggs, shelled and quartered lengthwise

½ cup drained Niçoise olives

1 jar, about 8 ounces, caper berries on the stem, drained

Position a rack in the middle of the oven and preheat to 400° F.

Wrap the beets tightly in a packet of aluminum foil. Set

HARICOTS VERTS—Haricots verts look like the skinniest baby green beans imaginable. They are, in fact, a special variety of green bean, with an intense, almost grassy flavor unlike that of all but the best American "string" beans. I occasionally find locally grown specimens, especially out on Long Island, but most are imported. They can be pricey, but their big taste and their automatically festive appearance make up for that. Because people don't always know what to do with haricots verts, the bin is sometimes full of tired and wilted-looking ones. Skip all but the freshest haricots verts, substituting when necessary regular green beans, thinly sliced lengthwise.

directly on the oven rack and bake until very tender, 1 hour to 1 hour and 15 minutes. Remove from the oven and cool the beets in the foil to room temperature. (The beets can be prepared to this point up to 1 day in advance. Refrigerate them in their foil, returning them to room temperature before proceeding.) Peel the beets and cut them into eighths.

On a sheet pan, toss the potatoes with the oil. Season lightly with salt and pepper. Roast the potatoes, stirring them occasionally, until they are tender and well browned, 30 to 40 minutes. Remove from the oven and cool.

Bring a medium pan of water to a boil. Add the artichokes and 2 teaspoons salt and cook uncovered, stirring occasionally, until tender when pierced with a fork, about 15 minutes. Drain well and cool. Quarter the artichokes vertically.

Bring a large pot of water to a boil. Add the haricots verts and 2 teaspoons salt. Cook until just tender, 2 to 3 minutes after the water returns to a boil. Drain the haricots verts, immediately transfer them to a bowl of iced water and let stand just until cool. Drain well.

Prepare a hot charcoal fire or preheat a gas grill (medium-high). When the fire is hot, distribute the wood chips if you are using them. Position the grill rack about 6 inches above the heat.

Spread one side of the tuna with half the tapenade. When the fire is hot, lay the fish on the rack, tapenade side down. Cover and grill for 4 minutes. Spread the upper side of the tuna with the remaining tapenade. Turn the fish and grill another 3 to 5 minutes for medium-rare, or until done to your liking. Transfer to a cutting board and cool slightly. Remove and discard the skin and cut the tuna into slices that are 2 inches long and about ½ inch thick. Season generously with freshly ground pepper.

In a medium bowl, toss the artichokes with 1 tablespoon of the vinaigrette. In a second bowl, toss the potatoes with 2 tablespoons of the vinaigrette. In a third bowl, toss the beets and red onions with 2 tablespoons of the vinaigrette. In a fourth bowl, toss the tomatoes with 2 tablespoons of the

 BALSAMIC VINEGAR—There is balsamic vinegar and then there is balsamic vinegar. This wildly popular wine-based product has been made in the Emilia-Romagna region of Italy for nearly a thousand years. Available in artisanal and industrial versions, it is a rich, dark-brown, mildly sweet vinegar with a mellow wine flavor. Of the former—complex-tasting and syrupy in texture, costing up to one hundred dollars for a few ounces—it can be said that it is unique. Not to be splashed indiscriminately around in salads by the quarter-cup full, but rather drizzled by the spoonful as a final seasoning over simple dishes of all sorts or even sipped as a restorative or liqueur, it is an experience no true lover of Italian cooking should be denied. The factory-made product, on the other hand, is the one most commonly found, for between five and ten dollars a bottle, in this country. The label should make it clear that it is from Modena, where pride in the local product extends even to these so-called *balsamicos industriales*. This is the kind of balsamic vinegar we use on The Market Table and the one you should use in the recipes in this book. Thinner and more acidic than artisanal *balsamico*, these vinegars are still sweeter and mellower than regular red and white wine vinegars and bring a unique flavor to the dishes in which they are used. Store all vinegars in a cool, dark place and use them up, after opening, within a few months.

vinaigrette. Season each vegetable to taste with salt and pepper and marinate for 30 minutes.

Mound the mesclun in the center of a large platter. Spoon the marinated artichokes, potatoes, beets, and tomatoes around (not on) the mesclun. Add the hard-cooked egg wedges to the platter and drizzle them with a tablespoon or two of vinaigrette. Arrange the tuna slices over the mesclun and drizzle the fish with 3 tablespoons of vinaigrette. Scatter the olives and arrange the caper berries decoratively over and around the various components and serve immediately. Pass the remaining vinaigrette at the table.

Balsamic Vinaigrette

Makes about 1¼ cups

3 tablespoons balsamic vinegar
1 tablespoon Dijon mustard
1 tablespoon minced shallot
1 teaspoon Tabasco Pepper Sauce

¾ teaspoon salt
1 cup cold-pressed extra-virgin olive oil
   Freshly ground black pepper

In a medium bowl, whisk together the vinegar, mustard, shallot, Tabasco and salt. Continue to whisk while adding the oil in a slow stream; the dressing will thicken. Add freshly ground pepper to taste, and adjust the seasoning. Use within an hour or so of completion.

Grilled Shrimp, Fennel and White Bean Salad with Sage Vinaigrette

Shrimp are wonderful party food, and never more so than in this pleasantly peasanty, Tuscan-feeling salad, a fine summer-lunch-on-the-deck one-dish meal. You may be familiar with shrimp and bean salads (it's a classic combination), but I feel sure that the addition of a roasted garlic marinade, grill-caramelized fennel and a pungent fresh sage-scented vinaigrette will make this version a new experience for you.

Serves 6 to 8

¾ pound dried white beans (cannellini or Great Northern), picked over
1½ pounds (about 30) medium-large shrimp, shelled and deveined
⅓ cup white wine
5 tablespoons olive oil
3 tablespoons Roasted Garlic Puree (page 162)
½ teaspoon crushed red pepper
   Salt
2 cups wood chips, preferably mesquite, optional

1 large fennel bulb, about 1 pound, fronds reserved, stems trimmed to 4 inches long
2 large sweet peppers, ideally 1 each of red and yellow, cut into quarters
⅓ cup cold-pressed extra-virgin olive oil
¼ cup minced fresh sage leaves
3 tablespoons white wine vinegar
¾ teaspoon Tabasco Pepper Sauce
   Sturdy, colorful mixed greens such as radicchio, frisée and red leaf

In a bowl, cover the beans with cold water and soak for at least 4 hours or overnight for convenience.

Drain the beans. In a large pot, cover them with fresh cold water. Set over medium heat and bring to a simmer. Tightly cover the pot, lower the heat and cook the beans, stirring occasionally, until just tender, about 30 minutes (bean cooking times vary widely; add additional boiling water and continue to cook the beans until tender if necessary). Remove from the heat and cool the beans in the water to room temperature. Drain well and transfer to a large bowl.

In a shallow nonreactive dish, stir together the shrimp, wine, 3 tablespoons of the olive oil, 1 tablespoon of the garlic puree, the crushed red pepper and ½ teaspoon salt.

Cover and let stand at room temperature, stirring occasionally for 1 hour.

Prepare a hot charcoal fire or preheat a gas grill (medium-high). When the fire is hot, distribute the wood chips if you are using them. Position the grill rack about 6 inches above the heat.

Quarter the fennel bulb vertically. Brush the fennel on all sides with the remaining 2 tablespoons olive oil. Lift the shrimp from their marinade, reserving the marinade, and slide them onto 4 or 5 flat metal skewers. Lay the skewered shrimp, fennel quarters and pepper quarters on the rack. Cover and grill, turning the shrimp skewers once and basting them often with the marinade and turning the peppers

and fennel 3 or 4 times, until the marinade is used up and the shrimp are just cooked through while remaining juicy, 7 to 8 minutes total, and the fennel is well marked by the grill and the peels of the peppers are lightly but evenly charred, 12 to 15 minutes total. Transfer the skewers and fennel to a cutting board. Transfer the peppers to a closed paper bag and steam until cool.

Core the fennel quarters. Cut the fennel into ½-inch pieces. Slide the shrimp from the skewers.

Mince the fennel fronds; there should be about 3 tablespoons. Rub away the burned peel, stem and core the peppers and cut them into thin strips. Add the shrimp, peppers, fennel and fennel fronds to the bowl with the beans.

In a food processor, combine the cold-pressed olive oil, sage, the remaining 2 tablespoons garlic puree, the vinegar, Tabasco and ½ teaspoon salt. Process until thick and fairly smooth.

Pour the vinaigrette over the contents of the bowl and toss. Adjust the seasoning. Serve within an hour or so of completion, spooned over a bed of the greens.

Note: The shrimp can be broiled or sautéed if desired, and the peppers roasted indoors by your preferred method. In this ungrilled version, the fennel could be used raw—and would be perfectly delicious. For variation, toss in a handful of small, unpitted green olives, such as picholines.

Sizzling Thai Beef Salad

Hot, tart, zesty, cool, crunchy, light and meaty all at once—is it any wonder Thai food is so interesting to cook and to eat? This is a take on beef yum *(or* yam*), a popular appetizer in Manhattan's Thai restaurants. I like it better as an entrée salad, and if the weather is sultry and no one feels like eating, this is what I cook—when that dressing begins to sizzle in the skillet, everyone's appetite returns with a vengeance! Drink Thai iced coffee (page 199) to cool the palate and offer chilled melon for dessert.*

Serves 6

1 small flank steak, about 1½ pounds

⅓ cup fresh lime juice

2 tablespoons plus ⅓ cup olive oil

3 tablespoons nam plah (Thai fish sauce, see below)

1 cup finely chopped cilantro

2 tablespoons finely chopped fresh ginger

3 garlic cloves, peeled and finely chopped

1 large fresh jalapeño chile, stemmed and finely chopped

1 tablespoon soy sauce, preferably tamari

1 medium head romaine lettuce, trimmed, washed and torn into bite-sized pieces

1 medium head red leaf lettuce, trimmed, washed and torn into bite-sized pieces

1 medium head curly endive, trimmed, washed and torn into bite-sized pieces

3 tablespoons minced fresh mint

3 tablespoons minced fresh basil

1 medium-sized red onion, peeled and cut into thin rings

2 large, ripe tomatoes, about 1 pound total, trimmed and cut into wedges

Half a large hothouse cucumber, peeled and cut into thin rounds

In a shallow, nonreactive dish just large enough to hold the flank steak comfortably, combine the steak with 3 tablespoons of the lime juice, 2 tablespoons of the oil and 1 tablespoon of the fish sauce.

NAM PLAH—This pale-brown sauce is an extract of tiny, anchovy-like fish, and is used more or less identically throughout Southeast Asia as a seasoning condiment. Among the powerful hot, sweet and salty flavors that make Thai food so compelling, this is one of the most important—if you don't like it, you probably don't like Thai cuisine. Because Thai cooking is increasingly popular, nam plah is now found in better supermarkets, though the brand that I find in Asian groceries, in a plastic bottle with its label entirely in Thai, <u>looks</u> more authentic, and I always seek it out. A tip: In a pantry emergency, nam plah can be substituted for the anchovies in a Caesar salad dressing.

In a food processor, combine the remaining ⅓ cup oil, half the cilantro, the remaining 3 tablespoons lime juice, the remaining 2 tablespoons fish sauce, the ginger, garlic, jalapeño and soy sauce. Process until smooth. Add 2 tablespoons of the pureed mixture to the marinating steak. Cover and let stand at room temperature for 2 hours, or in the refrigerator overnight. Return the steak to room temperature if chilled.

Heat a large, heavy skillet over medium-high heat until hot. Lift the steak from the marinade, reserving the marinade, and pat the steak dry. Lay the steak in the skillet and cook until well-browned, about 6 minutes. Turn and cook until well-browned on the other side, another 5 to 6 minutes for rare steak, or until done to your liking. Remove the skillet from the heat and transfer the steak to a cutting board. Off heat, add the remaining pureed mixture and the reserved marinade to the still-hot skillet. It will sizzle and boil up. Scrape the bottom of the skillet to dissolve any browned deposits. Cool the mixture to room temperature.

Cut the steak across the grain and at an angle into thin slices.

In a large bowl, toss the romaine, leaf lettuce, endive, remaining ½ cup cilantro, mint, basil and onion with about half of the dressing. Divide among 6 plates. Arrange the tomato wedges and cucumber slices around the dressed greens on the plates. Arrange the sliced steak over the greens. Serve, passing the remaining dressing at the table.

Left to right: Oil-Free
Wheat Berry Salad; Chick-
pea and Brown and Wild
Rice Salad with Moroccan
Spiced Dressing; Farfalle
and Spinach Salad with
Sun-Dried Tomato–Walnut
Pesto

Bean, Grain and Pasta Salads

There are times of the day when The Market Table is surrounded by people either on their way to the gym for a workout or all aglow after just finishing one. Either way, they're busy stocking up on the bean, grain and pasta salads that are our mainstays. It may seem at first that these healthy types are more interested in loading carbohydrates than in my kitchen's culinary skills. And indeed, these starches are energy-producing powerhouses. But when the same customers return without their gym bags and still head for the same dishes, I know it's because they like the earthy tastes and interesting textures that beans, grains and pasta supply, and they love the way these neutral ingredients take to the big, bold flavors with which we season them. I serve up these same satisfying salads at home, of course, in summer and winter, as solo accompaniments and as the stars of the meal, and my family and guests welcome them as much as I do. **Smoky "Baked" Bean Salad with Molasses-Mustard Vinaigrette • Tuscan White Bean Salad • Lentil and Roasted Red Pepper Salad with Walnuts and Grilled Green Onions • Chickpea and Brown and Wild Rice Salad with Moroccan-Spiced Dressing • New Year's Black-Eyed Pea Salad • Barley, Green Bean, Lima Bean and Corn Salad • Oil-Free Wheat Berry Salad • Cold Noodle and Vegetable Salad with Sesame-Soy Dressing • Brown and Wild Rice Salad with Cherries and Mangoes • Lemony Herbed Orzo with Tomatoes, Olives and Feta • Farfalle and Spinach Salad with Sun-Dried Tomato–Walnut Pesto**

Smoky "Baked" Bean Salad with Molasses-Mustard Vinaigrette

When you want the sweet and smoky taste of baked beans, but you don't want the fat and overheated kitchen that go with the traditional recipe, try this salad instead. Chipotle chiles rather than bacon supply the smoke, sun-dried tomatoes stand in for ketchup, and molasses sweetens the tangy vinaigrette, while through it all the cook stays cool. This salad can also be made with black beans.

Serves 4 to 6

2 cups (about ¾ pound) small dried white beans, such as Great Northern

¼ cup sherry vinegar

1 tablespoon yellow mustard seeds

¼ cup drained finely chopped oil-packed sun-dried tomatoes

3 tablespoons unsulphured molasses (page 207)

2 canned chipotle chiles (canned smoked jalapeños in sauce), with clinging sauce, finely chopped

½ teaspoon salt

⅓ cup cold-pressed extra-virgin olive oil

½ cup finely diced red onion

⅓ cup finely chopped flat-leaf parsley

In a medium bowl, cover the beans with cold water and let soak for at least 4 hours, or overnight for convenience.

Drain the beans. In a large pan, cover them with fresh cold water. Set over medium heat and bring to a simmer. Cover tightly, lower the heat and cook gently, stirring once or twice, until just tender, 35 to 45 minutes. Drain and cool.

In a small bowl, combine the vinegar and mustard seeds and let soak for at least 1 hour.

In a medium bowl, whisk together the soaked seeds and vinegar, the sun-dried tomatoes, molasses, chipotles and salt. Gradually whisk in the oil.

In a large bowl, toss together the beans, dressing, onion and parsley. Adjust the seasoning. Serve at room temperature, more or less immediately.

Tuscan White Bean Salad

I don't know that I've ever enjoyed beans more than in Italy. I used to think Italians had access to varieties we don't. This may be true, but I've learned that a simple mirepoix—a diced aromatic vegetable mixture—simmered with the beans adds tremendous flavor. That's especially important when the beans are served cold, as they are here. The mirepoix also adds a nice confetti of color to the salad.

Serves 6 to 8

2 cups (about 13 ounces) dried white beans, such as cannellini or Great Northern

½ cup chopped leek

½ cup chopped carrot

3 garlic cloves, peeled and chopped

4 sprigs fresh thyme

1 bay leaf

1 large, ripe tomato, about ½ pound, juiced, seeded and chopped

1 cup diced (½-inch) sweet pepper, ideally a combination of red, yellow and green

1 recipe Roasted Garlic Puree (page 162) or 6 garlic cloves, peeled and finely chopped

¼ cup seasoned rice wine vinegar

¼ cup cold-pressed extra-virgin olive oil

1¾ teaspoons salt

1¼ teaspoons Tabasco Pepper Sauce

1 cup finely chopped fresh basil
Freshly ground black pepper

In a medium bowl, cover the beans with cold water and let stand for at least 4 hours, or overnight for convenience.

Drain the beans. In a large, heavy pot, add cold water to cover them by at least 3 inches. Stir in the leek, carrot, chopped garlic, thyme and bay leaf. Bring to a boil. Tightly cover, lower the heat and simmer, stirring occasionally, until just tender, 30 to 40 minutes (bean cooking times vary widely; be prepared to add boiling water to the pan and continue to cook the beans until they are tender). Remove from the heat, add 2 cups cold water to the pan and let the beans stand in the cooking water until cool. Drain, discarding the thyme sprigs and bay leaf.

In a large bowl, toss the beans with the tomatoes and pepper. In a small bowl, whisk together the garlic puree, vinegar, olive oil, salt and Tabasco. Pour the dressing over the beans, add the basil and a generous grinding of pepper and toss again.

Serve the salad at room temperature, within an hour or two of completion.

SHERRY VINEGAR—Sherry vinegar is simply a vinegar that has been made from the nutty fortified Spanish wine called sherry. Brands vary, but all are darkly robust and quite powerful. The label of one brand I like warns, "Use sparingly—the flavor is rich and strong and comes through easily." True, but if you like sherry vinegar as much as I do, you won't be inclined to cut back much. If it proves difficult to find, good-quality red wine vinegar can be substituted.

Lentil and Roasted Red Pepper Salad with Walnuts and Grilled Green Onions

I love lentil salads, and of the many I have cooked up over the years, this is my favorite. Traditionally sold in French charcuteries as an accompaniment to pâtés, lentil salads are also satisfying alongside a cold roast chicken or as part of a buffet of meatless salads.

Serves 4 to 6

1 pound brown lentils, picked over and rinsed
½ cup cold-pressed extra-virgin olive oil
3 tablespoons red wine vinegar
3 tablespoons sherry vinegar
1 tablespoon fresh lemon juice
2 garlic cloves, peeled and crushed through a press
1½ teaspoons finely chopped fresh thyme
Salt
2 cups wood chips, preferably mesquite, optional
6 large, thick green onions, trimmed
1 teaspoon olive oil
1 large sweet red pepper
1 cup walnuts, toasted and coarsely chopped (page 114)
⅓ cup finely chopped flat-leaf parsley
Freshly ground black pepper

In a large pan, cover the lentils with cold water. Set over medium heat and bring to a boil. Partially cover, lower the heat and cook, stirring occasionally, until the lentils are just tender while holding their shape, 20 to 25 minutes. Drain well and transfer to a bowl.

Add the extra-virgin oil, the red wine and sherry vinegars, lemon juice, garlic, thyme and ¾ teaspoon salt to the hot lentils and toss. Cool to room temperature, stirring once or twice.

Prepare a hot charcoal fire or preheat a gas grill (medium-high). When the fire is hot, distribute the wood chips if you are using them. Position the grill rack about 6 inches above the heat.

Brush the onions with the 1 teaspoon olive oil. Lay the onions and pepper on the rack. Cover and grill the onions, turning them once, until they are lightly browned, 3 to 4 minutes total. Roast the pepper, turning it occasionally, until the peel is lightly but evenly charred, 10 to 12 minutes total. Transfer the onions to a cutting board. Steam the pepper in a closed paper bag until cool.

Thinly slice the green onions. Peel, stem and seed the red pepper and coarsely chop it. Add the onions, red pepper, walnuts, parsley and a generous grinding of black pepper to the lentils. Toss, adjust the seasoning and toss again. Serve at room temperature.

Note: If you don't want to light the grill, the pepper can be roasted indoors by your preferred method and the green onions can be used raw or roasted.

Chickpea and Brown and Wild Rice Salad with Moroccan-Spiced Dressing

Spicy and slightly exotic in the way of Moroccan food, this bean-and-grain salad is one of the store's most popular, and an enduring personal favorite of mine as well. It's good alongside plainly roasted or grilled cold meats such as lamb, chicken or ham, and essential when I'm putting out a meatless buffet or assorted cool salads for house guests to nibble on throughout a lazy summer day. Toasting the spices deepens and mellows their flavors, but this step can be omitted to save time if desired.

Serves 6

3 cups water
1 tablespoon soy sauce, preferably tamari
1 tablespoon unsulphured molasses
    (page 207)
½ cup wild rice, rinsed and drained
½ cup brown rice, rinsed and drained
    Salt
1 teaspoon ground turmeric
1 teaspoon ground coriander
1 teaspoon hot curry powder
1 teaspoon freshly grated nutmeg
¼ cup seasoned rice wine vinegar
¼ cup cold-pressed extra-virgin olive oil
2 tablespoons honey
2 tablespoons sugar
1 (15-ounce) can chickpeas (garbanzos),
    rinsed and drained
½ cup golden raisins
⅓ cup sliced unblanched almonds, toasted
    (page 114)

In a small saucepan, combine the water, soy sauce and molasses. Set over medium heat and bring to a boil. Add the wild rice, partially cover, lower the heat and simmer, stirring occasionally, until the rice is just tender, about 50 minutes (cooking times of wild rices vary widely; do not overcook). Drain well.

Bring a medium pan of water to a boil. Add the brown rice and 1 teaspoon salt. Partially cover, lower the heat and simmer, stirring occasionally, until the rice is just tender, about 30 minutes (rice cooking times vary widely; do not overcook). Drain well.

In a small, heavy skillet over low heat, combine the turmeric, coriander, curry powder and nutmeg. Cook, stirring often, until fragrant and lightly browned, about 6 minutes. Remove from the skillet immediately and cool.

In a small bowl, whisk together the rice wine vinegar, oil, honey, sugar and toasted spice mixture.

In a large bowl, combine the hot wild and brown rices, the chickpeas, raisins and dressing. Let stand, stirring occasionally, until cool. The salad can be prepared to this point up to 1 day ahead. Cover and refrigerate. Return to room temperature if chilled.

Stir in the almonds and adjust the seasoning. Serve at room temperature, no more than 30 minutes after adding the almonds.

New Year's Black-Eyed Pea Salad

Texans (and most other Southerners) eat some small portion of black-eyed peas for good luck as the New Year arrives. If you're throwing a New Year's Day open house, Super Bowl party or other buffet event, put this simple but good salad out along with the rest of the spread. (It can be eaten on corn tortilla chips, also, like a bean salsa.) Or, do as my mother did, and walk around the house with a bowl and a spoon, force-feeding it to your loved ones with a preventative mouthful against possible bad times ahead.

Serves 6 to 8

1 pound dried black-eyed peas, picked over, see Note

6 tablespoons cold-pressed extra-virgin olive oil

5 tablespoons white wine vinegar

1½ teaspoons Worcestershire sauce

1¼ teaspoons Tabasco Pepper Sauce

2 garlic cloves, peeled and crushed through a press

1½ teaspoons salt

½ small red onion, peeled and thinly sliced crosswise

In a medium pan, cover the peas with cold water. Set over medium heat and bring to a boil. Cover, lower the heat and cook gently, stirring once or twice, until just tender, about 25 minutes. Drain and transfer immediately to a medium bowl.

Add the oil, vinegar, Worcestershire, Tabasco, garlic and salt to the hot peas; toss well. Cool to room temperature. Stir in the onion and adjust the seasoning. Serve at room temperature.

Note: Six cups rinsed and drained canned black-eyed peas can be substituted.

TURMERIC—Turmeric (often mispronounced <u>toomer</u>-ick) is a bright yellow spice produced by drying and grinding the rhizome of a plant related to ginger. Used to make mustards yellow and in pickle mixtures like chowchow and piccalilli, turmeric is also a primary component of prepared curry powders. Despite its golden color and faintly medicinal taste, it's not a good substitute for saffron, though some cookbooks suggest it. Until you have used turmeric a few times, you may not like it, but it is a flavor that grows on you. The spice is always used dry, by the way, but in such small quantities that it's likely that if you do have some in the pantry, it's stale. Time to restock!

Barley, Green Bean, Lima Bean and Corn Salad

I love barley's nutty, mild flavor and satisfying chewy texture; it's good for you, too. Here is one of several summery salads based on barley that I make often. Its succotash-like main ingredients give it an attractive, homey quality while the sweet and spicy dressing adds contemporary flair. Serve it as an accompaniment to classic American barbecued chicken.

Serves 8

½ cup fresh lemon juice
1 tablespoon balsamic vinegar
1 tablespoon honey mustard
1 teaspoon ground cumin, preferably from
toasted seeds (page 4)
Salt
⅓ cup canola oil
Freshly ground black pepper
1⅓ cups pearl barley, rinsed and drained
½ pound green beans, trimmed and halved
1 cup baby lima beans, fresh or frozen and thawed
2 medium ears supersweet corn (or 1 cup well-
drained canned or thawed frozen corn)
½ cup diced red onion

In a small bowl, whisk together the lemon juice, vinegar, honey mustard, cumin and ½ teaspoon salt. Gradually whisk in the canola oil; the dressing will thicken. Season generously with pepper. Cover and let stand at room temperature for 1 hour to the develop the flavors. For conve-nience, the dressing can be prepared 1 day ahead, covered and refrigerated. Return to room temperature if chilled.

Bring a medium pan of water to a boil. Add the barley and 2 teaspoons salt. Lower the heat, partially cover the pan and cook, stirring once or twice, until just tender, about 30 min-utes. Drain. There should be about 4 cups cooked barley.

Bring a large pan of water to a boil. Add the green beans and 1 tablespoon salt and cook until crisp-tender, about 5 minutes. With a slotted spoon, transfer the beans to a bowl of iced water. Let stand just until cool, about 1 minute, then drain and pat dry.

Bring the pan of water back to a boil. Add the lima beans and ears of corn and cook until just tender, 3 to 5 minutes. (Canned or frozen corn does not require cooking.) Drain and cool. With a long, sharp knife, cut the corn kernels off the ears.

Just before serving, in a large bowl stir together the bar-ley, green beans, lima beans, corn kernels and red onion. Add the dressing and toss. Adjust the salt and season the salad generously with pepper. Serve at room temperature.

PEARL BARLEY—Pearl barley has been processed, like white rice, to remove several tough outer coatings. Some nutrient quality is lost when this happens, but the barley that results is still a powerhouse of protein. Thus pearl barley keeps longer on the pantry shelf, requires no presoaking and cooks up more evenly than pot and Scotch barley, which undergo less pro-cessing. This is one instance in which I do not hesitate to rely on a processed grain. Pearl barley can be found in most supermar-kets.

Oil-Free Wheat Berry Salad

Though we reduce the oil to the barest minimum in all our food (and especially our salads), a completely oil-free salad was one of my earliest goals. This is the result, a salad so crunchy, nutty and otherwise satisfying, no one misses what isn't there.

Serves 6

1½ cups raw wheat berries, rinsed and drained
    Salt
⅓ cup fresh orange juice
2 tablespoons soy sauce, preferably tamari
2 teaspoons Dijon mustard
1½ teaspoons sugar
¼ cup dried currants
¾ cup sliced green onion (tender tops included)
1½ teaspoons orange zest (colored part of peel, removed with a zester and minced)
    Freshly ground black pepper

Fill a medium-large pan with water and bring it to a boil. Add the wheat berries and 1 teaspoon salt. Partially cover, lower the heat, and simmer, stirring occasionally, until just tender, 50 to 60 minutes. Drain well.

Meanwhile, in a medium bowl, whisk together the orange juice, soy sauce, mustard, and sugar.

Add the hot wheat berries and the currants to the bowl and let stand, stirring occasionally, until cool. Stir in the green onion, orange zest and a generous grinding of black pepper. The salad can be prepared up to 1 day ahead. Cover and refrigerate. Let it come to room temperature and adjust the seasoning before serving.

Wheat berry is the cute name now given to whole unprocessed wheat—the grain that is ground for flour, cracked for cracked wheat, or precooked and then dried for bulgur. The popularity of wheat berries is on the rise, not surprising given how satisfyingly chewy and nuttily delicious they are. Many recipes for wheat berries recommend soaking them overnight, like dried beans, but I find this unnecessary. Wheat berries can be sprouted and baked into bread or used in stuffings, soups, salads, porridges and desserts. Shop for wheat berries in health-food stores and in some supermarkets. Like most whole grains, wheat berries turn rancid easily; store them in a cool dry place, even the freezer, and use them fairly promptly.

Cold Noodle and Vegetable Salad with Sesame-Soy Dressing

One of life's greatest pleasures, especially in a city like Manhattan, which seems to have a Chinese restaurant on every block, is curling up at the end of a hard day with a big white cardboard carton of cold sesame noodles. Coated with a typically rich and spicy peanut sauce, a delectable serving packs about the same number of calories as a pint of fudge ripple ice cream. Looking for a lighter way, I developed this salad, long on vegetables and without peanut butter, but otherwise equally habit-forming.

Serves 8 to 10

3 tablespoons sesame seeds
1 pound fresh snow peas, trimmed and stringed
18 ounces thin fresh noodles (such as Contadina brand linguine)
  Salt
2 tablespoons Asian dark sesame oil, from toasted seeds
3 tablespoons canola oil
¾ pound shiitake mushrooms, stems discarded, caps thinly sliced
½ pound cultivated cremini (brown) or white mushrooms, trimmed and thinly sliced
½ pound sunflower sprouts (also called sun sprouts, or substitute regular mung bean sprouts)
1½ cups thinly sliced green onion (1 large bunch with tender tops included)
  Sesame-Soy Dressing, recipe follows

In a small skillet over medium-low heat, toast the sesame seeds, stirring them often, until lightly browned, 8 to 10 minutes. Remove from the skillet and cool. The seeds can be toasted up to 3 days ahead. Store airtight, at room temperature.

Bring a very large pan of water to a boil. Add the snow peas and cook, stirring once or twice, until crisp-tender, 1 to 2 minutes. With a slotted spoon, transfer the snow peas to a bowl of iced water. Cool completely, then drain immediately and pat dry. The snow peas can be prepared several hours in advance. Cover and hold at room temperature.

Meanwhile, return the pan of water to a boil. Add the noodles and 1 tablespoon salt. Partially cover and cook according to package directions, stirring occasionally, until just tender, 2 to 3 minutes. Drain. Rinse thoroughly with cold water and drain again. In a large bowl, toss the noodles with the sesame oil. The noodles can be prepared several hours in advance. Cover and hold at room temperature.

In a large skillet over high heat, warm the canola oil. Add the shiitake and cremini mushrooms and cook, tossing and stirring occasionally, until barely tender, about 4 minutes. With a slotted spoon, transfer the mushrooms to the bowl with the noodles.

Just before serving, add the snow peas to the bowl with the noodles and mushrooms. Rewhisk the dressing and pour it over the salad. Toss well. Add the sprouts, green onion and 2 tablespoons of the sesame seeds and toss again. Turn the salad out onto a deep serving platter. Sprinkle the remaining sesame seeds over the salad and serve immediately.

Sesame-Soy Dressing

Makes about 1½ cups

¼ cup seasoned rice wine vinegar
¼ cup soy sauce, preferably tamari
2 tablespoons red wine vinegar
2 tablespoons Asian dark sesame oil, from toasted seeds
1 tablespoon fresh lime juice
2 garlic cloves, peeled and crushed through a press
1 tablespoon sugar
¼ teaspoon salt
¾ cup canola oil

In a medium bowl, whisk together the rice wine vinegar, soy sauce, red wine vinegar, sesame oil, lime juice, garlic, sugar and salt. Whisk in the canola oil.

Brown and Wild Rice Salad with Cherries and Mangoes

The contrast of juicy, sweet cherries and mangoes with crunchy rice makes for great and unexpected eating. In the winter substitute clementines and dried cranberries for the cherries and mangoes and scatter pomegranate seeds on top—a terrific complement to a smoked turkey or a big baked ham.

Serves 6 to 8

3 cups water

1½ tablespoons soy sauce, preferably tamari

1½ tablespoons unsulphured molasses (page 207)

¾ cup wild rice, rinsed and drained

¾ cup brown rice, rinsed and drained

Salt

½ pound sweet black cherries, stemmed, pitted and halved

1 medium-sized ripe mango, peeled and diced

1 cup (about 3 ounces) pecan halves, toasted and chopped (page 114)

½ cup golden raisins

½ cup thinly sliced green onion (tender tops included)

5 tablespoons cold-pressed extra-virgin olive oil

5 tablespoons raspberry vinegar

4 teaspoons orange zest (removed with a zester and minced)

Freshly ground black pepper

In a medium pan combine the water, soy sauce and molasses and bring to a boil. Add the wild rice, partially cover, lower the heat and simmer, stirring occasionally, until the rice is just tender, about 50 minutes (wild rice cooking times vary widely; do not overcook). Drain well and cool.

Bring a medium pan of water to a boil. Add the brown rice and 1 teaspoon salt. Partially cover, lower the heat and simmer, stirring occasionally, until the rice is just tender, about 30 minutes (rice cooking times vary widely; do not overcook). Drain well and cool.

In a large bowl, combine the wild rice, brown rice, cherries, mango, pecans, raisins, green onion, olive oil, vinegar, orange zest, ¼ teaspoon salt and a generous grinding of pepper. Toss well, adjust the seasoning and toss again. Serve at room temperature.

Cooking the wild rice with a touch of molasses and soy sauce in the water adds a deep, rich flavor that enhances the grain's natural goodness. It's an effect I especially like in rice salads.

Lemony Herbed Orzo with Tomatoes, Olives and Feta

One secret to making pasta salads that don't get soft and soggy is to use the smallest pasta shape possible, in this case orzo, which resembles a fat grain of rice. A pasta beloved by Greeks, here orzo is matched with other Greek favorites, including feta cheese and loads of fresh herbs. Try it alongside garlicky grilled shrimp or cold roast lamb.

Serves 8 to 10

1 pound semolina orzo pasta, preferably imported
Salt
6 tablespoons cold-pressed extra-virgin olive oil
6 tablespoons fresh lemon juice
3 medium-large ripe plum tomatoes (about ¾ pound), cored, seeded and diced
¼ pound pitted black Greek olives (Kalamatas), coarsely chopped
¼ pound drained feta, preferably Greek, crumbled
½ cup thinly sliced green onion, tender tops included
½ cup finely chopped flat-leaf parsley
2 tablespoons finely chopped fresh mint
2 tablespoons finely chopped fresh tarragon

2 teaspoons finely chopped fresh rosemary
2 teaspoons finely chopped fresh thyme
Freshly ground black pepper

Bring a large pot of water to a boil. Add the orzo and 1 tablespoon salt and cook partially covered, according to the package directions, stirring occasionally, until just tender, about 9 minutes. Drain and rinse thoroughly under cold running water. Drain again and transfer to a large bowl.

In a small bowl, whisk together the olive oil, lemon juice and ¼ teaspoon salt. Pour the dressing over the orzo and toss well. Add the tomatoes, olives, feta, green onion, parsley, mint, tarragon, rosemary, thyme and a generous grinding of pepper. Toss well and serve within an hour or so of completion.

Farfalle and Spinach Salad with Sun-Dried Tomato–Walnut Pesto

Even if you're tired of pasta salads, you'll find this one delicious. It's the pesto—packed with the flavors of sun-dried tomatoes, toasted walnuts and basil—that makes it work. Bow tie–shaped farfalle are fun to eat, but short fusilli or penne can be substituted.

Serves 6 to 8

¾ **pound dried semolina farfalle pasta, preferably imported**
Salt
1 **bunch flat spinach, trimmed, well rinsed, dried and coarsely chopped**
Sun-Dried Tomato–Walnut Pesto, recipe follows
½ **cup freshly grated Parmigiano-Reggiano cheese**

Bring a large pot of water to a boil. Add the pasta and 2 teaspoons salt and cook according to the package directions, stirring occasionally, until just tender, 10 to 12 minutes. Drain, rinse thoroughly under cold running water, and drain again.

In a large bowl, toss together thoroughly the pasta, spinach, pesto and ¾ teaspoon salt. Adjust the seasoning. Serve within an hour or two of completion, adding the cheese and tossing again at the last minute.

Sun-Dried Tomato–Walnut Pesto

This versatile and vibrantly flavored red pesto can also be used as an appetizer dip or spread. Try serving it in a crock, surrounded by bruschettas (page 14)—great with a glass of white wine before a summer meal from the grill.

Makes about 2 cups

1½ ounces sun-dried tomato halves
2 cups boiling water
1½ loosely packed cups coarsely chopped basil leaves
½ cup (about 2½ ounces) walnut pieces, toasted
    (page 114)
5 tablespoons cold-pressed extra-virgin olive oil
2 teaspoons red wine vinegar
2 teaspoons balsamic vinegar
1 garlic clove, peeled and chopped
½ teaspoon Italian red chile paste, optional
   Freshly ground black pepper
⅛ teaspoon salt

In a medium-sized heat-proof bowl, combine the tomatoes and boiling water. Let stand until the tomatoes are plump and fairly tender, about 15 minutes. Reserve 3 tablespoons of the tomato soaking water, then drain the tomatoes and chop them coarsely.

In a food processor, combine the tomatoes, basil, walnuts, olive oil, reserved tomato water, red wine vinegar, balsamic vinegar, garlic, chile paste, a generous grinding of pepper and salt. Process in short bursts of power, stopping several times to scrape down the sides of the work bowl. The mixture should be evenly chopped but chunky. The pesto can be prepared up to 3 days ahead; cover and refrigerate, returning it to room temperature before using.

Vegetable Salads

Left to right:
In large bowls—
Green Bean, New
Potato and Cherry
Tomato Salad
with Creamy
Vermouth Vin-
aigrette; Frisée,
Roquefort and
Pear Salad with
Pistachios; Winter
Salad of Grape-
fruit, Fennel and
Watercress

In my kitchens, salads are much more than greens. At Flavors, in fact, greens are problematical, tending to wilt, leading us to turn almost every other vegetable into salads instead. (Our wildly popular Caesar is the exception that proves the rule—and compels us to make it in small batches throughout the day to keep it crunchy.) The need for salads that start bright and stay bright occurs at home, too, as any cook with a crowd on the way can attest. My solution: Vegetables, at their respective seasonal peaks, minimally altered—often left raw—are adventurously combined, vividly seasoned and set out in a gorgeous array. When lightly dressed (no cloggy bottled dressings for me!) with best-quality vinegars and oils, and served at cool room temperature, their textures remain intact and their fresh flavors are readily apparent. Such salads actually are refreshing, which most foods are not, and they are satisfying as well. **Flavors' Bread, Tomato and Mozzarella Salad • Flavors' Caesar Salad • Carrot Salad with Thai Flavors • Frisée, Roquefort and Pear Salad with Pistachios • Winter Salad of Grapefruit, Fennel and Watercress • Beefsteak Tomato and Gorgonzola Salad with Toasted Walnuts and Basil • Mustardy Purple Cabbage and Carrot Slaw • Roasted Potato Salad with Rosemary and Asiago Cheese • Garden Herb New Potato Salad • Beet and Mango Salad with Curried Mango Dressing • Cucumber and Tomato Salad with Olives, Feta and Mint • Jicama, Green Bean and Sweet Pepper Salad • Sugar Snap Peas with Mint • Green Bean, New Potato and Cherry Tomato Salad with Creamy Vermouth Vinaigrette**

Flavors' Bread, Tomato and Mozzarella Salad

This is The Market Table take on panzanella, *the wonderful Tuscan salad of bread and tomatoes. Intended to use up leftovers of the crusty, flavorful bread for which Tuscany is famed, it is one of the great comfort foods. My Manhattan version begins with our big chile-flavored croutons, and combines them with* boccancini *(bite-sized balls of fresh mozzarella) and juicy sweet cherry tomatoes. This salad, and a piece of cool roast chicken, are all you need for a fine lunch on a hot summer's day.*

Serves 6

1 pound boccancini, drained and patted dry, see Note
¾ pound cherry tomatoes, preferably a combination of red and yellow, stemmed and halved
1 recipe Big Chile Croutons (page 145)
3 tablespoons cold-pressed extra-virgin olive oil
2 tablespoons balsamic vinegar
¾ cup coarsely torn fresh basil leaves
¼ cup coarsely chopped flat-leaf parsley
Salt
Freshly ground black pepper

In a large bowl, toss together the boccancini, tomatoes, croutons, oil and vinegar. Add the basil and parsley and season to taste with salt and pepper. Toss again and serve at room temperature, within an hour or so of completion.

Note: Some boccancini are actually bite-sized, while others amount to 2 or 3 bites. If you find only the larger (or if you must resort to full, 1-pound-or-so mozzarellas), just cut them into cubes about the right size. Low-moisture, part-skim supermarket mozzarella, perfect on pizza, is too bland, dry and rubbery for this sparkling salad.

Flavors' Caesar Salad

My Caesar dressing is not classic, but the flavor is authentic, and basing it on prepared mayonnaise rather than raw eggs relieves salmonella worries. Though I think this is one of the world's great first courses, it can be embellished into a pretty terrific main dish by adding strips of grilled chicken breast, cooked baby shrimp or lump crabmeat.

Serves 4 to 6

2 large heads romaine lettuce
  Caesar Dressing
1 cup grated Parmigiano-Reggiano cheese
24 Big Chile Croutons, recipe follows

Separate the heads of romaine, discarding any tough or browned outer leaves. Cut off the tough stems from the remaining leaves. Halve the leaves lengthwise, then cut them crosswise into 1½-inch pieces. There should be about 20 cups of lettuce pieces.

In a large bowl, toss the lettuce with the dressing. Add the cheese and the croutons and toss again. Divide the salad and the croutons among chilled plates and serve immediately, passing a pepper mill at the table.

Caesar Dressing

Makes about 1⅓ cups

1 cup mayonnaise
4 oil-packed anchovy fillets, chopped
4 teaspoons fresh lemon juice
2 large garlic cloves, peeled and chopped
½ teaspoon Tabasco Pepper Sauce
½ teaspoon freshly ground black pepper

In a food processor, combine the mayonnaise, anchovies, lemon juice, garlic, Tabasco and black pepper; process until smooth. Adjust the seasoning. The dressing can be prepared up to 3 days ahead. Cover tightly and refrigerate. Let the dressing come to room temperature before using.

CAESAR SALAD—This delicious, seemingly Italian recipe was created in Tijuana, Mexico, in the 1920s, by restaurateurs Caesar and Alex Cardini, reportedly in honor of pilots at an air base in nearby San Diego. Tijuana during Prohibition was a lively place and the salad is a fine symbol of racy good times. There are conflicting reports about whether anchovy was included in the authentic formula (or was the tiny amount of anchovy in the Worcestershire sauce sufficient?), but modern American diners expect anchovies, and so we include them, but pureed into the dressing as a subtle background flavor, not as whole fillets flung indiscriminately about. (When it's your salad, of course, you may do as you wish.) For adventurous friends, you might like to emulate Caesar's original serving method; use tender inner leaves of romaine, and serve them whole, encouraging guests to pick the dressed greens up with their fingers.

Big Chile Croutons

Worlds away from the dried-out and flavorless supermarket type, these big croutons are lightly crunchy and very spicy. They soak up the dressing in a particularly delicious way, and you will have to be sure you divide them evenly among your guests or quarrels may break out.

Makes 24

⅓ cup olive oil
1 tablespoon Italian red chile paste
2 garlic cloves, peeled and crushed through a press

24 1-inch cubes day-old crust-on, peasant-style bread, preferably semolina

Position a rack in the middle of the oven and preheat to 400° F.

In a large bowl, stir together the olive oil, chile paste and garlic. Add the bread cubes and toss well to moisten evenly. If necessary, let the cubes stand, stirring occasionally, until all the oil is absorbed.

Arrange the bread cubes in a single layer on a jelly roll pan. Bake, turning occasionally, until the croutons are lightly but evenly browned on all sides, 15 to 20 minutes.

Use warm, or wrap airtight and store at room temperature for up to 3 days or freeze for up to 1 month.

Carrot Salad with Thai Flavors

A salad that stays pretty and crunchy for hours, this one transforms sweet, simple carrots into something pleasantly adventurous. If you like your Thai food on the spicy side, add a little minced jalapeño or serrano chile to the dressing.

Serves 4 to 6

1½ pounds carrots, peeled and cut into 2-by-¼-inch batons
2 tablespoons cold-pressed extra-virgin olive oil
2 tablespoons fresh lime juice
1 tablespoon minced fresh ginger
1 teaspoon honey
1 teaspoon nam plah (page 122)
1 garlic clove, peeled and crushed through a press
Freshly ground black pepper
⅓ cup finely chopped cilantro

In a large bowl, toss together the carrots, olive oil, lime juice, ginger, honey, nam plah, garlic and a grinding of pepper to taste. Let stand at room temperature for 2 hours or refrigerate overnight.

Return the salad to room temperature if chilled. Add the cilantro and toss just before serving.

Frisée, Roquefort and Pear Salad with Pistachios

Slightly bitter frisée, sweet pears, potent Roquefort and nutty pistachios combine to make this winter salad lively and delicious. It is the sherry vinegar that pulls it all together, though in a pinch it can be made with red wine or even balsamic vinegar.

Serves 4 to 6

2 tablespoons sherry vinegar

1 teaspoon Dijon mustard

¼ teaspoon salt

¼ cup cold-pressed extra-virgin olive oil

6 ounces frisée
   Freshly ground black pepper

½ cup (about 4½ ounces) shelled pistachios, toasted and roughly chopped

¼ pound Roquefort cheese, preferably imported, crumbled

1 large ripe but firm pear, such as Bartlett, cored, peeled and cut into ½-inch chunks

In a small bowl, whisk together the vinegar, mustard and salt. Gradually whisk in the oil; the dressing will thicken.

In a large bowl, toss together the frisée and the dressing. Season generously with pepper.

Divide the salad among serving plates. Scatter the nuts, cheese and pear chunks over the salads and serve immediately.

FRISEE—Frisée, like radicchio and Belgian endive, is a member of the chicory family. It is indeed frizzy, but has been blanched (grown away from light) so that its leaves are a pale yellow-green and more tender than their spiky appearance would lead you to believe. Frisée is also not as bitter as other chicories. One of my favorite salad greens, it's worth seeking out, though except for the occasional leaf in a good batch of mesclun, it remains uncommon in much of the country. There's really no equivalent, though a combination of romaine, watercress and regular, unblanched curly endive or even escarole can be substituted.

Winter Salad of Grapefruit, Fennel and Watercress

Here is my variation on my Mom's famous romaine and grapefruit salad. You don't have to make it with Texas ruby-red grapefruit, but you really should.

Serves 6

3 medium pink grapefruits (1½ pounds total)
2 medium bunches watercress, tough 1½ inches of bottom stems trimmed
1 medium fennel bulb, very thinly sliced
1 small red onion, peeled, halved and thinly sliced crosswise
   Poppy Seed Dressing
   Freshly ground black pepper

With a serrated knife, cut a thick slice from the top and bottom of each grapefruit. One at a time, set the grapefruits on a cutting board, and with the serrated knife, cut downward toward the board, following the curve of the fruit, to completely remove the bitter white pith and the peel while leaving as much fruit behind as possible. Holding each grapefruit in your palm, cut downward between the segment dividers to remove the fruit sections.

Divide the watercress among 6 chilled salad plates. Mound the fennel and onion atop the watercress. Arrange the grapefruit segments over the salads.

Serve immediately, passing the dressing and a pepper mill at the table.

Poppy Seed Dressing

The inimitable Helen Corbitt, as head of a number of restaurants and clubs, including Neiman Marcus's tony Zodiac Room, had a profound influence on Texas cooks of the sixties and seventies. Her "American food with a Continental flavor" was sophisticated but approachable. I don't know if she invented poppy seed dressing, but she surely put it on the map.

Makes about 1⅓ cups

3 tablespoons apple cider vinegar
4 teaspoons Dijon mustard
1 tablespoon honey
¼ teaspoon salt
½ teaspoon freshly ground black pepper
1 cup corn oil
1 teaspoon poppy seeds

In a small bowl, whisk together the vinegar, mustard, honey, salt and pepper. Whisk in the oil in a slow, steady stream; the dressing will thicken. Stir in the poppy seeds. Adjust the seasoning. Use within an hour or so of completion.

Note: For a more authentic Corbitt-like flavor, add 1 or 2 tablespoons grated mild onion, including the juice.

Beefsteak Tomato and Gorgonzola Salad with Toasted Walnuts and Basil

A little different from other summertime tomato salads, this one points up the very obvious affinity between sweet basil and the delicious blue-veined Italian cheese, Gorgonzola. Be sure to purchase younger, softer, milder gorgonzola, which should be labeled dolcelatte, or sweet-milk; the aged cheese is too strong for this recipe.

Serves 8

4 large, ripe tomatoes, about 3 pounds total, preferably 2 each of red and yellow, trimmed and sliced crosswise into ½-inch-thick pieces

2 tablespoons cold-pressed extra-virgin olive oil

4 teaspoons balsamic vinegar

¼ teaspoon salt

½ cup packed fresh basil leaves

½ cup coarsely chopped walnuts, toasted (page 114)

½ cup coarsely crumbled Gorgonzola *dolcelatte* cheese

Freshly ground black pepper

Arrange the tomato slices in a slightly overlapping layer on a large platter. Drizzle the slices with the oil and vinegar. Sprinkle them with the salt.

Cover and let stand at room temperature for 30 minutes.

Tilt the platter several times to mix the oil, vinegar and rendered tomato juices. Tear the basil leaves into ½-inch pieces and scatter them over the tomatoes. Scatter the walnuts and Gorgonzola over the tomatoes. Season generously with pepper. Serve immediately.

TOMATOES—Tomatoes are the jewels of the garden and grow in wondrous array. Though some more than decent tomatoes can be located year-round (cherry tomatoes and Italian plum to name the most reliable), the best of them are summer glories, to be enjoyed precisely at that time of year when salad-making is at its frenzied peak. From tiny red-currant tomatoes to jumbo beefsteaks, in a rainbow of colors from yellow to red to pink to orange to green, tomatoes are far more varied and much more fun to eat than almost any other vegetable I know. Eventually, when the abundance overwhelms, I actually cook with these summer beauties, but for much of the tomato season I'm just glad to enjoy them raw. From sandwiches, where they add the squelch and acid, to big salad platters, either as the main ingredient or as a garnish, tomatoes are the best that summer offers.

Mustardy Purple Cabbage and Carrot Slaw

Tasty and pretty, this sweet mustardy slaw is never more delicious than when used on the barbecued chicken sandwiches on page 56. That said, it's also pretty good alongside grilled pork tenderloin, chicken or full-flavored fish, such as salmon. As usual, feel free to substitute fat-free versions of the yogurt and mayonnaise.

Serves 8

½ cup plain yogurt

½ cup mayonnaise

3 tablespoons whole-grain mustard

3 tablespoons sugar

2 tablespoons apple cider vinegar

1 teaspoon Tabasco Pepper Sauce

¼ teaspoon salt

6 cups thinly sliced purple cabbage

4 medium carrots, trimmed and coarsely shredded

¾ cup thinly sliced green onion, tender tops included

Freshly ground black pepper

In a medium bowl, whisk together the yogurt, mayonnaise, mustard, sugar, vinegar, Tabasco and salt.

In a large bowl, toss together the cabbage, carrots, dressing, green onion and a generous grinding of pepper. Let the slaw stand at room temperature for at least 30 minutes to mellow the flavors, or refrigerate overnight. Serve at room temperature.

Roasted Potato Salad with Rosemary and Asiago Cheese

For this mayonnaise-free salad (a great picnic take-along) the potatoes are oven-roasted. The wrinkly brown peels give it a wonderfully rustic look, while pungent rosemary and sharp Asiago (a granular grating cheese, similar to Romano) make it lively to eat. Like hot roasted rosemary potatoes, this is especially good with chicken or veal.

Serves 6 to 8

3 **pounds red-skinned new potatoes, well scrubbed and patted dry**
3 **tablespoons olive oil**
1 **teaspoon salt**
   Freshly ground black pepper
1 **tablespoon finely chopped fresh rosemary**
⅓ **cup shredded Asiago cheese**

Position a rack in the middle of the oven and preheat to 400° F.

Quarter the larger potatoes; halve the smaller ones. In a large bowl, toss the potatoes with the oil. Add the salt and a generous grinding of pepper and toss again. Transfer to a large jelly-roll pan or shallow roaster that will hold them more or less in a single layer. Roast the potatoes, stirring them occasionally, until they are crisply browned and tender, about 1 hour.

Remove from the oven and cool slightly. Transfer to a large bowl, add the rosemary and toss. Cool completely, add the Asiago and toss again. Serve at room temperature, preferably the same day the potatoes are roasted.

Garden Herb New Potato Salad

Here is a delicately crunchy and very herbal salad I first cooked in the Hamptons, the summer getaway area on the east end of Long Island. Vacation homes there are often set amid fields of potatoes, still one of the Hamptons' staple crops, and the local spuds—all sizes, shapes and colors—are incredibly delicious. Steamed to preserve their delicate texture and flavor, the tiniest "C-sized," or creamer, potatoes are served under a shower of summer garden herbs in a light vinaigrette. If you find no creamers, just use the tiniest, freshest potatoes available.

Serves 6 to 8

3 pounds small red-skinned new potatoes, well-scrubbed and trimmed
¼ cup apple cider vinegar
¼ cup cold-pressed extra-virgin olive oil
1½ teaspoons salt
Freshly ground black pepper
1 cup finely chopped celery
1 cup thinly sliced green onion, tender green tops included
¼ cup chopped drained cornichons (French gherkins)
¼ cup finely chopped fresh dill
2 tablespoons finely chopped fresh tarragon
2 tablespoons finely chopped fresh chives
2 tablespoons finely chopped flat-leaf parsley

Set a steamer basket in a pot and add about 1 inch water. Set the pot over medium heat and bring to a simmer. Halve the smaller potatoes; quarter the large ones. Add the potatoes to the steamer basket, cover the pot and cook just until tender, about 15 minutes.

Transfer the potatoes to a large bowl. While they are still hot, drizzle them with the vinegar and then the oil. Add the salt and a generous grinding of pepper. Toss gently. Add the celery, green onion, cornichons, dill, tarragon, chives and parsley and toss again. The salad is best when served still slightly warm, but it can be cooled and refrigerated overnight if necessary. Return it to room temperature before serving.

Note: Chopped fennel bulb can replace some or all of the celery. In addition, mince a tablespoon or two of fennel fronds and add them to the salad along with the herbs.

Beet and Mango Salad with Curried Mango Dressing

Here is a salad of vivid colors and intense flavors, perfect with a tropical or Asian-derived main course, especially the grilled duck breasts on page 66. When food is this beautiful, you hardly need to bother decorating the table.

Serves 8 to 10

1½ pounds (6 medium) beets, stems and tops
    trimmed to no more than ½ inch
Curried Mango Dressing
Salt
Freshly ground black pepper
⅔ cup diced red onion
12 cups bite-sized pieces of mixed sturdy salad
    greens, such as watercress, frisée and romaine
2 ripe mangoes, halved, pitted, peeled and cut into
    long strips

Position a rack in the middle of the oven and preheat to 400° F.

Tightly wrap 3 beets in each of 2 heavy-duty foil packets. Set the packets on the oven rack and bake the beets until they are tender, about 1 hour and 15 minutes. Cool the beets in the packets on a rack. The beets can be prepared to this point 1 day ahead. Refrigerate the beets in the packets, returning them to room temperature before proceeding.

Peel the beets and cut them into ¾-inch chunks. In a medium bowl, toss the beets with ¼ cup of the mango dressing, and salt and pepper to taste. Let stand for 30 minutes. Stir the onion into the beets.

Mound the greens on a platter. Spoon the beets onto the greens. Lay the mango strips over the beets. Serve immediately, passing the remaining dressing and a pepper mill at the table.

Curried Mango Dressing

I think this dressing requires a fairly hot curry powder in order to be really interesting to eat, but don't scorch your guests' palates. This can also be used to dress a fine, light chicken or turkey salad.

Makes about 2 cups

1 ripe, juicy mango, halved, pitted, peeled
    and cut into ½-inch chunks
⅓ cup apple cider vinegar
1 tablespoon Dijon mustard
1 tablespoon honey
1 teaspoon hot curry powder
½ teaspoon salt
½ teaspoon freshly ground black pepper
½ cup cold-pressed extra-virgin olive oil

In a food processor, combine the mango, vinegar, mustard, honey, curry powder, salt and pepper. Process until smooth. Add the oil and process to blend. Transfer to a medium bowl and let stand at room temperature for 1 hour, or refrigerate overnight, if desired. Return the dressing to room temperature if chilled.

Cucumber and Tomato Salad with Olives, Feta and Mint

Cool and refreshing, put together from a little garden abundance and a few pantry staples, this salad is wonderfully quick and easy. I know—I've made it on television, where they give you no time at all, and I make it at home nearly every summer weekend as well. Try it with the lamb sandwich recipe on page 60 for a nearly perfect hot-weather lunch.

4 to 6 servings

1 hothouse cucumber, about 1 pound, trimmed

¾ pound (3 medium) plum tomatoes

1 medium-sized red onion, peeled, halved and sliced

½ cup pitted black Greek olives (Kalamatas)

3 tablespoons finely chopped fresh mint

2 tablespoons cold-pressed extra-virgin olive oil

2 tablespoons seasoned rice wine vinegar
Salt
Freshly ground black pepper

5 ounces drained feta cheese, preferably Greek, crumbled

Halve the cucumber lengthwise. Angle-cut each half cross-wise into ½-inch pieces.

Core the tomatoes and halve them vertically. Scoop out the ribs and seeds. Cut each resulting tomato shell lengthwise into 5 or 6 ½-inch-wide strips.

In a large bowl, combine the cucumber pieces, tomato strips, onion slices, olives, mint, oil and vinegar. Toss well. Season lightly with salt (the feta will be salty) and generously with pepper and toss again.

Transfer the salad to a shallow serving bowl or deep platter if desired. Scatter the feta over the salad and serve immediately.

Jicama, Green Bean and Sweet Pepper Salad

Sweet and crunchy jicama stays that way all day long, making it an ideal base for this picnic or barbecue salad. Green beans and sweet peppers add colorful eye appeal. For a change of pace we use yellow sweet peppers, but any color—even green—will do.

6 to 8 servings

¾ pound green beans, trimmed and
    halved crosswise
    Salt
1 small jicama, about 1¼ pounds
1 large sweet pepper, preferably yellow
4½ teaspoons Dijon mustard
4½ teaspoons fresh lemon juice
½ teaspoon salt
¼ cup cold-pressed extra-virgin olive oil
¼ cup thinly cut fresh chives
    Freshly ground black pepper

Bring a medium pan of water to a boil. Add the green beans and 2 teaspoons salt. Cook uncovered, stirring occasionally, until the beans are just tender, 4 to 6 minutes. Drain and immediately transfer to a bowl of iced water. Let stand until cool, about 1 minute, then drain immediately and pat dry.

Peel the jicama and cut it into ¼-inch batons about 2 inches long.

Stem, seed and core the pepper. Cut it into ¼-inch-wide strips. Cut the strips crosswise into pieces about 2 inches long.

In a large bowl, toss together the beans, jicama batons and pepper pieces.

In a small bowl, whisk together the mustard, lemon juice and salt. Gradually whisk in the oil; the dressing will thicken.

Pour the dressing over the vegetables in the bowl. Toss well. Add the chives and a generous grinding of pepper and toss again.

If making the salad several hours in advance, reserve the green beans, adding them just before serving. This will prevent the dressing from discoloring them.

JICAMA—A light-brown legume that looks similar to a turnip, jicama (pronounced <u>hee</u>-ka-ma) is popular in Mexico and Central America and, with increasing frequency, is stocked by better greengrocers year-round. Once peeled, the crisp, white flesh tastes to me of apples crossed with water chestnuts. Good raw, it can be shredded for salads (try it as the base for a cabbage-free, Southwestern-style slaw) or thinly sliced and used as a dip scooper or in sandwiches. Adventurous cooks have been known to use it in desserts (combined with tropical fruits like papaya), in salsas, and even to deep-fry it into crisp chips. Good specimens are firm, heavy and free of soft spots. A good keeper, jicama does eventually spoil; try to use it within a week or so of purchase.

Sugar Snap Peas with Mint

I am one cook who can remember a time when sugar snap peas, edible pod and all, were a novelty. Now they're a staple, but still never less than satisfying to eat. One especially good way to enjoy them is in this easy, simple salad—crisp and crunchy and very fine alongside something hot and grilled or cool and roasted. Low- or nonfat sour cream and yogurt can be used, if desired.

Serves 4 to 6

1¼ pounds sugar snap peas, stemmed, stringed if necessary
2 teaspoons salt
1 cup sour cream
½ cup chopped red onion
¼ cup plain yogurt
2 tablespoons finely chopped fresh mint
¼ teaspoon ground cumin, from toasted seeds (page 4)
Freshly ground black pepper

Bring a medium pot of water to a boil. Add the sugar snaps and 2 teaspoons salt. Cook uncovered, stirring once or twice, until crisp-tender, about 1 minute. Drain and transfer to a bowl of iced water. When cool, drain immediately and pat dry.

In a medium-large bowl, whisk together the sour cream, onion, yogurt, mint, cumin, more salt to taste and a generous grinding of pepper. Add the sugar snaps and toss. Cover and refrigerate for up to 1 hour before serving.

Green Bean, New Potato and Cherry Tomato Salad with Creamy Vermouth Vinaigrette

This everything-from-the garden salad is one of my most reliable all-in-one summertime accompaniments. I serve it alongside a piece of grilled chicken, fish or beef, and all my work is done (okay, maybe I offer a little crusty bread and a glass of wine). There's nothing here you can't find in a good supermarket, but made with just-picked farm-stand produce, the salad becomes extra-special. It's also a good, neutral palette, to which you can add lots of fresh herbs, in amounts and combinations to taste.

Serves 8 to 10

1 pound red-skinned new potatoes, well-scrubbed and quartered
  Creamy Vermouth Vinaigrette, recipe follows
1 pound green beans, trimmed and cut crosswise into 2-inch pieces
2 12-ounce baskets cherry tomatoes (preferably 1 each of red and yellow), stemmed, rinsed and drained
1 medium-sized red onion, peeled and thinly sliced
  Salt
  Freshly ground black pepper

In a large pan, cover the potatoes with cold water. Set over medium heat and bring to a boil. Cook uncovered until the potatoes are just tender, about 6 minutes. With a slotted spoon, transfer to a large bowl; reserve the potato water. Add ⅓ cup of the vinaigrette to the hot potatoes and toss. Cool to room temperature.

Meanwhile, return the pan of water to a boil. Add the green beans and cook, stirring occasionally, until the beans are just crisp-tender, 4 to 6 minutes. Drain and transfer immediately to a bowl of iced water. When cool (about 1 minute), drain thoroughly and pat dry. The potatoes and beans can be prepared up to 1 day ahead. Refrigerate the potatoes, beans and remaining vinaigrette separately. Return to room temperature before proceeding.

Halve the tomatoes. Add the tomatoes, green beans, onion and half of the remaining vinaigrette to the bowl with the potatoes. Season to taste with salt and pepper and toss gently. Serve at room temperature, passing the remaining vinaigrette at the table if desired.

Creamy Vermouth Vinaigrette

This accommodating vinaigrette, light but clingy, is good over salad greens, more substantial vegetable salads, even marinated shrimp or chicken. Employing a French trick that I believe I learned from Madeleine Kamman, the vinegar is cut with a bit of vermouth, making the dressing less tart and thus more wine-friendly.

Makes about 2¼ cups

½ cup red wine vinegar
2 tablespoons Dijon mustard
2 tablespoons dry white vermouth
2 large egg yolks, brought just to room
   temperature
½ teaspoon salt
½ teaspoon freshly ground black pepper
1⅓ cups cold-pressed extra-virgin olive oil

In a food processor, combine the vinegar, mustard, vermouth, egg yolks, salt and pepper and process until smooth. With the motor running, add the olive oil through the feed tube in a fairly quick, steady stream; the dressing will thicken. Adjust the seasoning. The dressing can be refrigerated for up to 3 days. Let it come to room temperature before stirring and using.

Note: Nothing is more useful on a long weekend of lazy cooking and casual eating than a supply of leftover vinaigrette. If salmonella contamination is of concern to you, omit the egg yolks. The dressing will be thinner but will still taste good.

**Baked Vidalia Onions
with Goat Cheese and
Red Pepper Stuffing;
Grilled Asparagus with
Lemon Mayonnaise**

Side Dishes

Little vegetable sautés, smooth purées, spuds of all kinds, pilafs, pastas, stuffings and dressings—these are all on the side at Flavors. They are the loyal supporting players, not always getting the attention (at least from diners) that they deserve, but requiring planning, creativity and care all the same. Here is a chance for the cook to shine quietly, taking private satisfaction in how precisely al dente the vegetables have been cooked, at how moist the corn bread stuffing is, at how seductively creamy the mashed potatoes turned out. If glory is in the details, these side dishes are wonderful indeed.

Rosemary-Pancetta Potato Sauté • Roasted Garlic Mashed Potatoes • Secret Ingredient Sweet Potatoes • Sweet-and-Sour Glazed Shallots • Baked Vidalia Onions with Goat Cheese and Red Pepper Stuffing • Creamy Potato and Parsnip Gratin, after Madeleine • Succotash • Roasted Brussels Sprouts with Maple-Walnut Butter • Vegetables Glazed with Balsamic Vinegar • Oven-Roasted Vegetables • Grilled Asparagus with Lemon Mayonnaise • Cardamom Carrot and Pear Puree • Rosemary Millet Cakes with Sun-Dried Tomatoes • Saffron Couscous Pilaf with Roasted Vegetables • Noodles with Browned Caraway Butter • Corn Bread, Mushroom and Toasted Pecan Dressing • Fruited Sausage Stuffing with Fresh Sage • Gingered Pear Conserve with Cherries and Hazelnuts

Rosemary-Pancetta Potato Sauté

This quick little Tuscan-style stove-top potato dish is just the thing when the oven is tied up with a roast. Any herb that appeals to you will work in this dish (potatoes are pretty accommodating that way), but served with roast or stewed chicken or with veal, the rosemary is just right.

Serves 6

1 tablespoon extra-virgin olive oil
¼ pound diced (¼-inch) pancetta
12 whole garlic cloves, peeled
2¼ pounds (3 large) white-skinned boiling potatoes,
    peeled and cut into ½-inch dice
4 teaspoons minced fresh rosemary
    Salt
    Freshly ground black pepper

In a large (12-inch) heavy nonstick skillet over medium heat, warm the olive oil. Add the pancetta and cook, stirring often, for 4 minutes. Add the garlic and cook, stirring often, for 4 minutes. Move the garlic to the side of the pan, and with a slotted spoon, transfer the pancetta to a small bowl and reserve.

Add the potatoes to the pan and stir to coat with oil. Sauté the potatoes and garlic, stirring every 5 minutes or so, until the potatoes are crisp and golden outside and tender within and the garlic is cooked through, 25 to 30 minutes. Stir in the reserved pancetta and the rosemary, season with salt and pepper to taste, and serve immediately.

PANCETTA—Pancetta is pepper-and-spice-cured but unsmoked Italian belly bacon. Though it can be thinly sliced and eaten as is, it's really at its best cooked, where its sweetly nutty, pork-intense flavor is welcome in sautés, stews, pastas (particularly pasta carbonara), breads and even warm salad dressings. (It has less fat that way too.) There is no real substitute, but this potato sauté can be prepared (and will be equally good) with best-quality prosciutto.

Roasted Garlic Mashed Potatoes

Not all vegetable side dishes are lean, and not all self-indulgent treats are chocolate. I say this to justify these scrumptious and definitely very rich potatoes. There are few flavor pairings better than potatoes and garlic, and our customers have adored these since the first day we served them. Some luxuries—even in small portions—are worth the extra work at the gym.

Serves 8

4 pounds russet (baking) potatoes, peeled and cut into 2-inch chunks
1 cup whipping cream
½ cup Roasted Garlic Puree
    Salt
⅔ cup sour cream
1 teaspoon freshly ground black pepper
4 tablespoons (½ stick) unsalted butter, softened

In a large pan cover the potatoes with cold water. Set over medium heat and bring to a simmer. Partially cover and cook, stirring once or twice, until the potatoes are very tender, about 25 minutes. Drain, reserving ⅓ cup of the potato cooking water.

Meanwhile, in a small saucepan, combine the cream, garlic puree and 2 teaspoons salt. Bring the cream just to a simmer; remove from the heat and keep hot.

Immediately force the potatoes through a ricer or the medium blade of a food mill into the pan, or return them to the pan and mash them with a potato masher. Set the pan over low heat and stir the mashed potatoes constantly for 1 minute. Then gradually stir in the cream mixture, the reserved potato water, the sour cream and the pepper. Vigorously beat the potatoes for 30 seconds or so, adding the butter 1 tablespoon at a time as you beat. Add additional salt to taste. Serve immediately.

Roasted Garlic Puree

The mellowed but still enticing flavor of garlic that has been roasted is nearly addictive. So fundamental is this puree to my cooking, I nearly always put a few heads in the oven as soon as I walk into the kitchen, even before I completely make up my mind about what I'm going to prepare. This holds true even in the summer, when, in order to avoid heating up the house, I use a toaster oven. The puree can be stored in the refrigerator, topped by a thin layer of olive oil, for up to a week; you'll find yourself reaching for it often.

Makes about ½ cup

2 very large heads regular (not elephant) garlic, about ½ pound total
2 small sprigs fresh rosemary
2 tablespoons dry white wine
2 tablespoons extra-virgin olive oil
¼ teaspoon herbes de Provence, crumbled (page 9)

Position a rack in the middle of the oven and preheat to 350° F.

With a serrated knife, cut off the top quarter of the garlic heads, exposing the cloves inside. Set each garlic head in a 9-inch square of heavy-duty foil and partially draw up the sides. Lay the rosemary sprigs atop the garlic. Drizzle the wine and then the olive oil into and around the heads of garlic. Sprinkle the crumbled herbs over all. Enclose the garlic tightly in the foil.

Set the packets on the rack and bake until the garlic inside the peels is very tender, 1 hour to 1 hour and 15 minutes. Cool the garlic to room temperature in the foil. Squeeze the softened garlic out of the peels into a sieve. Set the sieve over a bowl and force the garlic through it with the back of a spoon. Or, the garlic can be pureed in a small food processor.

Use immediately, or drizzle with 1 teaspoon olive oil and refrigerate for up to 1 week.

Note: So popular has roasted garlic become, there is now at least one commercially available brand. From Consorzio, a maker of flavored oils, the puree, which comes in a medium-sized jar, is quite good, and can be substituted in any recipe calling for my homemade version.

Secret Ingredient Sweet Potatoes

My mother, Betty's, all-purpose flavoring agent is unreconstituted pineapple-orange juice concentrate. I honestly think she uses it more often than salt. I'm not so sure about all of the dishes she puts it in, but when it comes to sweet potatoes, she's definitely created a winner. In fact, this combination is so delicious, you can even skip the butter.

Serves 6 to 8

5   pounds (4 or 5 large) sweet potatoes
1   (12-ounce) container frozen pineapple-orange
     juice concentrate, thawed
½   cup packed golden-brown sugar
2   tablespoons unsalted butter, softened, optional
1   teaspoon salt
¾   teaspoon freshly ground black pepper

Position a rack in the middle of the oven and preheat to 400° F. Set the sweet potatoes directly on the oven rack and bake until very tender, about 1½ hours. Remove from the oven and cool. The potatoes can be baked up to 24 hours in advance. Hold unwrapped at room temperature.

Peel the potatoes, then mash them well in a bowl. Stir in the juice concentrate, brown sugar, butter if you are using it, salt and pepper. Transfer the puree to a 2-quart casserole dish with a lid.

Position a rack in the middle of the oven and preheat to 325° F. Heat the potatoes until steaming, 30 to 40 minutes. Serve hot.

Sweet-and-Sour Glazed Shallots

For this easy and delicious dish, whole shallots, with their onion-garlic flavor, are simmered in a mixture of port and stock and eventually glazed with tangy balsamic vinegar. Try spooning the shallots over sliced grilled steak, where they act as both sauce and garnish—delicious!

Serves 4

1 pound medium shallots, peeled
¾ cup tawny port
¾ cup Chicken Stock (page 45) or
    reduced-sodium canned chicken broth
1 tablespoon packed golden-brown sugar
1 tablespoon balsamic vinegar
1 tablespoon unsalted butter
1 teaspoon minced fresh thyme
    Freshly ground black pepper

In a medium-sized nonreactive saucepan, combine the shallots, port, stock, sugar, vinegar and butter. Set over medium heat and bring to a brisk simmer. Cook uncovered, stirring once or twice, until the shallots are almost tender, about 20 minutes. Add the thyme and a generous grinding of pepper and cook, stirring once or twice, until the liquid is reduced to a saucy glaze that lightly coats the shallots, another 5 to 7 minutes. Serve hot.

VIDALIA ONIONS—Vidalias are known in the onion biz as "specialty sweets," one of several crisp, mild, juicy onions mostly named after the region (Vidalia, Georgia; Walla-Walla, Washington; Maui, Hawaii) in which they are grown. Low in sulphur compounds, which makes them mild, they are also high in moisture, which makes them perishable. Since the Vidalia season (late spring to early summer) is short, as much as I would love to use them year-round, I can't. When the seasonal shipment arrives from my sister in Charleston, I store them at cool room temperature, with plenty of air circulation (hung from the ceiling in the legs of a pair of panty hose, for example), and enjoy them, raw or cooked, in a veritable Vidalia festival. I love to dress thick slices of tomatoes and Vidalias with red wine vinegar, olive oil and mint. They also make fabulous onion rings, and on a sandwich, like a hamburger, where you might use only a ring or two of ordinary onion, you can enjoy a whole slab of sweet Vidalia.

Baked Vidalia Onions with Goat Cheese and Red Pepper Stuffing

These stuffed onions are sweetly savory, especially fine as an accompaniment to unsauced roasted meats like chicken, pork or lamb.

Serves 8

8   medium Vidalia onions, about 6 pounds total, peeled

6   tablespoons (¾ stick) unsalted butter

1   large sweet red pepper, trimmed, cored and finely diced

6   garlic cloves, peeled and minced

4   teaspoons herbes de Provence, crumbled (page 9)

¼   pound soft goat cheese, such as Montrachet

3½   cups coarse, fresh crumbs from a white peasant-style loaf of sourdough bread

1   cup finely chopped flat-leaf parsley

1   cup (6 ounces) soft, moist domestic Parmesan cheese

2   teaspoons salt

1   teaspoon freshly ground black pepper

2½   cups Chicken Stock (page 45) or reduced-sodium canned chicken broth

Position a rack in the lower third of the oven and preheat to 350° F.

Cut a small slice off the bottom and a larger slice off the top of each onion. With a melon baller (or an ordinary teaspoon) and working from the top, scoop out the onions, leaving a shell about ½ inch thick all around.

Finely chop enough of the scooped-out onion to yield 1½ cups; reserve the remainder for another use. In a medium skillet over moderate heat, melt the butter. Add the chopped onion, sweet pepper, garlic and herbes de Provence and cook uncovered, stirring occasionally, until tender and lightly colored, 8 to 10 minutes. Stir in the goat cheese and cook until the cheese just melts, another 1 to 2 minutes. Remove from the heat. Add the bread crumbs, parsley, Parmesan cheese, salt and pepper and stir to combine. The stuffing will be moist and crumbly.

Spoon the stuffing into the hollowed onions, using it all. Pack the stuffing firmly into the cavities if necessary, and mound it above the tops of the onions if possible. Arrange the stuffed onions in a shallow baking dish just large enough to hold them comfortably. (The onions can be prepared several hours in advance. Drape with plastic wrap and hold at room temperature.)

Add the stock to the pan. Set the pan in the oven and bake, basting the onions and stuffing occasionally with the stock, until the onions are tender and the stuffing is lightly browned, about 1 hour and 15 minutes. Serve hot or warm.

Creamy Potato and Parsnip Gratin, after Madeleine

Of all the incredible dishes I tasted when I studied with the remarkable Madeleine Kamman, her opulent potato gratin stands out as one of the most delicious. Using her general technique and proportions, I make an equally delicious gratin combining potatoes and parsnips. The slightly bitter edge of the parsnip flavor tames the sweet richness of the cream—a spectacular dish.

Serves 6 to 8

1 garlic clove, peeled and halved
1 tablespoon unsalted butter, softened
3½ pounds (5 medium-large) russet or baking potatoes, peeled and thinly sliced crosswise
1½ pounds medium-large parsnips, peeled and thinly sliced
3 teaspoons salt
½ teaspoon freshly grated nutmeg
Freshly ground black pepper
1 quart whipping cream
¼ pound shredded Gruyère cheese

Position a rack in the middle of the oven and preheat to 325° F. With the cut sides of the garlic, thoroughly rub the inside of a 9-by-13-by-3-inch baking dish. Butter the dish.

In a colander under running water, rinse the potato and parsnip slices; drain well.

Alternately layer the potatoes and parsnips into the prepared dish, sprinkling each layer as you go with some of the salt, some of the nutmeg and a generous grinding of pepper. Pour the cream over the slices, tilting the dish several times to moisten them and distribute the seasonings evenly.

Bake uncovered for 30 minutes. With a metal spatula, press down on the top vegetable slices so that the cream comes up over them. Continue baking, pressing the upper slices down every 15 minutes, for another 45 minutes. Sprinkle the cheese evenly over the top vegetable layer and continue to bake until the vegetables are tender and the top is well browned, another 45 minutes. Let the gratin rest on a rack for 10 minutes. Serve hot.

In late summer, when all the various components can be found fresh in the market, succotash can easily become a meatless main course. It's particularly nice with a clove or two of garlic sautéed with the onion, a roasted red pepper chopped and simmered in and a handful of minced basil scattered over the top at the end.

Succotash

For a converted lima lover like me (I hated them as a child), this may well be the ultimate bean dish. The cream is optional but it does turn ordinary succotash into a real treat. Serve it on Thanksgiving to take advantage of its New England associations. Or, offer it as it was once served to me at Ovens, a restaurant in Tucson, Arizona, using the dish as a bed for sliced garlicky roast chicken. Don't hesitate to use frozen beans in this dish; limas freeze more successfully than almost any other vegetable.

Serves 6 to 8

Salt
½ pound green beans, trimmed and angle-cut crosswise into ½-inch pieces
½ pound frozen baby lima beans, thawed
2 tablespoons unsalted butter
1 cup finely diced yellow onion
2 medium zucchini (about ⅔ pound), scrubbed, trimmed, quartered lengthwise, cut crosswise into ½-inch pieces
½ pound thawed or canned corn kernels, drained
1 cup whipping cream
Freshly ground black pepper
2 tablespoons finely chopped flat-leaf parsley

SUCCOTASH—Just what is succotash, people often ask me, fearing, it seems, the worst. Or perhaps it's just the funny-sounding name. The word comes from several Narragansett Indian names for stew and corn, and reflects succotash's origins as a New England dish of fresh corn and lima beans, cooked with salt pork drippings and milk. Nowadays the combination includes green beans (probably for color) and sometimes, since frozen vegetable "medleys" are used, diced carrots. Improvisation is always welcome, but without the corn and lima beans, it just isn't succotash.

Bring a medium pot of water to a boil. Add the salt, green beans and limas and cook uncovered, stirring occasionally, until just tender, about 5 minutes. Drain. Transfer immediately to a bowl of iced water. Cool completely, then drain immediately and pat dry.

In a large, heavy skillet over medium heat, melt the butter. Add the onion, cover and cook, stirring once or twice, until the onion begins to color, about 4 minutes. Add the zucchini and cook, stirring occasionally, until the zucchini is lightly browned, about 5 minutes.

Add the green beans, lima beans, corn, whipping cream, ¾ teaspoon salt and a generous grinding of pepper. Cover and bring to a brisk simmer. Cook, stirring occasionally, until the cream has reduced by about half and is thickened slightly and the lima beans are tender, about 5 minutes. Remove from the heat and stir in the parsley. Adjust the seasoning. Serve hot.

Roasted Brussels Sprouts with Maple-Walnut Butter

Brussels sprouts have gotten a bad rap, possibly because too often they are overboiled and soggy. Roasting, however, transforms them into an entirely new vegetable—crunchy, caramelized and deeply flavorful. They're good that way, snatched piping hot right off the baking sheet, but they're even better with the sweet maple-nut butter melting over them—a quintessential Thanksgiving side dish.

Serves 6

⅔ cup chopped toasted walnuts (page 114)
4 tablespoons unsalted butter, softened
3 tablespoons genuine maple syrup (page 187)
Salt
Freshly ground black pepper
2 pounds brussels sprouts, trimmed
2 tablespoons canola oil

Position a rack in the middle of the oven and preheat to 450° F.

In a small bowl, stir together the walnuts, butter, maple syrup, a pinch of salt and a grinding of pepper. Hold at room temperature.

On a jelly-roll pan, toss together the brussels sprouts and oil. Season to taste lightly with salt and generously with pepper. Roast the brussels sprouts, shaking the pan and rolling them around every 5 minutes to promote even cooking, until they are richly browned and tender, 20 to 25 minutes total.

Transfer the brussels sprouts to a large bowl. Dollop the butter mixture over them and toss to mix. Serve hot.

Note: Pecans can be substituted for the walnuts.

Vegetables Glazed with Balsamic Vinegar

This quick and colorful vegetable side dish is especially good with simple roasted meats and with grilled entrées—wherever its sweet-and-sour glaze won't conflict with sauce or seasoning.

Serves 4

2 tablespoons olive oil

2 large sweet peppers, preferably one each of red and yellow, stemmed, cored and cut into ¼-inch-wide strips

1 small red onion, peeled and thinly sliced

2 zucchini, scrubbed, trimmed and cut crosswise into ½-inch-thick rounds

2 yellow summer squash, scrubbed, trimmed and cut crosswise into ½-inch-thick rounds
Salt

2 tablespoons balsamic vinegar

3 tablespoons finely chopped flat-leaf parsley
Freshly ground black pepper

In a large, heavy nonstick skillet over medium-high heat, warm the olive oil. Add the peppers and onion and cook uncovered, stirring once, until beginning to soften, about 4 minutes. Add the zucchini and yellow squash, season with ½ teaspoon salt and cook uncovered, stirring occasionally, until tender and lightly browned, another 8 to 10 minutes. Add the vinegar and boil until the liquid is reduced to a glaze and coats the vegetables, about 2 minutes.

Stir in the parsley and a generous grinding of pepper, adjust the seasoning and serve immediately.

Oven-Roasted Vegetables

Delicious hot, warm or cold, served on their own or used as an ingredient in pastas, pilafs—even sandwiches—these sweet, brown and tender roasted vegetables are a Market Table basic. Served up in a huge bowl (which empties repeatedly throughout the day), they are prepared from a changing array of vegetables, based upon the best the season has to offer. Lightly glossed with olive oil and their own reduced juices, seasoned with no more than salt and pepper, they are intensely flavored and irresistible. The list below can be augmented with quartered fennel bulb, chunks of winter squash, peeled sweet potatoes, eggplant slices, cubed rutabaga—any fairly firm vegetable, in fact, except beets, which are roasted separately, in foil, to keep their juices from coloring everything else.

Serves 6 to 8

5 firm plum tomatoes (about 1 pound), cored and halved lengthwise

3 large portobello mushrooms (about 1 pound), stems reserved for another use, caps cut into sixths

2 medium-large sweet peppers, preferably one each of red and yellow, stemmed, cored and cut into 1½-inch triangles

5 medium carrots (about ¾ pound), trimmed, peeled and cut into 1-inch chunks

1 medium-sized red onion (about ¾ pound), peeled and cut vertically into 6 wedges

2 medium zucchini (about ¾ pound), scrubbed, trimmed, halved lengthwise, then angle-cut crosswise ½ inch thick

1 medium yellow squash (about 6 ounces), scrubbed, trimmed, halved lengthwise, then angle-cut crosswise ½ inch thick

6 tablespoons olive oil

Salt

Freshly ground black pepper

Position racks in the upper and lower thirds of the oven and preheat to 450° F. Line 3 medium jelly-roll pans with foil.

In a bowl, one at a time, toss each vegetable type (treat the zucchini and yellow squash as one type) with 1 tablespoon of the olive oil. Season lightly with salt and pepper and then spread each vegetable over half of one of the prepared baking sheets.

Working in batches, roast the vegetables, stirring them every 8 to 10 minutes without mixing them, and exchanging the positions of the sheets on the racks from top to bottom and from front to back, until they are well browned and fairly tender. Times will vary from about 20 minutes for the tomatoes to about 40 minutes for the onions. As the vegetables reach their desired doneness, transfer them (and any juices) to a large bowl. When all are done, toss well and adjust the seasoning. Serve hot, warm or cool.

Grilled Asparagus with Lemon Mayonnaise

Asparagus hold up surprisingly well on the grill (placed crosswise on the rack so they don't fall through into the fire), picking up attractive markings and dehydrating slightly, which concentrates their sweet flavor. I think they hold up to the lightly smoky flavor of mesquite chips as well, but if you have doubts, just omit them. Grilled asparagus can be served at room temperature, as a salad; hot from the grill plated as a side dish; or even lukewarm as a passed appetizer, picked up in the fingers and dipped into the mayonnaise.

Serves 6

1 cup mayonnaise
1 tablespoon fresh lemon juice
1½ teaspoons lemon zest (colored part of peel, removed with a zester and minced)
1 teaspoon Roasted Garlic Puree (page 162)
½ teaspoon Dijon mustard
Salt
Freshly ground black pepper
2 pounds medium-thick asparagus (about 30 spears)
1½ tablespoons olive oil
2 cups mesquite wood chips, optional

In a medium bowl, whisk together the mayonnaise, lemon juice, lemon zest, garlic puree and mustard. Add salt to taste and season generously with pepper. Cover and hold at room temperature for up to 1 hour, or refrigerate for up to 3 days. Return to room temperature if chilled.

With a knife, trim off the toughest ½ inch or so from the ends of the asparagus. Using a swivel-bladed vegetable peeler, remove the tough peel from the lower third or so of each spear. On a jelly-roll pan or a large plate, toss the asparagus with the olive oil to coat evenly.

Prepare a hot charcoal fire or preheat a gas grill (medium-high). When the fire is hot, distribute the wood chips if you are using them. Position the grill rack about 6 inches above the heat.

Lay the asparagus on the rack, cover and grill, turning once, until the asparagus are smoky, well marked and tender, 6 to 8 minutes total. Transfer the asparagus to a platter. Season lightly with salt and fresh pepper to taste. Serve hot, warm or at room temperature, accompanied with the mayonnaise.

 Other suitable dipping sauces for the asparagus include Black Olive Aioli (page 18) and Saffron Aioli (page 17); the asparagus can also be served <u>au naturel</u>.

Cardamom Carrot and Pear Puree

Cardamom adds gingery presence to this delicate orange puree. Slightly sweet, it's especially good alongside pork or duck. The puree can be prepared entirely ahead; rewarm it just before serving.

Serves 4 to 6

1 pound (6 medium) carrots, peeled and
   cut into 1-inch chunks
2½ cups water
2 tablespoons unsalted butter
1 teaspoon sugar
¾ teaspoon ground cardamom, see Note
¾ teaspoon salt
½ teaspoon freshly ground black pepper
3 ripe Bartlett pears, about 1¾ pounds,
   cored, peeled and cut into 1-inch chunks

In a medium saucepan, combine the carrots, water, butter, sugar, cardamom, salt and pepper. Set over medium heat and bring to a brisk simmer. Cook uncovered, stirring occasionally, for 15 minutes. Add the pears and continue to cook uncovered, stirring often, until the carrots are tender and most of the liquid has evaporated (the pears will completely dissolve), about 25 minutes more.

Cool slightly, then force through the medium blade of a food mill or puree in a food processor. (The puree can be prepared up to 3 days in advance. Cool, cover and refrigerate.)

In a saucepan over low heat, rewarm the puree, stirring constantly, until steaming. Adjust the seasoning. Serve hot.

Note: An equal amount of Asian five-spice powder can be substituted for the cardamom.

MILLET—Millet may look like birdseed, but it is a nutritional powerhouse, second only to wheat in protein content and loaded with the essential amino acid lysine. In China, India and especially Africa, millet is widely cooked and eaten by humans, growing hardily despite adverse conditions and improving poor diets at low cost. In the U.S. you will find millet almost exclusively at health-food stores. Cook it into porridges, pilafs, soups and stews, where its nutty crunch and fluffy texture are most welcome. In <u>The Grains Cookbook</u>, Bert Greene recommends dry-toasting millet for even more flavor: Toss the tiny beads in a dry skillet over medium heat until they take on a deeper golden color and begin to pop, about 5 minutes. Proceed with the recipe as directed.

Rosemary Millet Cakes with Sun-Dried Tomatoes

Millet is a grain you may not have tasted before. It looks like birdseed—it is commonly used as such—but it is, in fact, quite delicious human food and is enjoyed by literally millions of people around the world, though not so much by Americans. If disbelievers could sample these crunchy, tomato-studded grain cakes, I think their minds would be changed. Serve the cakes alongside roast chicken and a simple green vegetable.

Makes 8 cakes, serves 4

5 tablespoons olive oil
2 garlic cloves, peeled and finely chopped
3 tablespoons finely chopped fresh rosemary
1½ cups Chicken Stock (page 45) or reduced-sodium canned chicken broth
1½ teaspoons salt
⅔ cup millet, available in health-food stores and some supermarkets, rinsed
2 large eggs
8 oil-packed sun-dried tomatoes (16 halves), drained and coarsely chopped
Freshly ground black pepper

In a medium saucepan over low heat, warm 2 tablespoons of the olive oil. Add the garlic and cook uncovered, stirring occasionally without browning, for 3 minutes. Add the rosemary and cook, stirring, for 1 minute. Add the stock and salt and bring to a simmer. Stir in the millet, cover and adjust the heat to low. Cook undisturbed until the millet has absorbed all the liquid and is tender, about 25 minutes. Remove from the heat and let stand, covered, for 5 minutes. Cool to room temperature. The millet can be prepared up to a day in advance. Cover tightly and refrigerate. Return to room temperature before using.

In a food processor, combine half the millet and the eggs and process until smooth. Stir the puree into the remaining whole millet. Fold in the tomatoes and season generously with pepper. Form the mixture into 8 2½-inch cakes.

In a large skillet over medium-high heat, warm the remaining 3 tablespoons olive oil until very hot (but not smoking). Gently set the cakes in the oil. Lower the heat slightly and cook, turning once, until crisp and golden brown on both sides, about 10 minutes total.

Formed into 4 slightly larger cakes (about 3½ inches in diameter), the millet mixture can be fried up into wonderful veggie burgers. Top each with a slice of provolone cheese, if desired, and let it melt, before serving on toasted sesame seed buns, along with a dollop of Black Olive Aioli (page 18) or Chipotle Rémoulade (page 17).

Saffron Couscous Pilaf with Roasted Vegetables

Here is a wonderful use for our oven-roasted vegetables. When they are on hand, simmering them up with instant couscous takes only minutes, though their rich flavor and the exotic spices will make it taste as if you've been cooking all day. Great with lamb, especially the braised shanks on page 92.

Serves 6

2 tablespoons olive oil
2 garlic cloves, peeled and chopped
¼ teaspoon crushed red pepper
⅛ teaspoon ground cinnamon
2¼ cups Chicken Stock (page 45) or reduced-sodium canned chicken broth
1½ cups chopped Oven-Roasted Vegetables (page 170)
1 teaspoon packed saffron threads
1 (10-ounce) box instant couscous (about 1⅓ cups if purchased in bulk)
⅓ cup finely chopped parsley

In a medium saucepan over low heat, warm the olive oil. Add the garlic, crushed red pepper and cinnamon and cook uncovered, stirring often without browning the garlic, for 5 minutes. Add the stock, vegetables and saffron and bring to a simmer. Remove from the heat, cover and let stand for at least 10 minutes to develop the saffron flavor.

Return the liquid to a simmer. Stir in the couscous, cover the pan and remove it from the heat. Let stand for 5 minutes. Stir the parsley into the pilaf. Serve hot.

Noodles with Browned Caraway Butter

This quick but flavorful side dish is perfect alongside the veal meatballs on page 91, but also good with pork or duck, particularly if there is a bit of sauce or gravy for them to absorb. Dried wide egg noodles can be substituted (use about ½ pound) if you can't find fresh fettuccine.

Serves 6

5 tablespoons unsalted butter

2 teaspoons caraway seeds

¾ pound fresh fettuccine noodles, halved crosswise

Salt

Freshly ground black pepper

In a small saucepan over medium heat, melt the butter. When it foams, add the caraway seeds. Lower the heat and cook, stirring often, until the caraway is fragrant and the butter is lightly browned, about 5 minutes. Remove from the heat.

Bring a large pot of water to a boil. Add the fettuccine and 2 teaspoons salt and cook until just tender, 3 to 4 minutes. Drain well.

Return the pasta to the pot. Add the caraway butter and set the pan over low heat. Cook, tossing and stirring, until the noodles are well coated with the butter and hot. Season generously with pepper. Serve immediately.

Corn Bread, Mushroom and Toasted Pecan Dressing

Here is a multicultural recipe that has come the long way around. It began in Michael's kitchen, as a Pennsylvania Dutch–inspired dish, but then was adapted to include both my Texas notions of how corn-bread dressing should be made as well as Chef Chris Siversen's memories of his Italian grandmother's stuffing. In final form it made a New York Times *roundup of great Thanksgiving recipes. I like the fact that it's wonderfully moist though it contains no eggs or stock; everyone likes the way it tastes. Make this with a corn bread that is on the sweet side, like the one that follows, for the proper balance of flavors.*

Serves 8 to 10

6 tablespoons (¾ stick) unsalted butter, plus
    softened butter for the baking dish
2 cups chopped yellow onion
1 cup finely chopped celery
1 cup finely chopped carrot
3 garlic cloves, peeled and minced
3 tablespoons finely chopped fresh thyme
1 tablespoon finely chopped fresh marjoram
1 tablespoon finely chopped fresh sage
½ pound (1 large) portobello mushroom, stem
    removed, cap cut into ½-inch chunks
½ pound shiitake mushrooms, tough stems
    removed, caps thickly sliced
½ pound oyster mushrooms, trimmed, clusters
    separated
    Salt
8 cups coarsely crumbled corn bread,
    recipe follows
3 cups milk
1 cup (about 4 ounces) pecans, toasted and
    coarsely chopped (page 114)

½ cup chopped flat-leaf parsley
1 teaspoon freshly ground black pepper

In a large, deep skillet over medium heat, melt the butter. Add the onion, celery, carrot, garlic, thyme, marjoram and sage. Cover and cook, stirring once or twice, until the vegetables are becoming tender, about 10 minutes. Add the mushrooms and 1 teaspoon salt, cover and cook, stirring once or twice, until the mushrooms begin to give up their juices, about 7 minutes. Uncover the skillet, raise the heat slightly and cook, stirring often, until the mushroom juices evaporate and the vegetables begin to brown, about 10 minutes. Remove from the heat and cool slightly.

Position a rack in the middle of the oven and preheat to 400° F. Butter a heavy, 4-quart baking dish with a cover.

In a large bowl, thoroughly combine the corn bread, mushroom mixture, milk, pecans, parsley and pepper. Spoon the dressing into the prepared baking dish. Cover and bake for 20 minutes. Uncover and bake until the top is lightly browned, 15 to 20 minutes. Let rest in the pan on a rack for 5 minutes before serving.

Corn Bread

Don't wait until turkey dressing time to make this sweet, moist corn bread—it has year-round appeal.

Serves 8

Solid vegetable shortening, for the dish
1⅓ cups yellow cornmeal
1⅓ cups unbleached all-purpose flour
1 tablespoon baking powder
1¼ teaspoons baking soda
¼ teaspoon salt
1 cup buttermilk, at room temperature
8 tablespoons (1 stick) unsalted butter,
    melted and slightly cooled
⅓ cup honey
2 large eggs, well beaten

Position a rack in the middle of the oven and preheat to 350° F. Lightly coat a 1¾-quart baking dish with shortening.

In a large bowl, thoroughly stir together the cornmeal, flour, baking powder, baking soda and salt. Add the buttermilk, butter, honey and eggs and mix until just combined. Do not overmix; a few lumps can remain.

Spoon the batter into the prepared dish. Cover and bake for 25 minutes. Uncover and continue baking until a tester, inserted in the center, comes out clean, about 30 minutes.

Serve hot or warm.

Fruited Sausage Stuffing with Fresh Sage

This old-fashioned fruit and sausage dressing gets extra zip from plenty of fresh sage and black pepper. Don't limit this to the Thanksgiving turkey; it's also good beside roast pork, duck and goose.

Serves 10

½ pound bulk sage breakfast sausage (or about 8 small links, casings discarded)

3 tablespoons unsalted butter, plus softened butter for the baking dish

3 medium-sized sweet apples (1 pound), such as McIntosh, cored, peeled and diced (½ inch)

2 cups finely chopped yellow onion

1 cup finely chopped celery

1 teaspoon dried thyme, crumbled

½ teaspoon dried marjoram, crumbled
   Salt

½ cup finely chopped fresh sage

10 cups cubed (¼-inch) crustless day-old firm good-quality peasant-style bread

1 cup coarsely chopped dried apricots, preferably Mediterranean or Turkish, see Note

⅓ cup golden raisins

2 large eggs, beaten

¾ cup Chicken Stock (page 45) or reduced-sodium canned chicken broth

¾ teaspoon freshly ground black pepper

Into a large skillet, crumble the sausage. Set the skillet over medium heat and cook, further breaking up the sausage, until it is lightly browned, 6 to 8 minutes. With a slotted spoon, transfer the sausage to paper towels to drain. Pour off any fat from the skillet but do not clean it.

Set the skillet over medium heat. Add the butter, and when it foams, add the apples, onion, celery, thyme, marjoram and ½ teaspoon salt. Cover and cook, stirring occasionally, until the vegetables are almost tender, about 12 minutes. Add the sage and cook, stirring once or twice, for 2 minutes. Cool to room temperature.

Position a rack in the middle of the oven and preheat to 350° F. Lightly butter a 4-quart baking dish with a lid.

In a large bowl, toss together the bread, apple mixture, sausage, apricots and raisins. Stir in the eggs, stock, pepper and ½ teaspoon salt. Spoon the dressing into the prepared dish.

Cover and bake for 20 minutes. Uncover and bake until the top is lightly browned, another 20 to 25 minutes. Let the dressing stand in the pan for 5 minutes. Serve hot.

Note: Mediterranean apricots are sweeter than Californian, and I like them better in this recipe. Feel free to use Californian if that is all you can find.

Gingered Pear Conserve with Cherries and Hazelnuts

A conserve is a chunky, chutney-like relish, often containing nuts. This one is not preserved by canning, merely refrigerated for a few days before it is served. Dried cherries plump up more dramatically, but at Thanksgiving, you may want to try making this with dried cranberries instead.

Serves 6

½ cup (about 2 ounces) raw, unblanched hazelnuts

2 pounds (5 medium) ripe, firm pears, such as Bartlett, peeled, cored and cut into ½-inch chunks

½ cup red wine vinegar

½ cup sugar

⅓ cup (about 4 ounces) sun-dried sweet cherries

2 tablespoons grated fresh ginger with juices

½ teaspoon freshly ground black pepper

¼ teaspoon salt

Position a rack in the middle of the oven and preheat to 350° F. In a shallow metal pan, such as a pie tin, roast the hazelnuts, stirring them several times, until the skins begin to loosen, about 12 minutes. Wrap the hot hazelnuts in a kitchen towel and let steam for 1 minute. Vigorously rub the towel-wrapped nuts to remove the peels. Shake the nuts in a colander to separate them from the peels. Cool completely. Store airtight at room temperature for up to 4 days.

In a medium, nonreactive saucepan, combine the pears, vinegar, sugar, cherries, ginger, pepper and salt. Set over medium heat and bring to a simmer. Cook uncovered, stirring occasionally, until thick, about 25 minutes. Remove from the heat and cool to room temperature. Cover and refrigerate for at least 24 hours, to mellow the flavors, and up to 3 days.

Return the conserve to room temperature. Coarsely chop the hazelnuts. Stir them into the conserve just before serving.

Sweet Things from Morning to Night

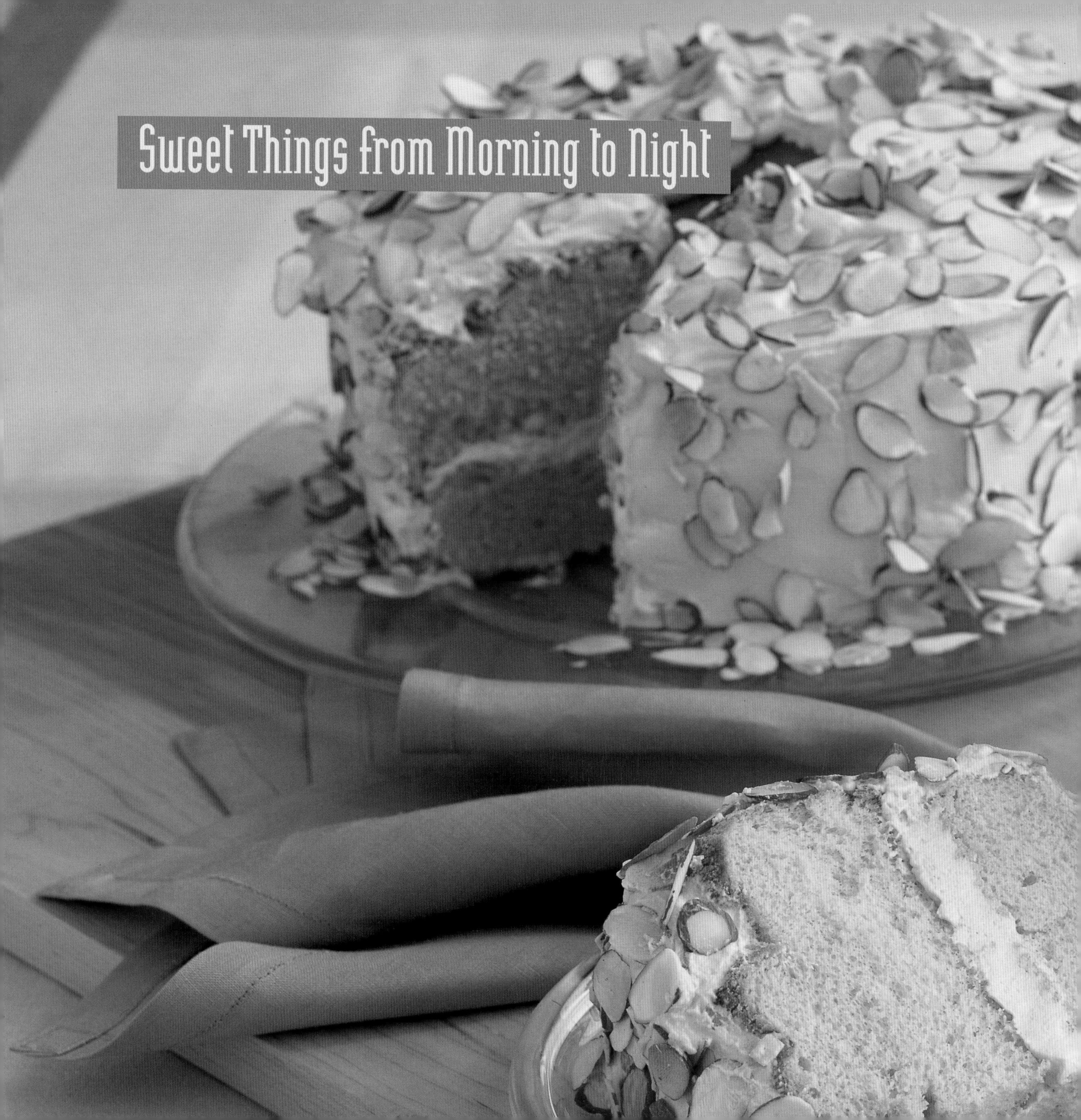

Left to right: Coffee
Angel-Food Cake; Mango
Lemonade; Mexican
Watermelon Quaff

The craving for a little something sweet cannot be denied. From breakfast right through to a midnight-or-later snack, few of us are immune to the siren call. Beginning with the morning's first bowl of granola and ending with a cup of hot chocolate before bed, there's not a moment of the day when a little something sweet can't brighten things up. Fortunately, my repertoire contains both lean and lavish treats, letting me—and you—take a balanced approach to sweet indulgence. Constant vigilance is just as stifling as constant excess; happiness is achieved when we're free to choose; through variety we can strike a happy medium. And after all, when it comes to the recipes in this chapter, happiness is what it's all about. **Flavors' Private Mix Granola • Sunberry Jam • Blueberry Gingerbread Pancakes • Baked Apples with Maple, Orange and Cinnamon • An Oatmeal "Bar" • Honeyed Banana Yogurt Cream • Dried Fruit Compote • Little Sticky Buns • Banana Bread with Ginger and Macadamia Nuts • Cinnamon-Currant Scones • Zucchini-Walnut Muffins with a Twist of Lemon • Cranberry-Pecan Tea Bread • Orange–Poppy Seed Mini-Muffins • Raspberry-Bran Muffins • Zach's Smoothie**

• Pamela's Eye-Opener • Chai (Indian Spiced Tea) • Thai Iced Coffee • Citrus-Glazed Pumpkin Squares • Walnut Brownies U.S.A. • Coconut Magic Bars • Granola Bars • Whiskey-Glazed Scotch Shortbreads • Almond-Orange Biscotti • Chocolate Double-Peanut Picnic Cookies • Extra-Spicy Gingersnaps • Bridge-hampton Café's Flourless Chocolate Cake with Tropical Fruit Sauce • Devil's Food Cake with Marshmallow Frosting • Grandma Rose's Marble Cake • Coffee Angel-Food Cake • Flavors' Apple Crisp • Very Lemony Pound Cake • Tequila-Glazed Pineapple and Nectarine Skewers with Orange Crème Anglaise • Semolina Bread Pudding with Warm Berry Sauce • Blackberry Crème Brûlée • Plums and Peaches in Blueberry-Vanilla Syrup • Wine-Poached Pear Crous-tades with Ice Cream • Cappuccino Mousse • Blushing Pear Granita • Espresso-Frangelico Granita • Marmalade-Glazed Fresh Fig and Mascarpone Tart • Banana-Chocolate Tartlets with Macadamia Praline Crunch • Harvest Nut Pie with a Touch of Bourbon and Chocolate • Pumpkin Cheesecake with Pecan Praline Sauce • Mexican Watermelon Quaff • Mango Lemonade • Mint Hot Chocolate

Flavors' Private Mix Granola

Granola is a powerhouse of slow-release, carbohydrate energy, as well as one of the most satisfying morning foods—at least when it's our private mix, one of the first recipes we developed for Flavors. At home, as at the store, I enjoy this crunchy treat as both a snack on the run and a breakfast meal with yogurt and fresh fruit. (And don't forget the Granola Bars on page 203.) It's not a low-fat food, however, so if that's a concern, treat granola as a topping or accent, rather than a grain dish to be eaten on its own.

Makes about 16 cups

8 cups old-fashioned (not quick-cooking) rolled oats

1 cup (about ¼ pound) hulled sunflower seeds (available in health-food stores and some supermarkets)

⅔ cup sliced unblanched almonds

⅔ cup coarsely chopped walnuts

1 cup honey

⅓ cup canola oil

5 tablespoons unsalted butter

4 teaspoons ground cinnamon

2½ teaspoons freshly grated nutmeg

1 teaspoon ground cloves

1⅓ cups (about 3 ounces) finely chopped dried apples

1⅓ cups golden raisins

⅓ cup dried cranberries

⅓ cup dried tart cherries

Position racks in the upper and lower thirds of the oven and preheat to 325° F. Line 2 12-by-18-inch jelly-roll pans with foil.

In a large bowl, stir together the oats, sunflower seeds, almonds and walnuts.

In a small saucepan, combine the honey, oil, butter, cinnamon, nutmeg and cloves. Set over medium heat and cook, stirring occasionally, until the butter has just melted. Gradually pour the hot honey mixture over the oat mixture in the bowl, stirring well to evenly moisten. Divide the granola between the two prepared pans and spread it evenly to the edges.

Bake the granola for 10 minutes. Stir thoroughly. Continue to bake the granola, stirring thoroughly every 5 minutes and switching the position of the pans on the racks from top to bottom and from front to back at the halfway point, until the granola is well browned, 25 to 30 minutes (the granola will become crisper as it cools).

Let the granola cool completely in the pans on a rack, stirring occasionally and scraping it up as it begins to stick to the foil.

In a large bowl, thoroughly stir together the cooled granola and the apples, raisins, cranberries and cherries. Transfer to a lidded container, cover and store airtight at room temperature; the granola will keep for a week or more, depending on the humidity.

Sunberry Jam

When I wanted both a homemade preserve that would recall those my mother used to put up as well as something conveniently quick to produce year-round, I developed this intense berry-flavored jam. Made with frozen and dried fruit, and merely refrigerated, rather than sealed in jars, it still sends the comforting message that "Mom is in the kitchen." Our morning regulars couldn't start the day without this on their croissants or muffins. Come summer, when fresh fruit is better (and cheaper) than frozen, don't hesitate to make the substitution.

Makes about 3½ cups

1 (16-ounce) bag unsweetened frozen strawberries, with their juices, or 2½ pints hulled, chunked fresh strawberries

1 (16-ounce) bag unsweetened frozen raspberries, with their juices, or 3 pints fresh raspberries, picked over

¼ cup sugar

3 tablespoons apricot preserves

3 tablespoons fresh orange juice

1 tablespoon fresh lemon juice

1¼ cups (about 6 ounces) dried sweet cherries

1¼ cups (about 6 ounces) dried cranberries

¾ teaspoon ground cinnamon

½ teaspoon vanilla extract

¼ teaspoon ground dried ginger

¼ teaspoon ground cloves

In a food processor, puree the strawberries and raspberries, leaving a few large pieces.

In a heavy, medium-sized nonreactive saucepan over moderate heat, combine the pureed fruit, sugar, apricot preserves, orange juice and lemon juice. Bring to a simmer. Partially cover and cook, skimming any foam from the surface of the fruit and stirring occasionally, until beginning to thicken, about 10 minutes. Add the cherries and cranberries, partially cover and cook, stirring often, until the preserves are thick and the dried fruit is fairly tender, another 10 to 12 minutes. Remove from the heat and cool to room temperature. Stir in the cinnamon, vanilla, ginger and cloves. Transfer to a container, cover and refrigerate for at least 24 hours before using. The jam will keep for at least 1 month.

Blueberry Gingerbread Pancakes

Gingerbread and blueberries are surprisingly affable partners, and since these spicy, molasses-sweetened flapjacks can be made with fresh or frozen berries, they can brighten any day all year-round. Maple syrup really makes these cakes, but the Honeyed Banana Yogurt Cream on page 189 is pretty wonderful on them, too.

Makes 12 5-inch pancakes, serves 4 to 6

2 cups unbleached all-purpose flour, see Note
1½ teaspoons baking powder
1½ teaspoons ground ginger
½ teaspoon ground cinnamon
¼ teaspoon freshly grated nutmeg
⅛ teaspoon ground cloves
¼ teaspoon baking soda
¼ teaspoon salt
¾ cup unsulphured molasses (page 207)
¾ cup buttermilk, at room temperature
2 large eggs, at room temperature
3 tablespoons corn or other flavorless vegetable oil, plus oil for the griddle
2 cups fresh blueberries, picked over, rinsed only if necessary
Genuine maple syrup and softened unsalted butter, as accompaniments

Position a rack in the middle of the oven and preheat to 200° F.

Onto a piece of waxed paper, sift together twice the flour, baking powder, ginger, cinnamon, nutmeg, cloves, baking soda and salt.

In a large bowl, whisk together the molasses, buttermilk, eggs and the 3 tablespoons oil. Add the dry ingredients and stir until just free of lumps. Fold in the blueberries.

Heat a heavy nonstick griddle or skillet over medium heat. Brush generously with oil. Working in batches, spoon the batter by quarter cupfuls onto the griddle and spread with the back of a spoon into 5-inch rounds. Cook until the undersides are lightly browned, about 2 minutes. Flip and cook until just done through, another 1 to 1½ minutes. Keep warm in the oven until all of the pancakes are cooked.

Serve with maple syrup and softened unsalted butter.

Note: To measure the flour, first stir it in the canister with a fork to lighten it, then spoon it into a dry-measure cup and sweep level. Do not scoop the cup into the flour; do not sift the flour into the cup.

To make mini-cakes, use about 2 tablespoons batter per cake, and since they're prone to stick, be sure the griddle is well oiled. The maple-nut butter from the brussels sprout recipe on page 168 also makes a fine pancake topper; just omit the salt and pepper.

Baked Apples with Maple, Orange and Cinnamon

Why is it that a baked breakfast apple seems so much more like a treat than many other kinds of fruit? Our customers love to start the day with these, prepared without the butter, but served with a dollop of plain yogurt. To transform them into the perfect dessert to follow a homey fall or winter supper, I substitute a scoop of premium vanilla or pecan ice cream for the yogurt.

Serves 6

6 large McIntosh apples (about 3 pounds total),
   cored completely through to create a
   ¾-inch-wide cavity
1½ cups dark or golden raisins
1 cup fresh orange juice
½ cup genuine maple syrup
1 teaspoon ground cinnamon
2 tablespoons butter, optional, cut into
   small pieces

Position a rack in the middle of the oven and preheat to 375° F.

With a swivel-bladed vegetable peeler, remove a 1-inch-wide band of peel from around the top of each apple. Arrange the apples in a shallow baking dish just large enough to hold them comfortably. Divide the raisins among the apple cavities, packing them in if necessary. Pour the orange juice and maple syrup over and around the apples. Sprinkle the cinnamon over and around the apples. Scatter the butter pieces, if you are using them, over all.

Set the dish in the oven and bake for 10 minutes. Baste with the pan juices and bake another 10 minutes. Baste again and bake until the apples are puffed and tender, maybe even a little collapsed-looking, another 10 to 15 minutes. Remove from the oven and let stand in the dish, basting occasionally, for 10 minutes. Transfer the apples to individual plates or shallow bowls. Spoon the sauce from the pan evenly over the apples. Serve warm.

MAPLE SYRUP—While there is considerable confusion about the various grades of maple syrup, that the real stuff is preferable to the fake is not in question. A uniquely American product, with a long history (Native Americans were using maple sap as a sweetener when the first European explorers arrived), genuine maple syrup is a delicious wonder that cannot be duplicated by combining artificial flavorings with corn syrup. To make the syrup, the sap is boiled down, concentrating the flavor and giving the liquid more body. (Further reduction creates solid maple sugar.) Now available is syrup from organically maintained trees, syrup cooked over wood fires and syrup flavored with cassis and other additions, but it is the plain old-fashioned thing that I cook with exclusively, both at the store and at home. Maple syrup grades are regulated by the government and are based on color, which is a reflection of how concentrated the syrup is. In general, lighter syrup is labeled A or AA and will have a more delicate flavor than the robust grade B. For me, only the big, molasses-like flavor of the latter will do.

An Oatmeal "Bar"

At the very heart of Flavors and The Market Table is the concept of giving people choices about foods and the way they combine them. In the morning that means the oatmeal bar, where hot milk-simmered steel-cut oats are available along with an array of delectable and healthful toppings. A little of each, a lot of one or just oats plain—however you want it, at Flavors that's how you can have it. The same tempting setup is easy to duplicate at home.

Serves 6 to 8

3 cups low-fat milk or water
1¼ cups steel-cut oats
½ teaspoon salt
Flavors Private Mix Granola (page 184)
Honeyed Banana Yogurt Cream (page 189)
Dried Fruit Compote (page 189)
Warm Berry Sauce (page 218)
No-work toppings, see Note

In a medium saucepan over high heat, bring the milk to a simmer. Add the oats and salt, lower the heat, partially cover, and simmer gently, stirring occasionally, until the oats are thick and tender, 15 to 20 minutes.

Serve immediately, accompanied by any or all of the suggested toppings.

Note: No-work toppings that can be offered instead of, or along with, the toppings listed in the recipe include brown sugar, maple syrup, honey, plain yogurt, raisins, unsweetened apple butter, marmalade and chopped toasted nuts.

STEEL-CUT OATS—Coarsely chopped or cracked, rather than flattened between rollers, steel-cut oats retain their nubbly, chewy texture even when cooked. Found in bulk in health-food stores or available as Irish oats in attractive tins in gourmet shops, steel-cut oats are an entirely new and delicious experience for Americans who have only eaten the mushy results rolled oats produce. They can also be cooked, risotto-like, with savory seasonings and served alongside the entrée.

Honeyed Banana Yogurt Cream

This easy mixture is so much better than purchased banana yogurts. It's also good on pancakes, waffles and scones.

⅓ cup plain low-fat yogurt
1 tablespoon honey
¼ teaspoon cinnamon
1 large, very ripe banana, peeled and diced

In a medium bowl, whisk together the yogurt, honey and cinnamon. Stir in the banana. Let stand, covered, at room temperature for about 1 hour, to develop the flavors. The cream can be prepared up to 1 day ahead. Cover tightly and refrigerate, returning to room temperature before using.

Dried Fruit Compote

A far cry from plain-old stewed prunes, this vanilla-scented compote is sweet-tart and rather luscious. Great on oatmeal, it's also very nice on its own, with just a dollop of plain yogurt on top. Conversely, warmed up with a bit of amaretto, or something like it, stirred in, it makes a lovely topping for vanilla ice cream.

Makes about 5 cups

2½ cups water
2 cups fresh orange juice
1 cup (about 6 ounces) quartered pitted prunes
1 cup (about 6 ounces) quartered dried apricots, preferably Mediterranean
1 cup (about 5 ounces) chopped dried Calimyrna figs
¾ cup sugar
½ cup golden raisins
½ cup dried tart cherries, blueberries or cranberries
1 vanilla bean, split
2 tablespoons fresh lemon juice

In a medium-sized nonreactive saucepan over moderate heat, combine the water, orange juice, prunes, apricots, figs, sugar, raisins and cherries. Scrape the seeds from the vanilla bean into the fruit mixture. Add the bean to the mixture. Bring to a simmer, then partially cover and cook, stirring occasionally, until the fruit is tender, about 25 minutes. Remove from the heat and stir in the lemon juice. Transfer to a container, cool to room temperature, cover and refrigerate at least overnight, to develop the flavors. The compote can be prepared up to 3 days in advance. Remove the vanilla bean and serve cool or at room temperature.

Little Sticky Buns

Jumbo-size sticky buns are an American tradition. I'm always amazed by the sight of these gargantuan pastries and wonder how anyone can even walk after eating one, much less get any work done. Perhaps they're brunch food, and meant to send the eater straight back to bed? Anyway, here is a recipe for schnecken, *the small-scale German-Jewish antecedents of those colossal treats, which I have adapted from Joan Nathan's book* Jewish Cooking in America. *They are just the right size, yet still sticky and very satisfying. Nice later in the day, too, with a cup of tea or coffee.*

Makes 18

Dough

- ¼ cup lukewarm water
- 1 package active dry yeast
- ½ cup granulated sugar
- 8 tablespoons (1 stick) unsalted butter
- ½ cup milk
- ½ teaspoon salt
- 1 large egg
- 1 large egg yolk
- 3¼ cups unbleached all-purpose flour
- 1 teaspoon canola oil

Topping and Filling

- 6 tablespoons (¾ stick) unsalted butter, melted and slightly cooled
- 6 tablespoons plus ½ cup packed dark-brown sugar
- 6 tablespoons honey
- 1 cup chopped pecans
- ½ cup dried currants
- ½ teaspoon cinnamon

To make the dough, in a small bowl stir together the water, yeast and ½ teaspoon of the granulated sugar. Let stand until foamy.

Meanwhile, in a small saucepan over low heat combine the butter, milk, remaining granulated sugar and salt. Heat, stirring once or twice, until the butter has just melted. Remove from the heat and cool to room temperature.

In a large bowl, whisk the egg and yolk. Whisk in the milk mixture and then the yeast mixture. Gradually stir in the flour. The dough will be soft and sticky. Knead it briefly in the bowl until it is fairly smooth. Coat the inside of a medium bowl with the oil. Add the dough, turning it to coat. Cover with plastic wrap and refrigerate overnight.

Position a rack in the middle of the oven and preheat to 350° F.

To make the topping, generously brush 18 cups of 2 muffin tins with some of the melted butter. Scatter 1 teaspoon packed dark-brown sugar in the bottom of each cup. Drizzle 1 teaspoon honey into each cup. Divide half the pecans among the cups.

To make the filling, on a lightly floured surface, roll the chilled dough out into a 7-by-18-inch rectangle. The dough will be stiff and will require some handling before it is responsive. Brush the remaining butter evenly over the dough. Sprinkle the remaining ½ cup packed dark-brown sugar evenly over the dough. Scatter the remaining pecans and the currants evenly over the dough. Sprinkle the cinnamon evenly over all. Starting with a long side, roll the dough up jelly-roll fashion. Slice the dough crosswise into 18 1-inch-thick pieces. Set each piece, with one of its cut sides down, in a prepared muffin cup.

Set the muffin tins on the rack and bake for 15 minutes. Lower the heat to 325° F. and bake until the dough is puffed and golden and the sugar mixture in the bottom of the cups is bubbling, another 12 to 15 minutes.

Invert the pan onto waxed paper. Scoop out any brown-sugar mixture remaining in the muffin cups and drizzle it over the buns. Serve warm or at room temperature.

Banana Bread with Ginger and Macadamia Nuts

Though the delicately spicy and tropical flavors of this recipe are at their best the day it is baked, it remains moist and can be enjoyed for several days. A slice with a little cream cheese and Sunberry Jam (page 185) is very nice with a cup of tea.

Makes 1 9-inch loaf

Solid vegetable shortening, for the
　　baking pan, see Note
2　cups unbleached all-purpose flour
1　teaspoon baking powder
1　teaspoon baking soda
1　teaspoon ground allspice
1　teaspoon salt
3　very ripe bananas
¼　cup buttermilk, at room temperature
2　teaspoons vanilla extract
8　tablespoons (1 stick) unsalted butter, softened
⅔　cup packed golden-brown sugar
½　cup granulated sugar
2　large eggs, at room temperature
1　cup coarsely chopped toasted macadamia nuts
　　(page 114)
3　tablespoons minced crystallized ginger

Position a rack in the middle of the oven and preheat to 325° F. Lightly coat the inside of a 9-by-5-by-3-inch loaf pan with shortening.

Sift together twice onto a piece of waxed paper the flour, baking powder, baking soda, allspice and salt. In a small bowl, mash the bananas. Stir in the buttermilk and vanilla extract.

In a large bowl, using a wooden spoon or an electric mixer if desired, cream the butter and sugars until light and fluffy. One at a time, beat in the eggs. Stir in the banana mixture; the batter may look grainy. Add the flour mixture, the macadamias and ginger and stir until just combined. Scrape the batter into the prepared pan. Bake until the loaf is puffed and just beginning to draw away from the sides of the pan and a tester inserted into the middle comes out almost clean, 1 hour to 1 hour and 10 minutes.

Cool in the pan on a rack for 10 minutes. Turn out and cool further on the rack. Serve warm or at room temperature.

Note: Goods baked in pans coated with shortening are less likely to stick than those baked in buttered pans; butter can be substituted if desired—just use plenty.

Cinnamon-Currant Scones

Warm and flaky from the oven (which is really when they are at their best), scones are the perfect accompaniment to a leisurely cup of tea. Enjoy them generously spread with good English marmalade or lemon curd, if desired.

Makes 16

Solid vegetable shortening, for the pans
3 large eggs
½ cup chilled buttermilk
3 cups unbleached all-purpose flour,
   plus extra for the work surface, see Note
¼ cup plus 2 teaspoons sugar
1¾ teaspoons baking powder
1 teaspoon ground cinnamon
¼ teaspoon salt
10 tablespoons chilled unsalted butter,
   cut into small pieces
¾ cup dried currants, see Note
1 teaspoon water

Position a rack in the middle of the oven and preheat to 375° F. Grease 2 9-inch round cake tins with vegetable shortening.

In a small bowl, whisk 2 of the eggs. Whisk in the buttermilk. Into a large bowl, sift together twice the flour, the ¼ cup sugar, baking powder, cinnamon and salt. With a pastry cutter, blend the butter into the flour mixture until pieces the size of peas form. Add the buttermilk mixture and the currants and stir until just combined; the dough will be crumbly. Lightly flour the work surface.

Turn out and knead the dough 10 or 12 times, just until a soft dough forms. Divide the dough in half and shape each half into a ball. Roll each ball out into an 8-inch round. Carefully transfer each round to one of the prepared pans. With a pizza wheel or a sharp knife, score each round into 8 wedges. In a small bowl, whisk the remaining egg with the water. Brush the glaze evenly and generously over the scones. Sprinkle evenly with the remaining 2 teaspoons sugar.

Bake until the scones are puffed and golden and the edges are crisp and lightly browned, 25 to 30 minutes. Remove the scones from the oven and cool in the pans on a rack for 5 minutes. Cut the scones into wedges along the score marks. Serve hot.

Note: To measure the flour, first stir it in the canister with a fork to lighten it, then spoon it into dry-measure cups and sweep level. Do not scoop the cup into the flour; do not sift the flour into the cup.

Other dried fruits, including cherries, cranberries, blueberries, raisins or finely chopped apricots can be substituted for the currants.

Zucchini-Walnut Muffins with a Twist of Lemon

Serve this party-sized batch of lemony muffins at a big brunch, or tuck some away in the freezer for casual nibbling.

Makes 24

Solid vegetable shortening, for the baking pans
2 cups unbleached all-purpose flour
2 teaspoons baking powder
1 teaspoon baking soda
1 teaspoon salt
¾ teaspoon freshly grated nutmeg
3 large eggs, at room temperature
1 cup granulated sugar
½ cup packed golden-brown sugar
1¼ cups corn oil
3 tablespoons lemon zest (colored part of peel, removed with a zester and minced)
1 teaspoon vanilla extract
2 cups grated unpeeled raw zucchini (from 2 medium), see Note
1¼ cups chopped walnuts

Position a rack in the middle of the oven and preheat to 350° F. Lightly coat the cups of 2 12-cup muffin tins with shortening.

Sift together twice onto a piece of waxed paper, the flour, baking powder, baking soda, salt and nutmeg.

In a large bowl, whisk the eggs. Whisk in the granulated and brown sugars and then the oil, lemon zest and vanilla extract. Stir in the zucchini. Stir in the flour mixture until almost combined. Add the walnuts and stir just until combined. Divide the batter between the prepared tins, filling each cup no more than three-quarters full.

Bake until the muffins are puffed and just beginning to pull away from the sides of the cups and a tester, inserted into the middle of a muffin, comes out clean, about 20 minutes.

Remove the pans from the oven and let the muffins stand in the tins on a rack for 10 minutes. Turn out and serve warm or at room temperature.

Note: The muffins can be made with 2 cups grated unpeeled raw apple in place of the zucchini.

Cranberry-Pecan Tea Bread

These not-too-sweet loaves are remarkably moist, especially considering they have less fat than almost any other quick bread I know. Don't overbake them or they will dry out, and do consider making up several batches to give away at the holidays. Leftovers are very nice toasted.

Makes 2 9-inch loaves

Solid vegetable shortening, for the
    baking pans
4 cups unbleached all-purpose flour
1 tablespoon baking powder
1½ teaspoons salt
1 teaspoon baking soda
4 tablespoons (½ stick) unsalted butter, softened
2 cups sugar
4 teaspoons orange zest (colored part of peel,
    removed with a zester and minced)
2 large eggs
1½ cups fresh orange juice
2 cups fresh cranberries, coarsely chopped
1 cup coarsely chopped toasted pecans (page 114)

Position a rack in the middle of the oven and preheat to 325° F. Lightly coat the inside of 2 9-by-5-by-3-inch loaf pans with shortening. Onto a piece of waxed paper, sift together twice the flour, baking powder, salt and baking soda.

In a large bowl, cream together the butter, sugar and orange zest. One at a time, beat in the eggs. Stir in the orange juice.

Add the cranberries and pecans to the flour mixture and toss to combine. Add the cranberry mixture to the butter mixture and stir until just combined; do not overmix. Divide the batter between the 2 prepared pans.

Bake the loaves until they are risen, lightly browned, just beginning to pull away from the sides of the pan and a tester, inserted into the middle of a loaf, comes out almost clean, about 50 minutes.

Cool the loaves in the pans on a rack for 15 minutes, then turn out and cool completely before slicing.

 For elegant little tea sandwiches, slice the loaf thin, spread half the slices lightly with stabilizer-free cream cheese and good marmalade, top with the remaining slices and trim the crusts.

Orange–Poppy Seed Mini-Muffins

Briefly dipped into fresh citrus juice while still warm from the oven, these muffins, already light and tender, become terrifically moist as well. It's an idea I learned from Elizabeth's Alston's little book, Muffins. *The poppy seeds add an attractive crunch and look nice too, but if you happen to be out of them, the muffins will still be good.*

Makes about 48

Nonstick vegetable spray, for the tins,
    see Note
8 tablespoons (1 stick) unsalted butter, softened
1 cup plus 3 tablespoons sugar
2 tablespoons orange zest (colored part of peel,
    removed with a zester and minced)
2 large eggs, at room temperature
1 teaspoon baking soda
1 cup buttermilk, at room temperature
2 cups unbleached all-purpose flour, see Note
1 tablespoon poppy seeds
⅓ cup fresh orange juice
4 teaspoons fresh lemon juice

Position a rack in the middle of the oven and preheat to 375° F. Lightly coat the cups of two 24-cup or four 12-cup mini-muffin tins with nonstick spray.

In a large bowl, with a wooden spoon or an electric hand mixer if desired, cream together the butter, 1 cup of the sugar and the orange zest until light. One at a time, beat in the eggs. Stir the baking soda into the buttermilk. Fold one-third of the flour and the poppy seeds into the butter mixture. Stir in half the buttermilk, the remaining flour and then the remaining buttermilk, stirring just to combine after each addition. Divide the batter among the prepared cups, filling them no more than two-thirds full.

Bake until the muffins are lightly browned and springy to the touch, 16 to 18 minutes.

Let the muffins cool in the pans on a rack for 5 minutes. Meanwhile, in a small bowl, stir together the orange juice, the remaining 3 tablespoons sugar and the lemon juice.

One at a time briefly dip the tops and bottoms of the muffins into the juice mixture, transferring them to a plate or napkin-lined basket as you go. Serve warm or at room temperature.

Note: Cups on mini-muffin tins come in various sizes, making the yield on this recipe a little imprecise. It's more important to fill the cups no more than two-thirds full than it is to arrive at a specific number of muffins (overfilled muffin cups make for flat-topped muffins).

You may use solid vegetable shortening or even butter on the tins if you prefer, but nonstick spray is really easier when the cups are this small.

To measure the flour, first stir it in the canister with a fork to lighten it, then spoon it into a dry-measure cup and sweep level. Do not scoop the cup into the flour; do not sift the flour into the cup.

Raspberry-Bran Muffins

Good-for-you high-fiber muffins get a little glamorous when fresh raspberries are added. Delicious as these are plain, they may be even better spread with a bit of excellent orange marmalade or Sunberry Jam (page 185).

Makes 18

Solid vegetable shortening or no-stick
   spray, for the muffin tins
2 cups unprocessed wheat bran
1½ cups whole-wheat flour, preferably stone-ground
1 teaspoon baking powder
1 teaspoon salt
¾ cup packed golden-brown sugar
½ cup canola oil
2 large eggs, at room temperature
1½ cups buttermilk, at room temperature
1¾ cups fresh raspberries, picked over

Position a rack in the middle of the oven and preheat to 400° F. Lightly grease or spray 18 of the cups from 2 standard muffin tins.

In a medium bowl thoroughly stir together the bran, whole-wheat flour, baking powder and salt.

In a large bowl whisk the brown sugar into the canola oil. One at a time, whisk in the eggs. Stir in the buttermilk. Add the dry ingredients and the raspberries and combine with a few swift strokes.

Do not overmix; a few lumps can remain. Divide the batter evenly among the prepared muffin cups, filling each level to the top.

Bake the muffins until they are puffed, the edges are browned and crisp, and a tester inserted into the middle of a muffin comes out clean, about 22 to 25 minutes.

Let the muffins rest in the pan on a rack for 5 minutes; serve hot or warm.

Zach's Smoothie

*This is the power breakfast I whip up for Zach every morn-
ing. Since the frozen berries act as a chilling agent, there is
no need for ice, which would dilute the flavors. A little honey
sweetens and smooths things out, but it's entirely optional.*

Makes 1 large or 2 medium drinks

1	ripe banana, peeled and chunked
10	large frozen strawberries, see Note
1	cup low-fat milk
1/3	cup fresh orange juice
1 to 2	tablespoons honey, to taste, optional

In a blender, combine the banana, strawberries, milk, juice
and the honey if you are using it. Puree until smooth. Pour
into 1 or 2 glasses and serve immediately.

Note: Frozen blueberries or raspberries can be substituted.
Use about 1 cup of either.

Pamela's Eye-Opener

*Though any number of fruit and vegetable combinations are
available at the Flavors juice bar, this is the one I choose
nearly every day. Cleansing, invigorating and shockingly peppery, it really starts my day off with a bang. If you don't have
a fully staffed juice bar at your disposal (a luxury I'm always
grateful for!) or own a juice machine, use purchased carrot
and apple juice. Finely shred the ginger on a vegetable grater
then press it in a sieve to extract the juice.*

Makes 1 drink

1/2	cup fresh carrot juice
1/2	cup fresh apple juice, see Note
1 to 2	teaspoons fresh ginger juice, to taste
	Ice cubes, optional

In a glass, stir together the juices. Add ice if desired. Serve
immediately.

Note: This is also good made with orange juice in place of
the apple juice.

GINGER—When I crave ginger it's nearly always fresh ginger, not dried or crystallized, though I use it plenty in those forms too. I own a book written in tribute to the seasoning, Bruce Cost's <u>Ginger East to West</u>, and in its foreword, Asian cooking expert Barbara Tropp describes ginger's effect, accurately, as "hot-clean-cool." Once available only in "ethnic" markets or at Christmas time, ginger has grown up into a year-round staple in most cities. What we buy is the rhizome or root-like underground stem of the plant, much of it grown in Hawaii and Fiji. Covered with a tough, papery peel, the flesh inside is crisply juicy (if properly fresh) and fibrous. Ginger is peeled and used sliced in stir-fries, minced and sautéed along with other aromatics like garlic and chiles, and grated or pressed to produce a pungent juice. No longer a rarity, ginger can be stored in the vegetable drawer of your refrigerator and should be used up in a week or so (if it begins to look shriveled, it's over the hill), or frozen for up to 1 month. From soup to dessert and from breakfast to suppertime, ginger is a versatile and compelling flavor.

Chai (Indian Spiced Tea)

Following hard on the coffee bar rage came the craze for chai. This spice-seasoned tea is now in such demand that flavoring syrups are made to help create it in quantity, and in some cities it can be purchased all ready to steam on the cappuccino machine and pour. As a spice lover and a tea drinker, I find it one of the mellowest ways to start the morning—and another cup midafternoon can get me through the last of the workday. Because of the spices it's especially nice in winter, but keep in mind when the weather gets hot that chai is terrific over ice too.

Makes about 4 cups, serves 2 to 4

4 cups skim milk
1 cup water
3 tablespoons best-quality Darjeeling tea,
    or to taste
1 teaspoon dried lemongrass
⅛ teaspoon Masala Chai
    Sugar or honey to taste

In a small, heavy saucepan over low heat combine the milk, water, tea, lemongrass and chai. Bring gradually to a simmer, stirring once or twice. Remove from the heat, cover and let steep for 5 to 10 minutes, depending on how strong you want the tea.

    Strain the tea into cups, add sugar or honey to taste and serve immediately.

Note: The lemongrass makes the chai especially stimulating, but it can be omitted if desired.

Masala Chai

This fairly traditional formula for the masala, or spice mixture, used for making chai, comes from a friend in Tucson, who learned to brew and love chai in India. Made up in quantity, the masala will keep fresh, if stored airtight, for several months. Use an electric spice mill, blender or a mortar and pestle to grind the spices.

Makes about ¼ cup

4 teaspoons freshly ground canela
    (a soft and fragrant type of cinnamon;
    canela chips are easiest to grind)
4 teaspoons freshly ground cloves
1 tablespoon freshly ground green (not white)
    cardamom pods
½ teaspoon whole cardamom seeds

In a small bowl, thoroughly stir together the canela, cloves, ground cardamom pods and whole cardamom seeds. Store airtight for up to 1 month at room temperature or freeze for up to 3 months.

Thai Iced Coffee

Thais acquired their taste for dark-roasted coffee from the French, who colonized the country. A small amount of sesame seeds and dried corn is roasted with the beans, which adds a pleasantly bitter note (rather like the chicory in New Orleans–style coffee). Brewed strong, then served cold and sweetened with condensed milk—one of the few dairy products that won't spoil in a tropical climate—Thai iced coffee can be drunk with food but is perhaps best enjoyed on its own, as a refresher in the middle of a scorching afternoon.

Serves 6

2 tablespoons sesame seeds
2 tablespoons stone-ground yellow
   cornmeal
⅔ cup French-roasted coffee beans
5 cups water
   About ¾ cup sweetened condensed
   milk, preferably skim

In a small, heavy skillet over low heat, combine the sesame seeds and cornmeal. Cook, stirring often, until lightly colored but not browned, about 6 minutes. Transfer to a bowl and cool.

In a blade-type (not burr action) coffee mill or a blender, working in batches and scraping down the sides of the container if necessary, finely grind the sesame mixture and the coffee beans. In a small bowl, stir them together thoroughly. Transfer the coffee mixture to the filter of an electric drip coffeemaker. Add 5 cups water to the reservoir and brew the coffee.

Transfer to a covered container and refrigerate until very cold, at least 2 hours or overnight for convenience.

Pour about ¾ cup chilled coffee into each of 6 tall glasses. Add condensed milk to taste (2 tablespoons is about right for authentic Thai sweetness; you may prefer a little less) and stir until thoroughly blended. Add ice to fill the glass. Serve immediately.

Citrus-Glazed Pumpkin Squares

Moist and packed with pumpkin flavor, nicely spicy and only lightly sweetened (the glaze brings them to life), these bars are the ideal solution to your holiday baking needs. My notes say "makes hundreds" and though that's not quite accurate, the yield is generous for the labor involved. Did someone say bake sale?

Makes 48

3 sticks (12 ounces) unsalted butter, melted and cooled slightly, plus butter for the baking pan

4¾ cups unbleached all-purpose flour

1 tablespoon baking soda

1 tablespoon ground cinnamon

2 teaspoons salt

1½ teaspoons freshly grated nutmeg

1 teaspoon ground ginger

¾ teaspoon ground cloves

3 large eggs

2½ cups granulated sugar

1 (29-ounce) can solid-pack pumpkin (not pie filling)

1 cup chopped walnuts

2½ cups lightly packed confectioners' sugar

3 tablespoons fresh orange juice

2 tablespoons fresh lemon juice

Position a rack in the middle of the oven and preheat to 325° F. Butter a 12-by-16-inch jelly-roll pan.

Sift together twice onto a piece of waxed paper the flour, baking soda, cinnamon, salt, nutmeg, ginger and cloves.

In a very large bowl, whisk the eggs. Gradually whisk in the sugar; stir in the pumpkin puree and the melted butter. Add the flour mixture and the walnuts and stir until just combined. Evenly spread the batter to the edges of the prepared pan. Bake until puffed and beginning to draw away from the edges of the pan and a tester, inserted into the center, comes out clean, 40 to 50 minutes. Cool completely in the pan on a rack.

In a medium bowl, whisk together the confectioners' sugar and orange and lemon juices until smooth. Spread evenly over the baked pumpkin mixture. Let stand a few minutes until set before cutting into 48 squares.

Note: Though the bars can be baked a day or two in advance (cover them tightly with plastic wrap and store them at room temperature) they should be cut and glazed shortly before serving. Don't cover them again after glazing or the wrap will pull off the glaze.

Walnut Brownies U.S.A.

Some things are too good to tinker with, among them the good old American brownie. This is more or less the standard formula, though I have increased the chocolate, to make the brownies even more moist and intense than usual. Best the day they are baked (I love the crunchy top and edges), these will keep, wrapped airtight, for several days, though I've never known them to last that long.

Makes 9

Solid vegetable shortening, for the pan
4 squares (4 ounces) unsweetened baking chocolate, chopped
8 tablespoons (1 stick) unsalted butter
2 large eggs
1 cup granulated sugar
1 tablespoon packed dark-brown sugar
1½ teaspoons vanilla extract
⅛ teaspoon salt
½ cup unbleached all-purpose flour
3 ounces (about ¾ cup) chopped toasted walnuts (page 114)

Position a rack in the middle of the oven and preheat to 350° F. Lightly coat the inside of an 8-inch square baking pan with the shortening.

In the top of a double boiler over hot (not simmering) water, combine the chocolate and butter. Heat, stirring once or twice, until just melted. Remove the top of the double boiler from the bottom and cool the chocolate mixture almost to room temperature.

In a medium bowl, using an electric mixer, beat the eggs just until foamy. Gradually beat in the granulated and brown sugars.

Beat in the vanilla and salt. Fold the chocolate mixture into the eggs until just combined. Add the flour and stir until just combined. Stir in the nuts; do not overmix. Scrape the batter into the prepared pan and spread it evenly to the edges. Bake the brownies until the edges are firm, while the center remains slightly soft, about 20 minutes. The blade of a knife inserted into the brownies 2 inches from the edge of the pan should come out with some clinging crumbs.

Cool the brownies completely in the pan on a rack. Carefully run a knife around the sides of the pan to release the brownies. Invert the pan onto a work surface; the brownies will drop out. Cut them, without turning them over, with a long sharp knife, into 9 squares (or rectangles of any size you desire); invert and serve.

Coconut Magic Bars

You can't really be a Texan if you don't like coconut (I couldn't tell you why). From a big, cool bowl of ambrosia to a triple-layered German chocolate cake, Texas celebrates coconut. From my own childhood (and from the back of the Eagle brand sweetened condensed milk can) comes this rich, sticky-sweet one we make regularly for our sophisticated New York customers. Not that it matters much, but you can get low-fat graham crackers as well as sweetened condensed low-fat or skim milk these days. It also helps to think of this as candy, rather than a dessert bar, and cut it into itty-bitty pieces.

Makes 24

8 tablespoons (1 stick) unsalted butter

1½ cups coarse graham cracker crumbs, preferably low-fat

1 14-ounce can sweetened condensed milk, skim or low fat

6 ounces (1 cup) semisweet chocolate chips

1 3½-ounce can sweetened flaked coconut

1 cup (4 ounces) coarsely chopped pecans

Position a rack in the middle of the oven and preheat to 350° F. (325° F. if you are using a glass baking dish).

In a 9-by-13-inch pan melt the butter in the oven. Sprinkle the graham cracker crumbs evenly over the melted butter. Drizzle the condensed milk evenly over the crumbs. Sprinkle the chocolate chips over the condensed milk. Scatter the coconut over the chocolate chips and sprinkle the nuts over the coconut.

Bake until the filling is bubbling and the edges are lightly browned, 25 to 30 minutes. Cool completely in the pan on a rack before cutting.

Granola Bars

Despite its inevitable health-food connotations, when transformed into these bar cookies, granola can only be thought of as an indulgence. It's nice to have the fiber and so on provided by the oats, but don't pretend that these are anything other than extremely rich and delicious little treats. The good news is that the bars can be cut any size you want, giving you at least some control over the fat and calorie content of them individually, if not collectively. Unfortunately, collectively is how you'll be inclined to eat them. These are good keepers and fairly solid—nice for lunch boxes and on picnics.

Makes 24

Solid vegetable shortening, for the baking pan
1½ cups Flavors' Private Mix Granola (page 184)
  or purchased premium granola with
  nuts and dried fruit
1½ cups semisweet chocolate chips
1½ cups chopped walnuts
1½ cups golden raisins
 1 cup old-fashioned (not quick-cooking)
  rolled oats
1¾ cups unbleached all-purpose flour
 1 teaspoon baking powder
 1 teaspoon baking soda
 ¾ teaspoon salt
 2 sticks (½ pound) unsalted butter, softened
 ¾ cup sugar
 ½ cup unsulphured molasses
 1 teaspoon vanilla extract

Position a rack in the middle of the oven and preheat to 325° F. Lightly grease a 9-by-13-inch baking pan, preferably metal (if using glass, lower the oven temperature by 25 degrees).

In a large bowl, stir together the granola, chocolate chips, walnuts, raisins and oats.

Onto a piece of waxed paper, sift together twice the flour, baking powder, baking soda and salt.

In a large bowl, with a wooden spoon or an electric mixer if desired, cream the butter. Add the sugar and beat until light. Beat in the molasses and vanilla (the mixture will appear grainy). Add the granola mixture and stir well. Add the flour mixture and stir well (the batter will be thick). Spoon the batter into the prepared pan and pat it firmly and evenly into place with your hands.

Bake until browned, just drawing away from the edges of the pan and a tester, inserted into the middle, comes out with a few clinging crumbs, 30 to 35 minutes. Do not overbake.

Cool completely in the pan on a rack. Cut into bars.

Whiskey-Glazed Scotch Shortbreads

It's hard to improve on classic Scotch shortbread. Tasting of nothing more than good butter and sugar, it is the simplest and most elemental of cookies. Still, I do like the edge my whiskey glaze gives these crisp shortbreads, making them somehow more grownup and certainly more apt to get special attention. Try one or two with a cup of smoky Lapsang Souchong tea, and see if you don't agree.

Makes about 20

8 tablespoons (1 stick) unsalted butter, softened
¼ cup granulated sugar
¼ teaspoon vanilla extract
1¼ cups unbleached all-purpose flour, plus extra
flour for the work surface
2 tablespoons yellow cornmeal, preferably
stone-ground
½ cup lightly packed confectioners' sugar
1 tablespoon Scotch whiskey
Drops of fresh lemon juice to taste

Position a rack in the middle of the oven and preheat to 300° F.

In a medium bowl, cream together the butter and granulated sugar until fluffy. Stir in the vanilla. Add the flour and cornmeal and work the dough until it begins to hold together. Shape the dough into a disk. Wrap tightly in plastic and refrigerate for 20 minutes. On a lightly floured work surface roll the dough out ⅛ inch thick. With a 2½-inch fluted round cutter, cut out the dough, transferring the rounds to an ungreased baking sheet. Gather the remaining dough, roll it out again and cut out the remaining cookies.

Bake until set and golden-brown, about 30 minutes. Transfer to a wire rack and cool completely.

In a small bowl, stir together the confectioners' sugar and Scotch. Stir in lemon juice to taste. Spread the glaze over the shortbreads. Transfer them to a plate and serve within an hour or so of glazing.

Almond-Orange Biscotti

The big jar of biscotti on the counter at Flavors needs frequent replenishing, so popular have these crunchy dipping cookies become. Despite their distinctive appearance, biscotti are wonderfully easy to make at home. You'll be delighted at how these come out looking just like biscotti the very first time you bake them, and you'll be thrilled to have your own jar to reach into whenever you need a treat. These are fragrant but not too sweet, perfect dipped into a cup of coffee or a glass of dessert wine.

Makes about 48

12 ounces (about 2¼ cups) whole,
    unblanched almonds
    Softened butter, for the baking pans
1¾ cups sugar
¼ cup minced orange zest (colored part of peel,
    removed with a zester and minced)
3 cups unbleached all-purpose flour
1 cup cake flour, not self-rising
1 tablespoon baking powder
½ teaspoon salt
6 large eggs
¼ cup canola oil
1½ teaspoons vanilla extract
1 teaspoon almond extract

Position a rack in the middle of the oven and preheat to 350° F. Spread the almonds in a single layer in a metal pan and toast, stirring once or twice, for 15 minutes. The almonds will become slightly browner and more flavorful but should not be completely toasted. Remove from the oven and cool.

Position racks in the upper and lower thirds of the oven. Lightly butter 2 baking sheets.

In a food processor, grind together half the almonds, the sugar and orange zest. Coarsely chop the remaining almonds. In a large bowl, stir together the all-purpose flour, cake flour, sugar mixture, chopped almonds, baking powder and salt. In a medium bowl, whisk the eggs thoroughly. Whisk in the canola oil, vanilla and almond extracts. Stir the egg mixture into the dry ingredients and mix thoroughly. The dough will be sticky. Divide the dough in half. Turn half out onto a well-floured work surface and, with floured hands, shape into a 14-by-3-inch log. With a long spatula carefully transfer the log to a prepared baking sheet. Reshape the log with your hands if necessary. Repeat with the remaining dough, transferring it to the second baking sheet.

Bake the logs, switching the position of the sheets on the racks from top to bottom and from front to back at the halfway point, until they are risen and golden brown and a tester, inserted into the center, comes out clean, about 40 minutes.

One at a time, transfer the logs to a cutting board. With a serrated knife, carefully saw the logs into ½-inch-thick cookies. Return the cookies to the sheets, laying them on their sides. Bake the biscotti, turning them once or twice, and switching the position of the baking sheets on the racks from top to bottom and from front to back, until the biscotti are crisp and lightly browned, 15 to 20 minutes (this will go faster with dark or blackened sheets than with shiny ones). Transfer to a rack and cool completely. Store airtight at room temperature.

Chocolate Double-Peanut Picnic Cookies

Chocolate and peanuts have such an affinity for each other that desserts combining them always taste, somehow, even better than you expect. (I think it's called synergy; I know the results are irresistible.) These cookies are picnic cookies not because they're especially portable—they're actually a bit fragile—but because they have a sweet, naive simplicity that I associate with eating outdoors. Semisweet chocolate chips or butterscotch chips can be substituted for the peanut butter chips, if you prefer.

Makes about 30 4-inch cookies

Solid vegetable shortening,
for the cookie sheets
½ pound semisweet chocolate, chopped
1¾ cups unsifted unbleached all-purpose flour
⅓ cup lightly packed unsweetened cocoa powder
1 teaspoon baking powder
½ teaspoon salt
2 sticks (½ pound) unsalted butter, softened
1 cup packed golden-brown sugar
½ cup granulated sugar
2 large eggs
2 large egg whites
2 teaspoons vanilla extract
6 ounces (about 1¼ cups) hulled salted peanuts
6 ounces (about 1⅛ cups) peanut-butter chips

Position a rack in the middle of the oven and preheat to 375° F. Lightly coat several cookie sheets with the shortening.

In the top of a double boiler over hot (not simmering) water, melt the chocolate. Remove and cool slightly.

Onto a piece of waxed paper, sift together the flour, cocoa, baking powder and salt. Sift the flour mixture a second time.

In a large bowl, with a spoon or with an electric stand mixer, cream the butter. Add the golden-brown and granulated sugars and beat until fluffy. One at a time, beat in the eggs and then the whites. Beat in the vanilla; the mixture may appear grainy. Add the dry ingredients and mix until almost combined. Add the peanuts and peanut-butter chips and mix in well; the dough will be soft.

For each cookie, scoop a scant ¼ cup of dough onto the prepared sheets, spacing about 2 inches apart. Working in batches, bake for 10 to 12 minutes, or until the cookies are just set in the middle. Let the cookies cool for 2 minutes on the sheets on a rack before transferring carefully to a wire rack.

Cool completely, then store airtight at room temperature for up to 3 days.

Extra-Spicy Gingersnaps

For a spice and molasses lover like me, these cookies are very nearly the perfect sweet treat. Crisp yet tender, and tingly with ginger, cinnamon, mustard, pepper and more, they inspire me to keep nibbling, cookie after cookie. I serve them alongside fruit desserts (they're ideal with poached pears) or enjoy them with a cup of tea. At Christmas, bake up several batches and pack them into tins to give as gifts—one rich and spicy whiff and the lucky recipients will know they've been given something truly special.

Makes about 40

Solid vegetable shortening, for the cookie sheets, plus ¼ cup shortening
2 cups unbleached all-purpose flour
2 teaspoons baking powder
2 teaspoons ground ginger
1 teaspoon ground cinnamon
½ teaspoon dry mustard
½ teaspoon ground white pepper
½ teaspoon ground cardamom
½ teaspoon salt
¼ teaspoon ground cloves
1 stick (4 ounces) unsalted butter, softened
1 cup packed dark-brown sugar
1 large egg
¼ cup unsulphured molasses
About 2 tablespoons granulated sugar

Position a rack in the middle of the oven and preheat to 350° F. Lightly coat several cookie sheets with solid vegetable shortening.

Onto a piece of waxed paper, sift together twice the flour, baking powder, ginger, cinnamon, mustard, pepper, cardamom, salt and cloves.

In a large bowl, cream together the butter and the ¼ cup shortening. Add the brown sugar and beat until light. Beat in the egg and then the molasses. Gradually add the dry ingredients and stir until well combined.

Portion the dough out by 1-inch balls, dredging one side of each as you go in the granulated sugar and then transferring it, sugar side up, to a prepared sheet, spacing the balls about 2 inches apart. Working in batches, bake the cookies until they have spread, are crisp and the tops have cracked, 10 to 12 minutes. Transfer to racks and cool completely. Store the cookies airtight at room temperature.

 UNSULPHURED MOLASSES—Dark, rich molasses is a by-product of sugar-making. After the cane is crushed and boiled in vacuum vats, the crystallized sugar and the molasses are centrifugally separated. The process is repeated several times, each successive extraction producing an ever darker, thicker and more bitter molasses. The final stage is black strap, beloved by health-faddists for its dietary iron content. During the later stages, sulphur fumes may be used to maximize the yield. Unsulphured molasses, then, is from the first extraction, and is sweeter, milder and much more suited to cooking.

Bridgehampton Café's Flourless Chocolate Cake with Tropical Fruit Sauce

Just down the road from my beach house is the stylish Bridgehampton Café. It's the perfect place to unwind after a big catering job, and let someone else do the cooking. Among the very best things on chef John DeLucie's menu is this perfect version of the classic flourless chocolate cake, which he has very nicely shared with me. Moist and dense, it's actually a fallen soufflé. Though a dollop of unsweetened whipped cream is really all the cake requires by way of adornment, I include a tropical fruit sauce to make it even more special. Serve tiny slices. It's rich!

Serves 12

Solid vegetable shortening, for the baking pan
Flour, for the baking pan
1½ pounds bittersweet Belgian chocolate
    (such as Callebaut), chopped
 4 sticks (1 pound) unsalted butter
2¾ cups sugar
12 large eggs, at room temperature
Tropical Fruit Sauce, recipe follows, optional
Unsweetened whipped cream, for serving

Position a rack in the middle of the oven and preheat to 325° F. Lightly coat the inside of a 12-inch round springform pan with vegetable shortening. Add some flour and tilt the pan to coat; tap out the excess.

In the top of a double boiler over hot (not simmering) water, combine the chocolate, butter and 1½ cups of the sugar. Heat uncovered, stirring occasionally until the chocolate is smooth and the sugar has dissolved. Remove from the heat and cool slightly.

Meanwhile, in an electric stand mixer (preferably equivalent to a KitchenAid in size and power) combine the eggs and the remaining 1¼ cups sugar and beat until the eggs have quadrupled in volume and are halfway to forming stiff peaks, about 4 minutes.

Fold the chocolate mixture into the beaten eggs until fully combined (the mixer bowl will be very full). Pour the batter into the prepared pan. Set the pan into a larger baking dish and add enough boiling water to come halfway up the sides of the cake pan.

Bake for 50 minutes. The top will be firm and a tester inserted into the center of the cake will come out clean but the cake should not have pulled away from the sides of the pan.

Remove from the oven and cool the cake in the pan on a rack to room temperature. Cover (do not let the wrap touch the top of the cake) and refrigerate until firm, at least 5 hours.

Dip a thin knife in hot water and dry the blade. Run the blade between the sides of the pan and the edge of the cake; remove the sides of the pan. Cut the cake into thin slices by dipping the knife in hot water and drying the blade between each cut. With a spatula transfer the cake slices to plates. Let the chilled cake soften at room temperature for a few minutes.

Spoon fruit sauce, if you are using it, beside each slice. Top with a dollop of whipped cream and serve immediately.

Tropical Fruit Sauce

This colorful sauce is good over everything from yogurt to ice cream—and wonderful with the flourless chocolate cake.

2 cups ripe papaya chunks (½ inch)
1 cup ripe mango chunks (½ inch)
½ cup fresh orange juice
5 tablespoons fresh lime juice
4½ tablespoons sugar
¾ teaspoon vanilla extract
2 kiwi, peeled and cut into ¼-inch cubes
4 strawberries, hulled and diced

In a food processor, combine the papaya, mango, orange juice, lime juice, sugar and vanilla. Process, stopping several times to scrape down the work bowl, until smooth. Transfer to a container, cover and refrigerate until cold, at least 2 hours.

Stir the kiwi and strawberry chunks into the sauce just before serving.

Devil's Food Cake with Marshmallow Frosting

One of my favorite purveyors of baked goods is Cheryl Kleinman. Her most successful product (as far as my happy customers are concerned) is this dark, moist cake, topped with fluffy frosting and curls of coconut. I'm so pleased she is sharing the recipe.

Solid vegetable shortening,
   for the pans
1¾ cups unbleached all-purpose flour
1¾ cups sugar
¾ cup sifted unsweetened cocoa powder
1½ teaspoons baking powder
1½ teaspoons baking soda
½ teaspoon salt
2 cups milk
½ cup vegetable oil
3 large eggs, lightly beaten
1 tablespoon vanilla extract
   Marshmallow Frosting, recipe follows
2 cups coconut chips, optional

Position a rack in the middle of the oven and preheat to 350º F. Lightly coat two 8-inch round cake pans with shortening. Line the pans with parchment or waxed paper.

Into a large bowl, sift together twice the flour, sugar, cocoa, baking powder, baking soda and salt. Gradually mix in the milk, oil, eggs and vanilla. Stir until just moistened. Do not overmix. Divide the batter evenly between the prepared pans.

Bake until the cakes are just pulling away from the sides of the pans and their tops spring back when lightly pressed, about 30 minutes. Cool in the pans on the rack for 10 minutes. Remove from the pans, peel off the parchment and cool on racks to room temperature.

Set 1 layer on a cake plate. Spread about ⅓ of the frosting over the layer. Scatter about ¾ cup of the coconut chips (if desired) over the frosting. Set the second layer in place. Frost the cake all over with the remaining frosting. Scatter the remaining coconut chips over the cake (press some into the sides as well, if desired).

The layers can be baked up to 1 day in advance (wrap the layers separately in plastic wrap and refrigerate), but the cake should be served within an hour of frosting.

Cut the cake into wedges for serving.

Note: For cupcakes, divide the batter among 20 greased muffin cups (fill each no more than ⅔ full). Bake until puffed and just pulling away from the sides of the muffin tins, 12 to 15 minutes. Cool slightly, then remove from the pans and cool completely. Frost with Marshmallow Frosting and top with coconut chips, if desired, or use your favorite chocolate icing.

Marshmallow Frosting

To me, marshmallow is one of the flavors of childhood. Teamed with the dark chocolate cake, it transports adults back to when all cakes were tall, all milk cold, all frosting sweet, every day special—yummy stuff. This recipe is adapted from Pillsbury's The Complete Book of Baking.

Makes about 4 cups, filling and frosting a 2-layer, 9-inch cake

½ cup sugar
2 tablespoons water
2 large egg whites
1 jar (7 ounces) marshmallow creme
1 teaspoon almond extract

In the top of a double boiler set over simmering water, beat together the sugar, water and egg whites until soft peaks form. Add the marshmallow creme and beat until stiff peaks form. Remove from the heat and beat in the almond extract.

Use immediately or cover and refrigerate overnight.

Grandma Rose's Marble Cake

Here is a marvelously easy and different dessert packed with sweet old-fashioned charm. It comes from my friend and publicist Peggy Tagliarino's grandmother, Rose Shulman, who never failed to bring a panful along to a family gathering, whether it was festive or somber. Don't wait for a christening or a funeral before baking this treat—it's nice at brunch and great during a coffee break.

Serves 12

Cake

    Solid vegetable shortening, for the pan
    Flour, for the pan
2½ cups cake flour (not self-rising)
1½ teaspoons baking powder
    Salt
2 sticks (½ pound) unsalted butter, softened
1½ cups granulated sugar
6 large egg yolks, at room temperature
1 cup milk, at room temperature
4 large egg whites, at room temperature

Topping

2 large egg whites, at room temperature
1 cup packed light-brown sugar
⅓ cup unsweetened Dutch-process cocoa powder, preferably Droste

Position a rack in the middle of the oven and preheat to 350° F. Grease and flour a 9-by-13-inch baking pan; tap out the excess flour.

To make the cake, into a medium bowl sift together the cake flour, baking powder and ½ teaspoon salt. Sift the flour mixture a second time.

In a large bowl cream together the butter and 1¼ cups of the granulated sugar until light and fluffy. One at a time, beat in the egg yolks. Add the flour mixture and the milk alternately to the butter mixture until well blended. Set the batter aside.

In a large bowl, beat the 4 egg whites until soft peaks form. Sprinkle on the remaining ¼ cup granulated sugar and a pinch of salt and continue to beat the whites until stiff peaks form. Fold the egg-white mixture into the batter. Do not overmix; some streaks of white may remain. Spoon into the prepared pan and spread to the edges.

To make the topping, in a medium bowl beat the egg whites until stiff peaks form. Add the brown sugar and cocoa and stir well. With a spatula, spread the topping over the cake. Using a knife, cut and swirl the topping into the cake to create a marbled pattern.

Bake the cake until a tester inserted into the center comes out clean, 50 to 60 minutes. Let the cake cool in the pan on a rack, then invert onto a platter. Or, the cake may be served directly from the pan. Serve warm or at room temperature.

Coffee Angel-Food Cake

Here is my mother's famous angel-food cake (which actually comes from my aunt Jeanne). Few special occasions at the Morgan household were held without this light but fabulously flavorful confection. The touch of maple flavoring adds just the right mysterious but balancing note to the coffee. Don't forget to let somebody lick the frosting bowl.

1 10-inch cake, serves 10

Cake

 1 cup cake flour
 1¼ cups superfine sugar
 2 tablespoons fine instant-coffee granules
 1½ cups (10 to 12) large egg whites, at room temperature
 1 tablespoon fresh lemon juice
 1½ teaspoons cream of tartar
 1 teaspoon vanilla extract
 1 teaspoon maple extract
 ½ teaspoon salt

Frosting

 2 cups whipping cream
 3 tablespoons confectioners' sugar
 1 tablespoon fine instant-coffee granules
 1 teaspoon maple extract
 6 ounces (about ⅔ cup) sliced unblanched almonds

Position a rack in the middle of the oven and preheat to 350° F.

For the cake, sift together twice onto a piece of waxed paper the flour, ½ cup of the superfine sugar and the coffee granules. In the bowl of an electric stand mixer, beat the egg whites until foamy. Add the lemon juice, cream of tartar, vanilla, maple extract and salt. Beat until soft peaks form. Two tablespoons at a time, beat in the remaining ¾ cup sugar until the whites are stiff and glossy. With a rubber scraper, fold one-third of the flour mixture into the whites. Repeat, folding in half the remaining flour at a time, until just combined. Spoon the batter into an ungreased 10-inch angel-food cake pan. Smooth the top. Bake until the cake springs back when pressed in the center, 35 to 40 minutes. Do not overbake. Invert the pan and let the cake stand upside down until cool.

Gently release the cake from the sides of the pan with a spatula. Invert the pan onto a plate; the cake will drop out. With a serrated knife, using a gentle sawing motion, cut the cake horizontally in half.

To make the frosting, in a medium bowl, whip the cream until soft peaks form. Continue to whip, sprinkling the confectioners' sugar, coffee granules and maple extract over the cream, just until stiff peaks form; do not overwhip.

Spread about one-fourth of the frosting over the cut surface of the bottom half of the cake. Set the top half in place. Spread the remaining frosting over the sides and top of the reassembled cake. Scatter the almonds evenly over the sides and top of the cake. Refrigerate until serving, not more than 2 hours after frosting.

Flavors' Apple Crisp

When I get a little tired of the exquisitely complex dessert creations that New York's pastry chefs are so good at making, when I want something light and simple yet satisfyingly sweet and comforting, I turn to Flavors' Apple Crisp. It's quick enough to make at the end of a long workday and it never fails to please.

Serves 4 to 6

3 medium-large Granny Smith apples (about 1½ pounds)
2 large McIntosh apples (about 1 pound)
3 tablespoons maple syrup
2 tablespoons fresh lemon juice
1 teaspoon lemon zest (colored part of peel, removed with a zester and minced)
Crunchy Oat Topping, chilled

Position a rack in the middle of the oven and preheat to 400° F.

Core, peel and thinly slice the apples. In a large bowl, toss the apple slices with the maple syrup, lemon juice and zest. Let stand 15 minutes.

Spoon the apple mixture and any juices into an 8-cup ovenproof serving dish. With the tines of a fork, break up the largest lumps of topping. Spoon the topping mixture evenly over the apples, using it all.

Set the dish in the oven and bake until the apples are tender, their juices are bubbling and the topping is crisp and brown, 35 to 45 minutes.

Let stand on a rack for at least 10 minutes. Serve hot, warm or cold.

Crunchy Oat Topping

This all-purpose topping can be prepared a day or two in advance and stored in the refrigerator. Only your imagination limits the kinds of seasonal fruit you bake beneath it. (For extra crunch, stir ½ cup chopped walnuts, almonds or pecans into the topping after processing.)

Makes enough for 1 batch of crisp

⅔ cup packed golden-brown sugar
½ cup unbleached all-purpose flour
½ cup old-fashioned (not quick-cooking) rolled oats
½ teaspoon ground cinnamon
¼ teaspoon salt
6 tablespoons (¾ stick) chilled unsalted butter, cut into small pieces

In a food processor, combine the brown sugar, flour, oats, cinnamon and salt and pulse to blend. Scatter the butter over the oat mixture and process until a soft, crumbly and lumpy cookie-type dough forms. The topping can be prepared up to 2 days ahead. Cover and refrigerate. Use directly from the refrigerator.

Very Lemony Pound Cake

I love just plain cake, the simpler the better, though I'll allow that a touch of lemon doesn't hurt a bit. Make that a lot of lemon, which this otherwise plain (but very moist) cake has in abundance. Nice with a cup of tea (toasted if it somehow becomes a little dry) and wonderful alongside fruit desserts, the cake is also great in a lunch box or eaten out of hand as a snack when on the run.

Makes 1 9-by-5-inch loaf

Solid vegetable shortening, for the baking pan
Flour, for the baking pan
2⅓ cups cake flour (not self-rising)
1 teaspoon baking powder
½ teaspoon salt
½ teaspoon freshly grated nutmeg
2 sticks (½ pound) unsalted butter, softened slightly
2¼ cups sugar
5 large eggs, at room temperature
1 tablespoon lemon zest (colored part of peel, removed with a zester and minced)
1 teaspoon vanilla extract
½ cup fresh lemon juice

Position a rack in the middle of the oven and preheat to 325° F. Lightly coat the inside of a 9-by-5-by-3-inch loaf pan with shortening. Add some flour and tilt the pan to coat; tap out the excess.

Sift the cake flour, baking powder, salt and nutmeg together onto a piece of waxed paper. Sift the flour mixture a second time.

In a large bowl with a spoon, or in an electric stand mixer fitted with the paddle attachment, beat the butter until soft and fluffy. Gradually add 2 cups of the sugar and beat until light and creamy. Add the eggs, one at a time, beating well after each addition. Add the lemon zest and vanilla.

By hand, or with the mixer on its lowest speed, gradually stir in the dry ingredients just until well blended. Turn the batter into the prepared pan. Bake until the cake is puffed and golden brown and a tester inserted into the center comes out clean, 1 hour to 1 hour and 5 minutes. Transfer the pan to a rack set on a baking sheet and let stand for 10 minutes. Turn the cake out of the pan and set it upright on the rack.

Meanwhile, in a small bowl, stir together the lemon juice and the remaining ¼ cup sugar. Gradually spoon the lemon mixture over the top of the still-hot cake, allowing it to be absorbed. Cool completely before cutting.

Tequila-Glazed Pineapple and Nectarine Skewers with Orange Crème Anglaise

Grilling doesn't cook fruit so much as it warms and caramelizes it, raising it to fragrant, juicy perfection. Though I usually serve the fruit with a rich orange-flavored custard sauce, you might prefer the low-fat Tropical Fruit Sauce on page 209 instead. Or just spoon the chunked fruit over macadamia praline ice cream.

Serves 6 to 8

¾ cup packed golden-brown sugar
⅔ cup tequila
1½ teaspoons vanilla extract
¼ teaspoon ground cinnamon
1 medium-large pineapple, peeled,
    cored and cut into 2-by-1-inch pieces
3 ripe but firm nectarines, pitted,
    each cut into 8 wedges
    Orange Crème Anglaise, recipe follows
    Raspberries, as optional garnish

In a small bowl, stir together the brown sugar, tequila, vanilla and cinnamon. Slide the pineapple and nectarine pieces onto 7 or 8 flat metal skewers.

Prepare a medium charcoal fire or preheat a gas grill (medium-low). Position the grill rack about 6 inches above the heat (see Note).

When the fire is hot, lay the skewers on the rack. Grill, basting the pineapple and nectarines with the tequila mixture and turning the skewers often, until the glaze is used up and the fruit is shiny and brown, 10 to 12 minutes total.

Spoon a pool of crème anglaise onto each of 8 dessert plates. Slide the fruit off the skewers onto the sauce. Scatter a few raspberries over the sauce on each plate. Serve immediately.

Note: When grilling fruit, be sure the grill rack is impeccably clean and free from other flavors.

Orange Crème Anglaise

Richly creamy and eggy, this sauce is one of the very best toppings for fruit desserts; it's especially fine with berries. But then again, it's also elegantly understated alongside a flourless chocolate cake like the one on page 208. You can even churn it into delicious ice cream, if you would like; double this recipe and follow the manufacturer's directions for your ice cream maker. Cover and freeze until serving.

Makes about 2½ cups

⅓ cup sugar
5 large egg yolks
2 cups half-and-half
3 tablespoons orange liqueur, such as Cointreau
½ teaspoon vanilla extract

In a medium, heatproof bowl, gradually whisk the sugar into the egg yolks.

In a heavy, medium saucepan over moderate heat, bring the half-and-half just to a boil. Whisk the egg mixture constantly while gradually dribbling in the hot half-and-half.

Return the mixture to the saucepan and set over medium heat. Cook, stirring constantly with a wooden spoon, until the mixture is steaming and the bubbles have disappeared from the surface, 2 to 4 minutes. An instant-read thermometer should register between 165° and 170° F. and a finger drawn across the back of the spoon should leave a track.

Remove the pan from the heat and immediately strain the sauce into a medium bowl. Cool to room temperature. Stir in the liqueur and the vanilla. Cover by pressing plastic wrap onto the surface of the sauce. Refrigerate until cold and slightly thickened, at least 2 hours. The sauce can be prepared up to 3 days ahead. Serve cold.

Semolina Bread Pudding with Warm Berry Sauce

I like the notion that bread pudding is a sensibly frugal way to use good bread that is somewhat past its eating prime. This holds true at Flavors, certainly, when unsold bread (particularly the light-golden Italian bread made from semolina, or pasta, flour) must get used up. At home, when I make this on purpose, I don't feel quite so frugal (and I don't always use semolina bread), but I am still impressed by what a good dessert I can make with a loaf of bread. Try to time this so that you can eat it barely warm from the oven—bliss.

Serves 6 to 8

Softened butter, for the baking dish
3 large eggs
¼ cup sugar
2 cups half-and-half
1 cup whipping cream
¼ cup fresh orange juice
2 tablespoons vanilla extract
1 teaspoon orange zest (colored part of peel, removed with a zester and minced)
1¼ teaspoons ground cinnamon
1¼ teaspoons freshly grated nutmeg
8 cups 1-inch cubes crustless, day-old bread, preferably semolina
1½ cups quartered hulled fresh strawberries
1½ cups blackberries
Confectioners' sugar
Warm Berry Sauce, recipe follows

Position a rack in the middle of the oven and preheat to 325° F. Lightly butter a 2½-quart ovenproof serving dish about 4 inches deep.

In a large bowl, whisk the eggs. Whisk in the sugar. Whisk in the half-and-half and cream. Whisk in the orange juice, vanilla, orange zest, cinnamon and nutmeg.

Scatter half the bread cubes over the bottom of the prepared dish. Scatter half the strawberries and half the blackberries over the bread cubes. Scatter the remaining bread cubes over the berries. Scatter the remaining berries over the bread cubes. Pour the egg mixture over the bread cubes and berries. Lay a sheet of plastic wrap directly onto the surface of the pudding. Weight it with 2 or 3 small ramekins or saucers so that the bread is completely immersed in the egg mixture. Let stand for 10 minutes.

Remove the weights and the plastic wrap. Set the pudding in the oven and bake until the top is lightly browned and the custard is set but not firm when the dish is jiggled, 50 to 60 minutes. Let the pudding rest in the dish on a rack for at least 10 minutes.

Sift confectioners' sugar through a sieve onto the bread pudding and serve hot or warm, accompanied by the berry sauce.

Warm Berry Sauce

Though definitely at its best made with fresh berries, this can be pretty good prepared from frozen fruit as well. Don't limit it to topping the pudding—it's nice on pancakes, waffles, oatmeal and yogurt and simply divine on vanilla ice cream.

Makes about 2 cups

1 cup fresh or frozen blueberries,
   picked over if fresh
1 cup fresh or frozen raspberries,
   picked over if fresh
1 cup fresh or frozen blackberries,
   picked over if fresh
1 cup fresh or frozen strawberries,
   hulled and quartered if fresh
3 tablespoons sugar
1 tablespoon fresh lemon juice

In a small, nonreactive saucepan, combine the blueberries, raspberries, blackberries, strawberries, sugar and lemon juice. Let stand until any frozen berries are fully thawed.

Set the saucepan over medium heat and bring to a simmer. Cook, stirring, for 2 to 3 minutes, or until juicy.

The sauce can be prepared several hours in advance. Rewarm gently over low heat before using.

Blackberry Crème Brûlée

Traditional crème brûlée gets a nice, summery twist when whole blackberries are baked in. Diners dig down through crackly brown-sugar topping and tender custard to discover a puddle of berries and juice at the bottom of the dish: great eating!

Serves 6

2 containers, 6 ounces each, fresh blackberries, picked over
3 tablespoons plus ½ cup granulated sugar
1 teaspoon orange liqueur, such as Cointreau
5 large egg yolks
2⅓ cups whipping cream
Pinch of salt
1 teaspoon vanilla extract
⅓ cup packed golden-brown sugar

Position a rack in the middle of the oven and preheat to 325° F.

In a medium bowl, stir together the blackberries, 3 tablespoons of the sugar and the liqueur. Let stand for 15 minutes.

Divide the berries and any rendered juices among 6 ¾-cup broiler-proof serving dishes.

Meanwhile, in a large bowl, whisk together the egg yolks and the ½ cup sugar.

In a medium pan over moderate heat, combine the cream and salt. Bring to a boil. Gradually whisk the hot cream into the yolks. Stir in the vanilla. Divide the cream mixture among the 6 dishes, pouring it gently to mix it as little as possible with the berries.

Transfer the small dishes to a 9-by-13-inch baking pan. Add enough very hot tap water to the pan to come halfway up the sides of the dishes. Set the pan in the oven. Bake until the custards just bubble gently around the edges, about 35 minutes. They will not be firmly set. Cool the custards in the pan of water on a rack to room temperature. Cover and refrigerate at least 5 hours or up to 2 days.

If serving the crème brûlées warm, let them come just to room temperature. Position a rack about 4 inches below the heat source and preheat the broiler. Force the brown sugar through a coarse sieve over the tops of the custards in an even, fluffy layer.

Working in batches to maintain control, set the dishes under the broiler and broil until the sugar topping turns crisp and brown, about 1 minute. Serve immediately, warning diners that the edges of the dishes will be hot.

Or, return the crème brûlées to the refrigerator and serve them cold, within a few hours of broiling.

Plums and Peaches
in Blueberry-Vanilla Syrup

Less is more in this very easy, very pretty summer fruit-based dessert, in which uncooked ripe plums and peaches swim in a vanilla-scented blueberry syrup. All sorts of prime fruit can join or replace the plums and peaches, depending on what you find in the market and like to eat. Serve it after a picnic lunch, accompanied with a lightly toasted slice of Very Lemony Pound Cake (page 214).

Serves 8

1 cup fresh or frozen blueberries,
   picked over if fresh
1 cup sugar
½ cup dry white or red wine
½ cup water
1 vanilla bean, split lengthwise, halved crosswise
1 pound (5 medium) ripe, juicy plums, such as
   Santa Rosa, pitted and cut into eighths
2 pounds (5 medium) ripe, juicy peaches or
   nectarines, pitted and cut into eighths
3 tablespoons fresh lemon juice
2 tablespoons finely chopped mint

In a small, nonreactive saucepan, combine the blueberries, sugar, wine and water. Scrape the seeds from the vanilla bean pieces into the pan; add the vanilla bean pieces to the pan. Set over medium heat, partially cover and bring to a brisk simmer. Cook, stirring occasionally, until the mixture has reduced and is slightly syrupy, about 7 minutes. Remove from the heat. Transfer the syrup to a heat-proof bowl and cool to room temperature. Cover and refrigerate until cold, at least 5 hours, or overnight for convenience.

Remove the vanilla bean pieces from the syrup. In a food processor, puree the syrup.

In a large bowl, stir together the plums, peaches, syrup and lemon juice. The dessert can be served immediately or it can be refrigerated for up to 1 hour.

Spoon the fruit mixture into dessert bowls, dividing the syrup evenly and using it all. Sprinkle each portion with some of the mint and serve immediately.

 Though delicious to eat as is, a scoop of complementary fruit sorbet (such as lemon or raspberry) can be floated in the syrup along with the plums and peaches. Garnish the dressed-up dessert with a whole sprig of mint.

Wine-Poached Pear Croustades with Ice Cream

Although croustade *most often refers to a crisp casing carved out of bread to hold a savory filling, or to a rustic fruit tart, the name can be applied to any crunchy supporting player. Here, it is the toasted pound cake that accompanies the spicy, wine-poached pears. Though light, this fruit dessert is intensely flavored and full of textural and temperature contrasts—lively eating, and a nice ending to a bistro-style autumn dinner.*

Serves 6

4½ cups red wine, such as Merlot

¾ cup sugar

18 whole black peppercorns

2 6-by-1-inch strips orange zest (colored part of peel, removed with a zester and minced)

1 tablespoon grated fresh ginger with juices

½ teaspoon ground cardamom

1 bay leaf

3 firm but ripe Bosc or Bartlett pears, cored, peeled and halved lengthwise

1½ tablespoons fresh orange juice

1½ tablespoons cornstarch

6 ½-inch-thick slices Very Lemony Pound Cake (page 214) or substitute purchased plain pound cake

Premium vanilla ice cream, softened slightly

In a large, nonreactive saucepan over medium heat, stir together the wine, sugar, peppercorns, orange zest, ginger, cardamom and bay leaf until the sugar dissolves. Raise the heat to high and boil, uncovered, for 5 minutes. Add the pears, lower the heat, partially cover the pan and gently simmer the pears, turning them once or twice, until they are just tender, about 10 minutes. Transfer the pears and poaching liquid to a heatproof bowl and cool to room temperature. Cover and refrigerate until cold, at least 5 hours or overnight for convenience.

With a slotted spoon, transfer the pears to a plate. Strain the liquid into a small, nonreactive saucepan; discard the solids. Set the pan over medium-high heat and cook the poaching liquid briskly until it is reduced to 1½ cups, about 8 minutes. In a small bowl, whisk the orange juice into the cornstarch. Whisk the juice mixture into the reduced poaching liquid. Simmer, stirring often, until the sauce boils and thickens, about 1 minute. Remove from the heat and cool slightly.

Lightly toast the pound cake slices. Cut them in half diagonally. Thinly slice the pears lengthwise. Arrange 2 pound cake triangles and 1 sliced pear half on each of 6 plates. Top each with a small scoop of the ice cream. Drizzle generously with the sauce and serve immediately.

Cappuccino Mousse

This sophisticated coffee-chocolate mousse, with its attractive streaks of cream, perfectly embodies one of my favorite flavor combinations and always garners raves at the table. All the whipping, whisking and bowl-using get done well in advance, making this a perfect party dessert.

Serves 6 to 8

1½ cups whipping cream
 4 large eggs, separated, at room temperature
½ pound bittersweet chocolate, chopped
 4 teaspoons instant espresso powder
⅛ teaspoon cream of tartar
¼ cup sugar
¾ teaspoon vanilla extract
 Unsweetened whipped cream,
   as optional topping

In a small saucepan whisk together ¼ cup of the cream and the egg yolks. Set over low heat and cook, whisking constantly, until the mixture thickens, about 2 minutes. Add the chocolate and espresso powder and stir just until smooth. Remove from the heat.

In a large bowl whisk the egg whites until foamy. Whisk in the cream of tartar. Continue to whisk until the whites begin to mound. Gradually add the sugar while whisking constantly, until stiff peaks form. Fold the chocolate mixture into the whites, blending well.

In a chilled medium bowl, whip the remaining 1¼ cups whipping cream to soft peaks. Whisk in the vanilla extract. Fold the whipped cream into the chocolate mixture just until barely blended, leaving visible streaks of white.

Spoon the mousse into a 6-cup serving dish, or divide it among 6 or 8 individual dishes. Cover carefully with plastic wrap to avoid marring the surface of the mousse and chill until set, about 5 hours for the individual servings or overnight for the bowl.

Spoon the mousse from the large bowl onto dessert plates. Garnish each serving with a dollop of the cream, if desired, and serve immediately.

Spoon the mousse into demitasse cups and chill. Transfer the whipped cream to a pastry bag fitted with a medium star tip. Pipe a rosette of whipped cream onto each portion of mousse. Center a chocolate-covered coffee bean in each rosette and serve immediately.

Blushing Pear Granita

Easy to make, and requiring no special kitchen machinery, granitas are rustic desserts, icier and more granular than sorbets. Delicately pink ("white" zinfandel is actually pale pink), this beautiful confection is intensely pear-flavored. Many foods are described as "refreshing" but this is one of the few that actually are. Serve it, Italian-style, as a midmorning or midafternoon snack on a hot day, or enjoy it as a light dessert, accompanied by biscotti (page 205) or other crisp cookies.

Serves 8

1⅔ cups white zinfandel wine
½ cup sugar
3 tablespoons fresh lemon juice
2 pounds (4 large) *very ripe* pears,
    such as Bartlett, cored, peeled
    and cut into ½-inch chunks

In a small, nonreactive saucepan combine the wine, sugar and lemon juice. Bring to a simmer, stirring to dissolve the sugar, and cook briskly for 2 minutes. Remove from the heat and cool to room temperature.

In a food processor, puree the pears until smooth. In a storage container with a tight-fitting lid thoroughly stir together the pear puree and the cooled wine mixture. Cover and freeze until solid, preferably overnight.

With a metal spoon, break the frozen pear mixture into 1-inch chunks. In a food processor, working in batches if necessary, process the granita with short bursts of power until it is chopped and just becoming slushy. Divide among 8 dessert bowls and serve immediately.

Note: Choose a container large enough to hold the granita in a layer no thicker than 2 inches, or it may be impossible to break it into chunks as directed.

Espresso-Frangelico Granita

Unlike the pear granita, which is delicate enough to stand alone, this vividly coffee-flavored sweet actually welcomes a dollop of unsweetened whipped cream, by way of palate relief. Again, this can be enjoyed as a quick, invigorating snack or as a full-fledged dessert.

Serves 8

1¼ cups freshly ground espresso coffee
6 cups water
1 cup plus 2 tablespoons sugar
¼ cup Frangelico (Italian hazelnut liqueur)
1 tablespoon fresh lemon juice

In an electric drip coffeemaker (or equipment of your choice), brew the coffee with the 6 cups water. There should be about 5½ cups strong, dark coffee. Stir the sugar, Frangelico and lemon juice into the coffee and cool to room temperature. Transfer to a covered container and freeze until solid (due to the alcohol in the Frangelico, this may take up to 12 hours).

To serve, break the granita into 1-inch chunks. In a food processor, with short bursts of power, chop the granita into an icy slush. Spoon into bowls and serve immediately.

Note: Choose a container large enough to hold the granita in a layer no thicker than 2 inches, or it may be impossible to break it into chunks as directed.

Marmalade-Glazed Fresh Fig and Mascarpone Tart

Fresh figs are so lusciously sweet and beautiful, they require no cooking and, in fact, little embellishment. This easy but spectacular-looking tart, in which the raw figs are halved and arranged over a simple filling of the rich Italian cream cheese called mascarpone, is a good case in point. An ideal summer dessert, the tart's crisp shell can be baked early in the day, leaving plenty of time for the house to cool down for company.

Makes 1 9-inch tart, serves 6

½ pound mascarpone (rich Italian cream cheese),
    at room temperature
3 tablespoons confectioners' sugar
1 fully baked Sweet Tart Shell
15 ripe, fragrant figs, preferably Black Mission,
    stemmed and halved vertically
½ cup orange marmalade
1½ teaspoons orange liqueur, preferably
    Grand Marnier
½ teaspoon fresh lemon juice
2 tablespoons pine nuts, toasted (page 114)

In a medium bowl, stir together the mascarpone and confectioners' sugar. Spread the mascarpone mixture evenly into the tart shell. Beginning at the outer crust, arrange the figs, cut sides upward, in concentric circles over the mascarpone. In a small bowl, combine the marmalade, orange liqueur and lemon juice. Brush the marmalade mixture over the figs, using it all. Sprinkle the tart with the pine nuts. Serve within an hour or so of completion.

Sweet Tart Shell

Makes 1 9-inch shell

1½ cups unbleached all-purpose flour
2 tablespoons sugar
    Pinch of salt
5 tablespoons unsalted butter,
    well chilled and cut into small pieces
¼ cup solid vegetable shortening,
    well chilled and cut into small pieces
    About ¼ cup iced water

In a food processor, combine the flour, sugar and salt. With pulses of power blend in the butter and shortening until the mixture resembles coarse meal. With short bursts of power, blend in the water 1 tablespoon at a time until a crumbly dough forms. Turn out onto a lightly floured work surface and gather and press into a disk. Wrap tightly in plastic and chill at least 2 hours, or overnight for convenience.

    Soften the dough briefly at room temperature if it is hard. On a lightly floured work surface, roll it out into a

⅛-inch-thick round. Fit the dough into a fluted 9-inch tart pan with a removable bottom and trim the edges. Chill for 1 hour.

Position a rack in the middle of the oven and preheat to 400° F. Line the tart shell with parchment or waxed paper and fill it with pie weights or dried beans. Bake until set, about 10 minutes. Remove the weights and waxed paper. Prick the shell lightly all over with the tines of a fork and flatten any steam pockets. Bake until golden and cooked through, another 8 to 10 minutes. Cool completely on a rack. Remove the sides of the tart pan and slide the shell onto a plate. Fill and serve as directed.

Banana-Chocolate Tartlets with Macadamia Praline Crunch

Adapted from a recipe by Beth Hirsch, these elegant and delicious little tarts are wonders of sweet flavor and texture. The praline melts slightly (the rum helps get things started), leaving the bananas topped with a sensational combination of caramel sauce and crunchy praline.

Makes 8 4-inch tartlets

¾ pound semisweet or bittersweet chocolate, chopped
¾ cup whipping cream
2 tablespoons dark Jamaican rum, such as Meyers's
8 fully baked 4-inch tartlet shells, recipe for Tart Dough follows
  Macadamia Praline, recipe follows
4 large ripe bananas, thinly sliced

In the top of a double boiler over hot (not simmering) water, heat the chocolate, uncovered, stirring occasionally, until almost melted. Remove the top of the double boiler from the bottom and stir the chocolate once or twice more, until just smooth.

Meanwhile, in a small saucepan over medium heat, warm the cream until steaming (do not boil). Add the cream all at once to the chocolate and stir until smooth. Stir in 1 tablespoon of the rum. Spoon the chocolate mixture into the tartlet shells. Transfer them to a baking sheet and refrigerate until set, about 2 hours. Add banana slices.

Chop the praline. Sprinkle it evenly over the bananas on the tarts, using it all. Drizzle the praline with the remaining 1 tablespoon rum. Refrigerate until the rum begins to dissolve the praline slightly, about 4 hours, before serving.

Tart Dough

2 sticks (½ pound) unsalted butter, chilled
2¼ cups unbleached all-purpose flour,
    plus flour for the work surface
1 tablespoon plus 1 teaspoon sugar
¼ teaspoon salt
⅓ cup iced water

Cut the butter into ¼-inch pieces. Freeze until firm, about 15 minutes.

In a food processor, combine the flour, sugar and salt and pulse to blend. Add the butter and process until the mixture is finely granular, resembling grated Parmesan cheese. Add the iced water and pulse just until there is no loose flour in the bottom of the work bowl. Do not overprocess.

Turn out onto a large piece of plastic wrap. Shape the dough into a rectangular slab. Wrap tightly and chill for at least 1 hour. The dough can be refrigerated for up to 1 week or frozen for up to 1 month.

Remove the chilled dough from the refrigerator and let it stand about 10 minutes to soften slightly. On a well-floured surface, roll the dough out into an approximately 12-by-24-inch rectangle. Cut the rectangle into 8 6-inch squares. Roll each square out into a rough round about 7 inches in diameter. One at a time, drape a round of dough over a 4-inch false-bottom tartlet pan. Repeat with the remaining dough. Run the rolling pin over the top of the tartlet pans to trim off the excess dough. With your thumb, gently press the remaining dough into the tartlet pans; the dough will come up slightly higher than the edge of the pan. Prick the tartlet shells all over with the tines of a fork. Chill the tartlet shells for 30 minutes.

Position a rack in the middle of the oven and preheat to 350° F.

Set the chilled tartlet shells on a baking sheet. Cut 8 8-inch squares of foil. Line each shell with foil, then fill with metal pie weights or dried beans. Set the sheet in the oven and bake for 15 minutes. Remove the weights and then the foil. Bake the tartlet shells until they are golden brown and just cooked through, another 20 to 30 minutes. Cool completely in the pans on a rack. Remove the sides of the tartlet pans and slide the tartlet shells from the bottoms. The tartlet shells can be baked several hours before being filled.

Macadamia Praline

Don't wait until baking a batch of banana-chocolate tartlets before making this glorious praline. It will transform store-bought ice cream (especially chocolate and coffee) or even sliced fresh fruit, such as peaches or pineapple, into an elegant dessert.

1 tablespoon unsalted butter, softened
¾ cup sugar
1 cup lightly salted macadamia nuts

Butter a heatproof dish, such as a glass pie plate.

In a small, heavy saucepan over low heat, melt the sugar, stirring occasionally, about 10 minutes. Add the nuts and continue to cook until the mixture is golden brown and the nuts are lightly toasted, another 3 minutes or so. Immediately pour the mixture onto the prepared plate.

Cool to room temperature. Break the praline into large chunks and store airtight at room temperature. In dry weather the praline will keep at least 1 week.

Harvest Nut Pie with a Touch of Bourbon and Chocolate

A whole harvest's worth of crunchy nuts is found in this rich treat, a flavor-boosted variation on old-fashioned pecan pie. A splash of good bourbon and a hint of chocolate make for a less-sweet pie, a change I find very welcome.

1 9-inch pie, 6 to 8 servings

4 ounces bittersweet (not unsweetened) chocolate, melted and cooled slightly

1 unbaked, 9-inch pie shell, chilled

3 large eggs, at room temperature

⅔ cup packed dark-brown sugar

¾ cup dark corn syrup

¼ cup bourbon, such as Maker's Mark

4 tablespoons (½ stick) unsalted butter, melted and slightly cooled

2 teaspoons vanilla extract

¼ teaspoon salt

½ cup coarsely chopped pecans

½ cup coarsely chopped unblanched almonds

½ cup coarsely chopped walnuts

Unsweetened whipped cream, for serving

Position a rack in the middle of the oven. If you are not using a glass pie dish, set a metal baking sheet on the rack. Preheat the oven to 350° F.

Spread the chocolate evenly over the bottom of the prepared pie shell.

In a large bowl whisk the eggs. Whisk in the brown sugar, corn syrup, bourbon, butter, vanilla and salt. Stir in the pecans, almonds and walnuts. Pour the filling into the pie shell. Bake the pie until the top is browned and the fill-ing is uniformly but not firmly set, about 50 minutes.

Remove from the oven and cool on a rack to room temperature before cutting. Serve the pie with a dollop of whipped cream.

Pie Shell

A combination of butter and solid vegetable shortening makes a pie crust that is tender, flaky and flavorful. For a two-crust pie, just double the ingredients.

For 1 9-inch, single-crust pie

2 cups unbleached all-purpose flour, plus flour for the work surface

¼ teaspoon salt

⅓ cup chilled vegetable shortening, cut into pieces

5 tablespoons chilled unsalted butter, cut into pieces

About ⅓ cup iced water

In a food processor, combine the flour and salt and pulse to blend. Add the shortening and butter and pulse until bits the size of corn kernels form. With the motor running, add just enough of the water through the feed tube to form a loose, granular dough.

Lightly flour the work surface. Turn out the dough and gather and press it into a disk. Wrap the disk of dough tightly in plastic and refrigerate for at least 1 hour or up to 3 days.

Soften the dough briefly at room temperature if it is hard. Lightly flour the work surface. Roll the dough out into a 14-inch round, about ¼ inch thick. Transfer the dough to a 9-inch pie pan. Trim the edges, then crimp and flute them decoratively if desired. Wrap the pie shell in plastic and refrigerate for at least 1 hour or up to 1 day before using.

Pumpkin Cheesecake with Pecan Praline Sauce

An unexpectedly welcome alternative to pumpkin pie on the Thanksgiving menu, this light and creamy cheesecake with its delicate pumpkin flavor and crisp gingersnap crust is also good from the first day of fall to the last day of winter.

Serves 12

36 gingersnap cookies
3 tablespoons plus ¼ cup granulated sugar
4½ tablespoons unsalted butter, melted and cooled slightly
1 pound cream cheese, at room temperature
1 can (16 ounces) solid-pack pumpkin puree (not pie filling)
5 large eggs
¾ cup packed golden-brown sugar
¾ cup Amaretto liqueur
1 teaspoon ground cinnamon
1 teaspoon vanilla extract
½ teaspoon ground ginger
¼ teaspoon freshly grated nutmeg
¼ teaspoon ground cloves

1 container (16 ounces) sour cream
Pecan Praline Sauce, recipe follows

In a food processor, grind the gingersnaps together with the 3 tablespoons granulated sugar into fine crumbs. With the machine running, gradually add the butter. Press the mixture firmly into the bottom of a 9-inch springform pan and refrigerate until hard, about 30 minutes.

Position a rack in the middle of the oven and preheat to 350º F.

In a food processor or mixer, combine the cream cheese, pumpkin, eggs, brown sugar, ½ cup of the Amaretto, the cinnamon, vanilla, ginger, nutmeg and cloves. Process, stopping once or twice to scrape down the sides of the workbowl, until just combined; do not overmix. Pour the filling into the prepared pan and bake until the edges of the cake just begin to pull away from the sides of the pan, 40 to 45 minutes. The center of the cake will not be firm.

Meanwhile, in a bowl whisk together the sour cream, the remaining ¼ cup granulated sugar and the remaining ¼ cup Amaretto.

Without removing the cake from the oven, pour the topping evenly over it, starting with the edges. Spread the topping evenly. Bake the cake another 8 to 10 minutes, or until the edges of the topping just begin to bubble. Cool the cake in the pan on a rack. Cover (avoid marring the topping) and chill until firm, at least 12 hours.

Carefully run a knife between the edge of the cake and the sides of the pan; release and remove the sides. With a thin, sharp knife, dipped into hot water and wiped dry between cuts, cut the cake into serving pieces. Transfer to plates and let stand at room temperature for 20 minutes. Spoon a bit of the praline sauce over and beside each piece just before serving.

PUMPKIN—I share Linus's excitement as summer eases into fall and the fields in the Hamptons not used for growing potatoes are suddenly aglow with thousands of fat, orange pumpkins. Other signs of seasonal change may give mixed signals, but spotting pumpkins (if not The Great Pumpkin) is a sure indication summer is over. At home I use big pumpkins as jack-o'-lanterns, while for catered affairs they serve as vases for huge bouquets of harvest foliage on buffet tables. Tiny baby pumpkins are scooped out and baked or steamed, to hold individual portions of pumpkin soup. Here's a tip: The pumpkins grown for jack-o'-lanterns ("face" pumpkins) are very different from those grown to make canned pumpkin ("cheese" pumpkins), which is why, after years of sweaty disappointment, I've stopped trying to puree my own. This is one of the few times when canned is actually better than homemade.

Pecan Praline Sauce

Leftovers of this sauce, should such an unlikely event occur, are delicious over scoops of vanilla ice cream.

Makes about 1¾ cups sauce

1 cup packed golden-brown sugar
7 tablespoons unsalted butter
7 tablespoons water
2 eggs, well beaten
½ cup chopped pecans
1 teaspoon vanilla extract

In a heavy, medium saucepan over moderate heat, combine the sugar, butter and water. Bring just to a boil, stirring occasionally.

In a medium bowl, whisk the hot syrup into the eggs. Return the mixture to the pan, set over low heat and cook, stirring constantly, until the mixture thickens, 1 to 2 minutes.

Remove from the heat and cool to room temperature. Stir in the pecans and vanilla. Use at room temperature.

Mexican Watermelon Quaff

This is an agua fresca, *one of a whole class of Mexican drinks made from little more than fresh fruit puree or juice, water and, optionally, sugar. In Mexico, in stands in the markets and along the streets, these drinks are sold from big barrel-shaped glass jars, usually with a block of ice floating therein. Agua frescas are among the simplest and most refreshing drinks on a hot day (or with spicy food), and made with the right ingredients, they can be the most flavorful, too. Choose a deep red, properly ripe and juicy watermelon, and you'll be surprised at how intensely good something so easy to make can be.*

Makes about 5½ cups, serves 4

8 cups chunked watermelon, with or without seeds, chilled
6 ice cubes (from a regular household tray)
Wedges of lime, as accompaniment

In a food processor or blender, working in batches, pulse the melon chunks just until liquefied but without chopping the seeds. Transfer to a pitcher. Add the ice cubes and stir until they are partially melted and the drink is very cold. Divide among tall glasses and serve; drink with a straw in order not to swallow any seeds.

Mango Lemonade

While lemon and mango are popular agua fresca *flavors individually, they can also be combined for a more unusual and tart refresher. Or, lime juice can be substituted for the lemon (fragrant Key or Mexican limes are especially wonderful); adjust the sugar upward slightly if desired. The lemonade can also be mixed with vodka or tequila. When something smoky and spicy is on the grill in the summer, there is always a pitcher of this lemonade on my table.*

Makes about 7 cups, serves 4 to 6

2 large mangoes, about 2 pounds total
2½ cups water
1½ cups fresh lemon juice (from about 6 medium lemons)
⅓ cup plus 2 tablespoons sugar
Fresh mint sprigs, as optional garnish

Peel, pit and chop the mangoes. In a food processor, puree the mango, stopping once or twice to scrape down the sides of the work bowl. There should be about 2 cups puree.

In a pitcher, combine the mango puree, water, lemon juice and sugar; stir well to dissolve. Cover and refrigerate until very cold, at least 5 hours and preferably overnight.

Taste and add additional sugar if desired. Pour the lemonade over ice in tall glasses. Garnish with mint if desired and serve immediately.

Mint Hot Chocolate

This hot chocolate is good and different and will warm the tummies of you and yours on a cold winter's day. Adjust the sugar to taste, and feel free to omit the whipping cream and to use low-fat milk in place of regular; the beverage is (almost!) as good without it. Suitable garnishes include whipped cream and a dusting of grated chocolate or a sprinkle of crushed peppermint stick.

Serves 4

3	cups milk (low-fat milk can be used)
1 to 2	teaspoons sugar, to taste
¾	cup semisweet mint chocolate chips
¼	teaspoon vanilla extract

In a medium-sized heavy saucepan over moderate heat, combine the milk and sugar. Bring just to a brisk simmer. Pour the hot milk mixture into a blender. Add the chocolate chips and vanilla. Cover the blender, pressing a towel firmly on the cover. Blend the mixture, first on a low speed until combined, then on a high speed until very frothy.

Divide the hot chocolate among 4 mugs and serve immediately.

Some Seasonal Menus

WINTER MENUS

Olive Mélange with Fennel and Orange
Provençal Marinated Leg of Lamb with Pan Vegetables
Creamy Potato and Parsnip Gratin, after Madeleine
Wine-Poached Pear Croustades with Ice Cream

Roast Pork Loin with Savory Spinach Stuffing
Rosemary-Pancetta Potato Sauté
Sweet-and-Sour Glazed Shallots
Cappuccino Mousse

SPRING MENUS

Salmon Brûlée with Tarragon-Mustard Cream
Baked Vidalia Onions with Goat Cheese
and Red Pepper Stuffing
Grilled Asparagus with Lemon Mayonnaise
Coffee Angel-Food Cake

Pernod-Scented Artichokes with Black Olive Aioli
Herbed Lamb and White Bean Ragout
Crusty French Bread
Mesclun with Creamy Vermouth Vinaigrette
Devil's Food Cake with Marshmallow Frosting

SUMMER MENUS

Grilled Eggplant-Tomato Dip
Oven-Baked Pita Chips with Za'atar
Cumin-Grilled Sea Bass with Preserved-Lemon Sauce
Chickpea and Brown and Wild Rice Salad
with Moroccan-Spiced Dressing
Tomato and Cucumber Salad with Mint and Feta
Marmalade-Glazed Fresh Fig and Mascarpone Tart

Marcella's Fava Bean Spread
Chile Pita Chips
Cold Red Pepper and Fennel Soup with Summer Herbs
My Tuna Salad Niçoise
Plums and Peaches in Blueberry-Vanilla Syrup
Almond-Orange Biscotti

Mango Lemonade
Baja Beach Clams Steamed in Beer
BBQ Chicken Breast Sandwiches with Mustardy Slaw
Smoky "Baked" Bean Salad with
Molasses-Mustard Vinaigrette
Tequila-Glazed Pineapple and Nectarine Skewers
with Orange Crème Anglaise
Extra-Spicy Gingersnaps

Thai Red Seafood Curry
Jasmine Rice
Beet and Mango Salad with Curried Mango Dressing
Thai Iced Coffee
Coconut Magic Bars

FALL MENUS

Savory Pumpkin Bisque with Fresh Sage
Polenta-Crusted Deep-Dish Cheese
and Roasted Vegetable Tart
Flavors' Caesar Salad
Cappuccino Mousse

Frisée, Roquefort and Pear Salad with Pistachios
Spice-Braised Lamb Shanks with Figs
Roasted Potato Salad with Rosemary and Asiago Cheese
Flavors' Apple Crisp
Vanilla Ice Cream

Crab and Corn Cakes with Chipotle Rémoulade
Hot and Smoky West Texas Barbecue Meat Loaf
Roasted Garlic Mashed Potatoes
Succotash
Citrus-Glazed Pumpkin Squares
Blushing Pear Granita

THANKSGIVING

Flavor's Sweet and Spicy Cocktail Nuts
Squash, Apple and Ginger Soup
Red Chile–Rubbed Roast Young Turkey
Corn Bread, Mushroom and Toasted Pecan Dressing
Secret Ingredient Sweet Potatoes
Roasted Brussels Sprouts with Maple-Walnut Butter
Gingered Pear Conserve
Pumpkin Cheesecake with Pecan Praline Sauce
Harvest Nut Pie with a Touch of Bourbon and Chocolate

NEW YEAR'S DAY

Gravlax with Sweet Mustard-Dill Sauce
Pumpernickel Bread, Capers and Onions
Bourbon- and Mustard-Glazed Country Ham
Secret Ingredient Sweet Potatoes
Winter Salad of Grapefruit, Fennel and Watercress
Poppy Seed Dressing
Bridgehampton Café's Flourless Chocolate Cake
with Tropical Fruit Sauce

PICNIC

Smoky White Bean Spread
with Roasted Garlic and Basil
Creamless Corn Soup
Crisp Unfried Chicken
Oil-Free Wheat Berry Salad
Beefsteak Tomato and Gorgonzola Salad
with Toasted Walnuts and Basil
Very Lemony Pound Cake
Walnut Brownies U.S.A.
Fresh Berries

STEAK COOKOUT SUPPER

Two Tomato-Basil Bruschettas
Flavor's Caesar Salad
Grilled Steaks with Peppery Lemon-Herb Marinade
Green Bean, New Potato and Cherry Tomato Salad with
Creamy Vermouth Vinaigrette
Plums and Peaches in Blueberry-Vanilla Syrup

Index

granita, blushing pear, 223
granita, espresso-Frangelico, 224
granola, Flavors' private mix, 184
granola bars, 203
grapefruit, fennel, and watercress, winter
    salad of, 147
gravlax with sweet mustard-dill sauce, 22–23

ham, bourbon- and mustard-glazed, 82
ham sandwiches with Dijon-Brie spread, 58
haricots verts, 118
hash, brisket, 95
hazelnuts, gingered pear conserve with cherries
    and, 179
herbes de Provence, 9
honeyed banana yogurt cream, 189
honey-ginger glaze, spice-rubbed grilled quail
    with, 71

jam, sunberry, 185
jicama, green bean and sweet pepper salad, 154

lamb:
    herbed, and white bean ragout, 95–96
    Provençal-marinated leg of, with pan
      vegetables, 72–73
    roast leg of, sandwiches with smoky white
      bean spread, 60
    spice-braised shanks with figs, 92–93
lavash with herbed cream cheese and smoked
    salmon, 20–21
lemon(s):
    herbed orzo with tomatoes, olives and feta,
      137
    -herb marinade, peppery, grilled steaks with,
      75
    mango lemonade, 231
    mayonnaise, grilled asparagus with, 171
    preserved, cumin-grilled sea bass with sauce
      of, 89–90
    quick preserved, 90
    very lemony pound cake, 214
    zucchini-walnut muffins with a twist of,
      193
lemongrass, 87
lentil and roasted red pepper salad with walnuts
    and grilled green onions, 129
linguine with tuna, green olives, sun-dried
    tomatoes and capers, 99

macadamia nuts:
    banana bread with ginger and, 191
    praline, 227
    praline crunch, banana-chocolate tartlets
      with, 226–27

magrets, 67
mango(es):
    and beet salad with curried mango dressing,
      152
    brown and wild rice salad with cherries and,
      136
    lemonade, 231
    melon, and peach soup, cold, 31–32
maple, baked apples with orange, cinnamon
    and, 187
maple syrup, 187
maple-walnut butter, roasted brussels sprouts
    with, 168
marble cake, Grandma Rose's, 211
marmalade-glazed fresh fig and mascarpone
    tart, 225–26
Marsala wine, 78
marshmallow frosting, 210
masala chai, 198
mascarpone and fresh fig tart, marmalade-
    glazed, 225–26
mayonnaise:
    lemon, grilled asparagus with, 171
    pesto, 61
    wasabi, 81
meat loaf, hot and smoky West Texas BBQ, 74
melon, mango, and peach soup, cold, 31–32
menus, seasonal, 233–34
mezze, 5
millet, 172
millet rosemary cakes with sun-dried tomatoes,
    173
mint:
    cucumber and tomato salad with olives,
      feta and, 153
    hot chocolate, 232
    sugar snap peas with, 155
molasses, unsulphured, 207
molasses-mustard vinaigrette, smoky "baked"
    bean salad with, 127
mousse, cappuccino, 222
mozzarella, bread and tomato salad, 143
muffins:
    orange-poppy seed mini-, 195
    raspberry-bran, 196
    zucchini-walnut, with lemon twist, 193
mushroom(s):
    corn bread and toasted pecan dressing,
      176–77
    dried, 40
    duck and barley broth, 39
    grilled portobello hero loaf with smoky
      tomatoes, ricotta and arugula, 52–53
    portobello, 53
    removing gills from, 101

three-cheese pasta gratin with radicchio
    and, 100–101
    wild, soup, 40–41
mustard:
    and bourbon-glazed country ham, 82
    Dijon-Brie spread, Black Forest ham sand-
      wiches with, 58
    -dill sauce, 23
    -molasses vinaigrette, smoky "baked" bean
      salad with, 127
    purple cabbage and carrot slaw, 149
    slaw, BBQ chicken sandwiches with, 55
    -tarragon cream, 80

nam plah, 122
nectarine and pineapple skewers, tequila-
    glazed, with orange crème anglaise,
    215–216
noodle(s):
    with browned caraway butter, 175
    chicken and corn soup with saffron, 36–37
    and chicken salad with peanut dressing,
      Chinese, 111–12
    cold, and vegetable salad with sesame-soy
      dressing, 134–35
nuts:
    Flavors' sweet and spicy cocktail, 13
    harvest pie with a touch of bourbon and
      chocolate, 228
    toasting of, 114
    see also specific nuts

oatmeal "bar," 188
oat topping, crunchy, 213
olive(s):
    black, aioli, 18
    cucumber and tomato salad with feta,
      mint and, 153
    green, pantry linguine with tuna, sun-dried
      tomatoes, capers and, 99
    lemony herbed orzo with tomatoes, feta
      and, 137
    mélange with fennel and orange, 15
    pitted, 7
    and tomato tapenade, 6–7
onion(s):
    baked Vidalia with cheese and red pepper
      stuffing, 165
    caramelized, 8
    green, -tequila marinade, 108
    grilled green, lentil and roasted red pepper
      salad with walnuts and, 129
    Vidalia, 164
orange:
    -almond biscotti, 205